D0148703

The CULTURE HISTORICAL METHOD *of* ETHNOLOGY

The CULTURE HISTORICAL METHOD *of* ETHNOLOGY

The Scientific Approach to the Racial Question

By

WILHELM SCHMIDT

Translated by S. A. SIEBER

GREENWOOD PRESS, PUBLISHERS
WESTPORT, CONNECTICUT

Library of Congress Cataloging in Publication Data

Schmidt, Wilhelm, 1868-1954.
The culture historical method of ethnology.

Reprint of the 1939 ed. published by Fortuny's, New York.
Translation of Handbuch der Methode der kulturhistorischen Ethnologie.
1. Ethnology--Methodology. I. Title.
GN33.S252 1974 572'.07'2 73-10761
ISBN 0-8371-7036-2

Originally published in 1939 by Fortuny's, New York

Reprinted in 1973 by Greenwood Press, Inc.
51 Riverside Avenue, Westport, CT 06880

Library of Congress catalog card number 73-10761
ISBN 0-8371-7036-2

Printed in the United States of America

10 9 8 7 6 5 4 3 2

PREFACE

FATHER SCHMIDT has done me the honor of asking me to write a few words introducing the English translation of his definitive treatise on the culture historical method in ethnology. I accede to this request of my revered teacher with great pleasure, for I have long been convinced that only an extended publication *in English* would dissipate the lamentable confusions and misunderstandings as to the culture historical school which have been all too current among English-speaking ethnologists. "Graebner" and "Schmidt" are names which enter rather often into the small talk of my professional brethren in this country and England, but—if I may be quite candid—it is a rough induction from my field notes on such conversations that these authors have been more talked about than read! It is fact as well as folk-lore that we of English speech (scholars included) avoid reading in foreign languages except in sheer necessity. There are, to be sure, individuals who, by virtue of some accident of training or experience or perhaps following some inborn predisposition, continue to read widely in German after they have passed the reading examinations for their doctorate, but these are surely far from the mean or mode of this curve of dispersion. The annual output of ethnological literature has assumed horrendous proportions in recent years, and one is hard put to digest those works which converge upon one's own principal research interests. Small wonder if we tend to limit our "general" reading to books in our own language. Thus, while still unfortunate, it is understandable that many English and American ethnologists have too often disposed of Graebner, Schmidt, and Koppers with a few pat but superficial and misleading phrases learned while they were cramming for their doctoral examinations.

This translation will remove any vestige of excuse for such a situation. There is a diligent exegesis of Graebner with a detailed elucidation of many involved points. Father Schmidt's own corrections, modifications, and supplements are given their most recent formulation and the whole provides a complete and convenient guide to all aspects of the culture historical method. The numerous and excellent examples, applying the abstract in the concrete, should resolve all doubts as to the operations which this group feels should become standard in ethnological procedure. I hope that this work will be painstakingly and sympathetically studied by my co-workers. I find it singularly timely and potentially useful, for I think its strongest points are precisely the weakest points of our anthropology in this country (so far as one may generalize). We are proud (with reason, I feel) of our scrupulous field work. But library (and, to some extent, also museum) research has been done far less extensively and intensively than in Europe and with far less attention to canons of procedure. This is surely the most exhaustive treatise on those sensitive precisions of criticism of source material and of the logic of inference which we have observed put into practice in so many excellent articles in *Anthropos* and elsewhere. Similarly, I welcome the present translation as likely to stimulate English-speaking cultural anthropologists into greater articulateness and more systematic consideration of questions of method and theory. I think the late Professor Sapir was penetratingly right when he used to remark something of this sort: "In scholarly work neatness should be a tendency rather than accomplished fact. Reality is a continuum—not a symmetrical set of categories such as our systematic minds would often wish to make it appear. There should always be 'give' in any intellectual system." Now I would venture the opinion that Father Schmidt's views on method may verge too much on the polarity of "neatness." Nevertheless I hold it certain that American anthropology has typically approached the opposite polarity far too nearly.

We American ethnologists are definitely individualists in our work and particularly in our methodological and theoretical approaches. Perhaps, as Professor Schmidt intimates, we are so too much. In view of that fact, however, it seems unlikely that the publication of this translation will bring about any sudden or totalitarian acceptance of the culture historical method. If I may be pardoned the personal note, it is perhaps not irrelevant to state that I am not (as certain readers of my article on the method and theory of this group have inferred) a "follower" (in any rigorous sense of that word) of the culture historical school. It so happens that my own research interests are not those which are likely to lead to scholarly productions of the sort which emanate from those who rigorously put into practice the principles set forth in this book. In English parlance I am "descriptive ethnographer" and "social anthropologist" by interest far more than "ethnologist." But at the same time I recognize the abiding significance of culture historical studies for my tasks in descriptive ethnography and social anthropology. Moreover, I cannot forget that I learned, as a student of Professor Schmidt and Professor Koppers, certain phases of method common to all studies in cultural anthropology better, I honestly believe, than I should have from any other teachers.

It is from such considerations and in such a spirit that I warmly recommend the reading and the study of this book. Whether at a given point one agrees not at all or only with many reservations makes little difference. To follow the argument (often of intricately reasoned structure) surely means an enrichment of one's perspectives on techniques, method, theory, and methodology. Almost every paragraph appears to me to offer sharp insights and profound subtleties. These have, in general, the more value for being couched in an idiom which is more a part of the pattern of European than of American scholarship.

Ethnologists are too prone to neglect to apply their science to themselves and to forget that their own views on method and theory are cultural products. To expose oneself, then, to another intellectual climate is in itself a valuable exercise in the preservation of that perspective by cultural relativity which is perhaps the greatest contribution of cultural anthropology to the main stream of intellectual life. In one respect, however, the fact that this treatise follows a somewhat different set of traditions of scholarship may interfere somewhat with the communication of its central ideas. "The Outline History of the Historical Method in Ethnology" seems to me chiefly remarkable for that erudition which has made Dr. Schmidt world famous. I am sure that its author would be the last to claim that it was a presentation without bias. Professor Schmidt, ever keen in dispute, has used plain speech in his discussion of various American and English ethnologists. It is much to be wished that this forthrightness (which at times strikes a challengingly controversial note) will not annoy readers into neglect of the more dispassionate exposition of the method proper. Even if one feels that this is at times over-schematic and cannot assent to every detail, there can be no doubt that this systematic development of method in the later chapters is worthy of the most patient and careful study.

Clyde Kluckhohn, Ph.D.
Assistant Professor of Anthropology,
Harvard University

TABLE OF CONTENTS

FOREWORD

The value of a new exposition of the method of ethnology is made evident by the fact that, since 1911, the year when Graebner's *Methode* appeared, ethnology has made significant progress in every respect. Such progress has served to develop and to perfect the method itself, and this development in method in turn has increased the possibilities of further profitable ethnological investigation. The need for a revised exposition has long been felt, because the treatise of Graebner, which is sometimes overconcise, too replete with overlapping steps in the development of the argument and not infrequently obscure, is difficult for even German-speaking people to follow.

Long years of academic experience has only too well convinced Professor Koppers and myself of these facts, and already in my lectures at the University of Vienna in the year 1932–1933 I endeavored to supply this need. I could not bring myself to publish these lectures as long as Fr. Graebner, though for some time mentally dead because of an undiagnosed disease, still lingered among the living. After death had released him from his tragic fate, (1) I thought I should no longer oppose the pressure put upon me from many quarters to publish these lectures. In this exposition Professor Koppers has also undertaken important sections; namely, section six of the Introduction, "Historical and Ethnological Methodology" (pp. 13-19), and the whole second chapter, "The Sources of Ethnology and Their Methodical Treatment" (pp. 81-124). Moreover, we have discussed the whole manuscript together, and I am greatly indebted to him for a whole series of valuable suggestions and additions. I wish in particular to record my indebtedness to him for an important correction in the conception of the criterion of the Degree of Cultural Relationship.

Of the "Historical-Critical Section" of Graebner (pp. 77-104) I have already included the first part, "Theories of Evolution," in the Introduction. I purposely shortened it because there is no longer any necessity today to treat the matter at length. Some things are taken up again in Chapter I of this book; namely, all that has served in some way or other, positively or negatively, as a preparation for the historical method.

Furthermore, my "Outline History of the Genesis and Spread of the Historical Method of Ethnology" is, understandably, more extensive than that of Graebner, for the simple reason that, at that time, Graebner had hardly a decade of the history of the culture historical school behind him, while today some thirty-five years have gone by. Besides this greater span of time there is also to be taken into consideration the greater expansion of the subject. Since Graebner's time and hence, unknown to him, there has been a wide diffusion of the historical idea in other countries, an account of which must be given.

I was long in doubt whether I should prefix this historical part to the exposition of the method, or whether I should allow it to come later. The fact that most of the authors treated here only appeared on the scene long after Graebner's book speaks for the last procedure. Even weightier is the consideration that the greatest part of the criticism given these authors can only then be understood completely and appreciated after acquaintance of the Culture Historical Method has been made. Nevertheless, I decided to put the entire historical section before the exposition of the method, because in a certain sense it forms an introduction to it. However, I do not deny that it will be useful to read this historical part again after the Culture Historical Method itself has been studied.

Naturally, I have also made use of the exposition of the Culture Historical Method which H. Pinard de la Boullaye gave in his work, *L'Étude comparée des religions.* (2) I have pointed out the advantages of Pinard over Graebner elsewhere before, as well as the former's high degree of originality. However, I did not fail to recognize Graebner's superiority to Pinard in other matters. (3) Chief among the advantages to be found in the work of Graebner is the manner in which he combined the single parts of his *Methode* in a broad universal system. Pinard, on the other hand, places his different criteria loosely beside one another, simply enumerating them one after the other. Finally, Pinard's exposition is also given with considerable less detail and consequently in a much more summarized form than Graebner's *Methode*.

In like manner, the *Beiträge zur Methode der Völkerkunde* (4) of G. van Bulck has also been used. He drew largely from both Graebner and Pinard as well as from my own writings, but he endeavors to improve upon them as the following quotation indicates: "I soon had to confess that I was unable to find Graebner's criteria adequate as he had proposed them *ex professo* for the 'migrations of peoples,' when I wanted to investigate and determine the other diffusions of culture." (5) He had undertaken an intensive study on "Haus und Hütte in Afrika," and in addition thereto he investigated many other culture elements of Africa. Now, since Graebner takes the illustrative material for his *Methode* principally from his special field of study, Oceania, and van Bulck is almost exclusively interested in Africa, the work of the latter would thus be a good complement to Graebner's book. However, between Graebner and van Bulck's supplement there is not only an external inessential difference, but also an internal and essential one which should not be overlooked in our evaluation of van Bulck's book. I will give a brief discussion of this difference in what follows.

Graebner's attention was at all times strictly concentrated upon the principal goal he set for himself; namely, the formulation of a method whereby the cultural contacts of peoples without written documents may be grasped in their spatial, temporal, and causal relations. But he does not give an exposition of the culture itself. For this reason Radin is obviously mistaken when he attributes to Graebner "the laws that govern culture growth." (6) The treatment of this question, which is not to be found in Graebner, forms almost the main part of the book of Dr. G. van Bulck: the two parts, "Life of Culture" and "Picture of Culture," cover one hundred and thirty-eight pages (pp. 33-170), while the two methodological parts, "Elements of Culture" (7) and "Investigation of Culture," only sixty-seven pages (pp. 171-238). In itself there is nothing objectionable in this mode of procedure; the first part could serve as a useful supplement, whereas the second would be a shorter summary of Graebner and Pinard, with a few critical comments. But this division is not consistently retained throughout by van Bulck, for already in the section which describes the life and picture of culture he often mixes in methodological rules for determining culture and its history, thus disrupting Graebner's compact exposition; *e.g.*, p. 59, s., p. 62, ss., p. 66, s., p. 72, s., pp. 105, 140, 143, ss., p. 147, s., p. 195, s., p. 170, s. Although I do not consider this confusion to be an advance, there may be some of the opinion that van Bulck's real contribution to the method consists in the exposition of the different kinds of "Culture Diffusion and the Cultural Changes and Overlays resulting therefrom" (pp. 33-169), which is indeed the opinion of van Bulck himself. Whether that is really the case, and especially whether it contains essentially new and more comprehensive rules than Graebner's, we shall have occasion to investigate in the course of this work.

Van Bulck also devotes a great deal of his book to a very useful, detailed, and practical introduction to research as such, beginning with directions for the collection of material. This, however, has nothing to do with theory or method.

W. SCHMIDT.

Salzburg, August 15, 1936.

I take the welcome opportunity of offering my most sincere thanks to Her Serene Highness Countess Salm and to Professor W. Moock for their careful reading of the proof sheets as well as for many important suggestions. I wish also to record my indebtedness to two of my pupils, Dr. Frederick Borneman and

A. Burgmann, for the carefulness with which the former prepared the subject and object index and latter the other indices, all of which are very important for a work of this kind.

Perhaps I may dare to hope that this somewhat more comprehensive, clearer, and more extensive exposition of the method of culture historical ethnology will relieve it of and protect it against many misunderstandings and obscurities and be the means of finding for it an easier and more sympathetic appreciation.

To mention but a single particular case of what I mean, let us take the explanation which I gave with regard to the standpoint of antievolutionistic culture historical ethnology on the question of evolution. The special usefulness of this can be seen from several recent statements of Professor Lowie concerning the way in which I set forth the developmental sequence of the different phases of mother-right in my lecture, "The Position of Woman with Regard to Property in Primitive Society." (8) He writes: "In accepting the independent repetition of terminological features where social concomitants are repeated, we avowedly admit 'evolution.' However, it is a strictly empirical parallelism, which does not pretend to sketch cultural history as a whole, but merely to account for specific resemblances. It is, indeed, very difficult to deal with cultural phenomena and fail to recognize certain organic bonds between phenomena. As Father Schmidt has recently explained, aprioristic evolutionism must be eschewed, but it is quite proper to make a quite logical deduction from the very nature of things and men, to arrange them (cultural measures) in a certain series of phases of development." (8) In a different passage he thinks that I avoided the word evolution here but not the concept. He is far from criticizing me for that; in fact, he welcomes the idea, "for anthropologists are at times confronted with phenomena which are organically related and some of which indubitably precede others." It seems to him to be "certainly significant that thinkers with such diverse starting points as Father Schmidt, Thurnwald, and Radcliffe-Brown should converge towards the acceptance of a qualified evolutionism."

Now Professor Lowie and others will see from my exposition of method that I not only make use of the word, but also even recognize the concept and fact of evolution. As a matter of fact, together with the whole culture historical school I frankly and openly accept evolution, but now as well as before I stand in opposition to evolutionism. Neither do I want to be bedfellow of a "qualified evolutionism" or some kind of "neoevolutionism." For it is not only the fact that we reject aprioristic evolutionism. For us, the matter is rather, as Professor Lowie well remarks, a case of "a strictly empirical parallelism"; *i.e.,* we would never trust ourselves to support a whole series of phases of development merely on "quite logical deductions" if they were not at the same time supported and developed by such a state of affairs in all the single stages of development geographically and spatially throughout the region. This will thus make it possible for us to work out the historical chronological sequence legitimately with the aid of the criteria and rules of our method, as I endeavored to do in the article on the development of mother-right mentioned above. In other words, also in this matter we shall continue to cultivate culture *historical* ethnology.

W. SCHMIDT.

Budkau, January 1, 1937.

(1) See my obituary in *Anthropos,* XXX (1935) pp. 203-214.

(2) Paris, Vol. I (1922); Vol. II (1925). (Third ed. of both volumes in 1929.) See Vol. II, pp. 243-304.

(3) W. Schmidt, *Ursprung der Gottesidee,* I (1934), pp. 790-804.

(4) *Wiener Beiträge zur Kulturgeschichte und Linguistik,* II (1931), pp. 1-256.

(5) Van Bulck, *op. cit.,* p. 6. We shall see in the course of this work that this interpretation of Graebner is not reliable.

(6) P. Radin, *The Method and Theory of Ethnology* (New York and London, 1933), p. 80.

(7) An unhappy term for "Criteria of Research" ("Forschungskriterien") in which the discordant nature of the whole exposition manifests itself.

(8) *American Anthropologist,* N. S. XXXVII (1935), pp. 244-256.

TRANSLATOR'S PREFACE

SCIENTISTS of the most divergent views are agreed that the work and theories of Wilhelm Schmidt are well worthy of respectful consideration. Other members of the Vienna School of Ethnology and Father Schmidt himself have often complained, however, that many English-speaking ethnologists have misinterpreted or misunderstood much of their work and more so the theories they defend. This translation of his *Handbuch der Methode der kulturhistorischen Ethnologie* will serve, we hope, in making known to the English-speaking world not one or the other of their statements, but the whole system of the school of culture historical ethnology.

It was a great help to me in understanding the German text of the original that I translated this book in a German atmosphere as a student of Professor Schmidt at the University of Vienna, while a revision undertaken in a milieu where my mother tongue was spoken was meant to improve upon the literary form. There is no one more conscious than myself, however, that despite these advantages, the translation contains many defects. It might be well, therefore, not to exonerate myself, but simply to clarify matters, if I briefly describe some of the difficulties that confronted me and my efforts to arrive at a solution.

In the two books of Wilhelm Schmidt that have appeared in English, (1) there are some fifty pages that deal with method. Consequently, the terminology of this school (and it is very much their own creation) has not been given equivalents in the English language. One of the reasons that urged Dr. Schmidt to write his book on method was the difficulty in understanding Graebner's work (even for German-speaking people) on the same subject. Now since almost every line of this difficult book of Graebner is quoted in the course of Schmidt's book, it demanded of me a translation into English also of a text that was in many cases too hard for those who speak German to follow. It was also impossible for me to give a freer translation of these passages, since the subsequent comment upon them (often involving every word) forced one to give the Graebner text as literal as possible. Many have advised a freer translation bordering on adaptation as was done for the last chapter of Graebner's book in V. F. Calverton's Modern Library compilation, but I can only say that neither was I given the license for such an adaptation nor did I presume to rate myself capable of the task. And surely one would rather read what Schmidt and Graebner, experienced and tried scholars, had to say, for instance, on some mooted point, than be presented with the views of some toddling abecedarian in the field of ethnology.

Ethnological people are in general those who have not attained the use of writing. From this aspect as well as from other features of their culture (*e.g.*, food-gathering stage, primitivity, uncivilized conditions, nearness to nature, etc.) ethnologists have created a whole host of terms to designate these people. In this book ethnological peoples are called "the primitives." Since Father Schmidt has given the word "Primitive" a specific place in his terminology by applying it to the first of his culture circles, I have capitalized the word whenever he refers to the oldest culture circle or to any culture element characteristic of, or specifically pertaining to, this group (Primitive) or to the people embraced by this classification (Primitives). Otherwise, the term "primitives" (not capitalized) designates and includes all ethnological peoples. Moreover, especially in the section contributed by Dr. Wilhelm Koppers, these peoples are contrasted with those of literary history. Wherever reference is being made, therefore, to the primitives as people without the art of writing, I have called them preliterates in contradistinction to literate peoples. The present book as well as all the works of Wilhelm Schmidt shoud convince everyone that it is about time to put an everlasting taboo on the word "savage."

It is the urgent wish of the Vienna School that for the sake of uniformity their "Kulturkreise" always be translated by "culture circles."

The term "Beziehungen" (most used in combined forms; such as, "Kulturbeziehungen," "Raumbeziehungen") was rendered for the most part by "relations" (culture relations, spatial relations) and only rarely by the more common word "relationship," because the latter term is also used by the author in a specific sense to designate one of the auxiliary criteria, the criterion of the degree of relationship.

For the disjunctive subdivision of the species of acculturation, I selected "marginal acculturation" (already in English usage), in which there is culture contact merely along the borders of two cultures, and coined the expression, "planitional acculturation" *(planities:* Latin for a surface or plane), in which the contact involves a large geographical area. Similar disjunctives in the book are: local and distant interpretation, unilateral and multilateral (or reciprocal) interpretation, internal and external development. Other such expedients will be found in the book. These examples are sufficiently numerous to illustrate the principles of translation followed in this book.

I wish to record my indebtedness to Dr. Wilhelm Schmidt himself, Dr. Wilhelm Koppers, Dr. Fritz Borneman, and Professor Stanislaus Marusczyk for their painstaking efforts to enable me to understand the German text. I take the welcome opportunity of offering my most sincere thanks to Professor Clark Wissler, Mr. Clyde Kluckhohn, Dr. Lawrence Mack, and Rev. Robert Hunter, who critically read the manuscript and whose many valuable suggestions concerning the terminology and literary form of the book have been embodied in the text. My thanks are also due to Miss Emma Heeks and Mrs. N. Deyell for typing the whole manuscript. I owe a special debt of gratitude to the hundreds of interested people whose advance subscriptions made this first edition of Father Schmidt's book in English possible. Finally, it would be an unforgiveable oversight on my part should I fail to acknowledge my indebtedness to those faithful friends whose enthusiasm and moral or financial support urged me to continue the work and bring it to completion. As for myself, I shall feel amply repaid if this communication of Father Schmidt's ideas to English-speaking scientists should prove to be a stimulus and an aid to them in unraveling the manifold threads of man's early history and thus help to clarify the "archaeological, linguistic and ethnological tangle" of human culture by uniting into one harmonious whole the universal and "only proper study of mankind, the study of man."

Oakland, California, June 1, 1939. S. A. SIEBER.

(1) W. Schmidt, *The Origin and Growth of Religion,* translated by H. J. Rose (New York: The Dial Press, 1931), pp. 219-250; W. Schmidt, *High Gods in North America* (Upton Lectures in Religion, Manchester College, Oxford, 1931), (Oxford University Press, 1933), pp. 1-21.

The CULTURE HISTORICAL METHOD *of* ETHNOLOGY

THE NATURE, AIM, AND METHOD OF ETHNOLOGY

1. THE NECESSITY OF A METHOD FOR ETHNOLOGY

It is essential to true science that it strive after certainties, that it aim at certitude. A study that rests content with probabilities and possibilities, that consists of mere hypotheses and theories would not be a science. Of course, it is but natural to every science that it does not attain certitude everywhere and always, but in many cases must be satisfied with possibilities and probabilities. But even then, true scientific method demands that at least *this* certitude be demonstrated, that for the time being—or even definitely—complete certainty is not possible in the case in question. But if a science lead *only* to such negative certainties, or if the greater part of its proven conclusions would be of such a negative quality, it would accordingly fall into discredit and lose its authority.

I. Assured results are only obtained by pursuing the goal with understanding and perseverance along a certified way: that is the μέθοδος, the method of a science. Method is the foundation of its existence and worth. A real science without a method is unthinkable, howsoever many particular data it may have heaped together. It is not only that it all remains uncertain, because no solid and certain way was followed, and that to obtain these single results all was left to chance, to "finder's luck," to a false "intuition"; but there is also the fact that you could not lead others along such routes (which are really not routes at all) in order that they also might come to the same conclusions, and thus on the basis of them advance further.

In other words, such a science without method simply cannot be taught. This difficulty, of teaching a science without a method, is all the greater in ethnology, because of the unending diversity of its material as a consequence of the great number of peoples and the variegated riches of their cultures which constitute the object matter of ethnology. Thus, as it were, from an *embarras de richesse* we get rather a *richesse d'embarras.*

Ethnology found itself in such a condition for a long time. Real sciences, that have solid methods, have on that account frequently eyed ethnology with suspicion and have not considered it a full-fledged science. For a long time this utter lack of method brought to naught all its efforts to obtain chairs of ethnology in universities. It is remarkable to note that ethnology was supported in this endeavor by the natural sciences, such as geology, physical anthropology, anatomy, etc., because the ethnology of that time had borrowed a part of the method of those natural sciences; while, on the other hand, it was especially the historical and philological sciences which for a long time disputed its scientific character especially as a branch of the university curriculum.

II. But it is also not sufficient for a science to have any kind of method whatsoever; the method must correspond to the nature of the science. Hence the method of the natural sciences which served ethnology for a time was as good as no method at all for it. It was not only not a way for it, but also it was, in fact, a false way. That ethnology ever adopted the method of the natural sciences was due to various reasons:

1. When ethnology began to develop,(1) idealistic philosophy, which might have produced a method for a science of the mind, had crumbled in its exaggerations, while the natural sciences dominated the field with splendid discoveries and inventions.

2. Materialism, which came forward at the same time, explained the intellectual as but a mere function and emanation of matter.

3. The greatest part of the ethnologists of those days had come from the natural sciences and had begun their scientific expeditions as physicians, zoologists, botanists, geologists, and only during the course of these expeditions did they become ethnologists.

4. The literary historians (*i.e.*, historians making use of written sources exclusively) had their hands full merely to protect their field against the deluge of the natural sciences and materialism. Hence they did not find time to make the Primitives the object of their research as a continuation of the historical peoples backward.

2. THE SO-CALLED PSYCHOLOGICAL METHOD

In like manner, A. Bastian, who gave such a strong theoretical impulse to the ethnology of his day, was originally a physician, but soon turned to philosophy, to a philosophy, to be sure, that was closely related to the natural sciences. We shall not enter into a special treatment of Bastian here, but only point out the role he played as the go-between of a peculiar compromise between Idealism and Materialism. This compromise became important for the ethnology of the time, since he endeavored to produce a suitable method for it.

Bastian was a pupil of Herbart, whose philosophy stood close to natural science. Other pupils of Herbart were Lazarus and Steinthal, the founders of the "Zeitschrift für Völkerpsychologie und Sprachwissenschaft." From them Bastian took the conception of the social psyche, the productions of which appear in custom, law, society and beliefs; according to Bastian, all of these are based fundamentally on "elementary ideas" ("Elementargedanken"), which as such are common to all peoples because of the essential identity of their spiritual nature. In this Bastian appears to be an idealist and a spiritualist, though also a positivist. He certainly was not a downright materialist. In fact, he at times made fun of the fanatical materialism of Vogt, Büchner, and Moleschott. However, he joins the ranks of the materialists when he claims that the different peoples arise from the "folk ideas" ("Völkergedanken") of the different geographical provinces, which for him are in the main materialistically formed through the climatic factors, as well as the fauna and flora of the different regions in which they live. The importance of migration is indeed recognized, but this is for the most part nullified by the doctrine that all the travel routes were determined by nature. (2)

Here, in this peculiar mixture of psychism and materialism, we find the root of that shallow psychologizing which for so long a time and even today constitutes the ostensibly "deeper" foundation for the explanation of cultural elements and happenings for some ethnologists in England, France, and Holland. A change in this matter in Germany, Austria, and North America has gone so far that this "psychological" method can no longer dare to pretend to be the only method of ethnology, for the historical method had here conquered too extensive regions for that. But in certain circles, especially in England, they now teach: both methods are valid and each one valuable in its own way; according as one feels or finds it useful he may use now this, now that; a person with historical interests can undertake the study of culture relations and migrations; on the other hand, a person psychologically inclined will explain cultural phenomena from the psyche of the contemporary carriers of the culture and from their environment. Here we must pause a moment in order to subject these opinions to a critical examination.

This approach does not deserve the name "psychological" at all; for it investigates almost exclusively the influences of the *material* environment on the mind and neglects almost entirely the study of the interactions of mind upon mind, from one people to another, which are twofold and withal fully psychological. We find influences between individual minds already within the tribe: the influences of parents on children, grandparents upon parents, between husband and wife, and vice versa, talented upon the untalented, leader upon followers. The tribe did not fall out of the open sky all complete and then constantly remain in its own one area; it migrated, and in the course of its migration it came into contact not only with different material environments, but also with different human beings, tribes, and cultures, directly or indirectly, which have certainly left their effects in the minds of the tribe. Hence the mind of each tribe and people is thus full of such influences received from time immemorial.

The tribe does not receive all this passively, but rather grasps it actively after its own peculiar individuality, whereby a continuous transformation takes place, which is already a work of its own creation. Often the influences received from without merely give an impulse to productions which are almost entirely the property of the soul of the recipient people. These creations of the tribe, however, owe their nascent beginnings to these stimuli, which came to them by means of migrations.

All that taken together constitutes the full and rich content of this individual spirit, of the spirit of the tribe or a people.

But how can we grasp and understand this complete content in the dissimilarity of its origins and in the complexity of its developments if we do not trace out the currents of their wanderings and study the incidents of their history? For all those impressions and reactions of the distant past are historical realities and are now in some way or other garnered among the contents of the human spirit.

3. ETHNOLOGY A SCIENCE OF THE MIND, OF SPATIAL AND TEMPORAL RELATIONS

From all these reflections three conclusions may be drawn:

1. Ethnology is a science of the mind. All that it deals with has proceeded from the mind, has gone through the mind and bears its impress, and it is precisely through this process that it becomes a culture object. A mere object of nature as such does not belong to the field of investigation of ethnology. Through this derivation from the mind the object indeed is fashioned, but also and even more so the mind itself. This formation of the mind is the proper and real culture, and not the external

culture goods that encompass it: "The soul of the culture is the culture of the soul," according to the profound utterance of a prince of the church (Cardinal Faulhaber).

Therefore the objections which Fr. Krause raises against the ethnology of the culture historical school; namely, that it does not consider man but only his culture (3) goods are without foundation. That was refuted by my definition of ethnology which I had already formulated before 1914; namely, "a science which has for its object the study of the development of the mind and of the exterior rational activity of man in racial life." (4) Of course, the formation of the mind can only be grasped by us in its external expressions; that is, in the culture goods it produces, because under no circumstances can we see into the souls of others, and in our very own but imperfectly. Among "external culture goods" are to be understood not only the objects of the so-called material culture, but also the products of culture we find in poetry, customs, law, and religion.

If ethnology is a science of the mind, then its method must also be that of the mental sciences and not of the natural sciences: it must be able to grasp and to appreciate person, the individual, and free will, which so often seem to have disappeared in the mass; though within it talented individuals and geniuses are at work on its content, and leaders on its form. This method must have a means to grasp alongside the collective also the particular, the individual. It should not stop at the "typical" or the "average," but must be idiographical. It must endeavor and be prepared to grasp and appreciate the individual.

2. The different minds and tribes and peoples live and come into contact with one another in the proximity of space and thus influence one another. Hence ethnology is also a science of spatial relations, a geographical science, not in the mere sense of the so-called physical geography, that it teaches how to recognize the influences of the physical earth and its different factors (climate, soil, flora, fauna) upon man, but it is a geographical science far more in the sense of anthropogeog-

raphy, pointing out, as it does, also the influences of people living in one district upon those living elsewhere. In this regard, it is very significant that Ratzel, the creator of anthropogeography, was also one of the founders of culture historical ethnology. (5)

Spatial relations are accompanied by a sort of time relation; namely, contemporaneity, which is an important prerequisite for cultural influence. The requisite for the mutual influence of two human beings or two tribes upon each other is that they be contemporaneous; there can be no influence at all on the past, nor yet on the future, except indirectly through the influence of something now present. It is not permissible, therefore, to bring elements of different time periods together in direct historical relation. All questions of individual relation of culture elements and the gathering of many such relations in one culture circle must always again and again go back to this contemporaneousness of geographical proximity. Therefore, through investigation we must find the same time when two or more individuals or tribes came so near one another spatially that through their mutual contact they influenced and fashioned one another.

3. Both the internal self-development of the mind or of a human group, as well as their external active and passive influence, take place chronologically in the succession of events and become thereby historical. Consequently ethnology is essentially an historical science. The specific task of ethnology in history is something exceedingly valuable, in fact, something absolutely necessary, which no other science can accomplish in such vivid fullness. Ethnology and ethnology alone is called upon to enter beyond all the thousands of years which are illustrated by written history and to go still further back into the most distant millenia of the beginnings of human history, into which no written document even remotely reaches. Ethnology shares this privilege with prehistory; but it surpasses the latter through the incomparable richness and the full life of the different peoples it presents to us, while prehistory can but offer the Lifeless and the Maimed data, which become all the more

rare, the further back the people go and the older they are. (6)

But how can ethnology reach back into those dark and distant times? In what particular way does ethnology gain an exact objective proof of the temporal and causal succession of culture, since there is a lack not merely of written documents, but also of the means prehistory enjoys; namely, the stratification of prehistoric culture strata?

4. EVOLUTIONISM AS THE ALLEGED MEANS FOR THE DETERMINATION OF TIME

Here progressive evolutionism offered itself as a convenient expedient. It was proposed already by the French Girondists(7) as well as in Herder's *Ideen zur Philosophie der Geschichte der Menschheit* and in Schiller's "Was heisst und zu welchem Ende studiert man Universalgeschichte?" The evolutionistic theory was not generally accepted in ethnology till about the middle of the nineteenth century. Also about this time these ideas gradually attained a more concrete form and one more acceptable to the times through H. Spencer, (8) Darwin's "Origin of Species" (1859) and Huxley's "Evidence As to Man's Place in Nature" (1860, 1863). Ethnology and evolutionism were then for a long time close traveling companions, as bearers of an apparently highly obvious doctrine with the following methodological principles: Development proceeds on the whole always from the bottom upward, from the lower to the higher, from the more simple to the more complex, from the poorer to the richer—consequently the first of these two members is always the older, the second the younger.

Therewith a most simple time measure seemed to have been found also for the oldest times of mankind. Naturally, it took quite a while till these principles were built up into detailed theory; but Graebner (9) had shown that this theory was presented almost completely in L. Morgan's *Ancient Society* (1878) at first as a mere practical undertaking, but then also theoretically developed in McLennan's *Studies in Ancient History* (1886, 1896).

We now know that this time measure fails. The reasons that have led us to the recognition of this, are, in short, the following:

1. The development in all fields simply does not always proceed from the lower to the higher. In this matter prehistory has often been the cause of much misunderstanding through its rude forms of the oldest and the ever more perfect forms of the later implements, because it did not take into consideration the fact that even the most highly intellectual human being in his working of his material would produce extremely rude forms at first.

2. There is also a simplicity due to impoverization, a poverty due to degeneration, which therefore is younger than the previous more perfect condition.

3. The development in its entirety does not at all proceed in an ascending line, but rather, even when starting from one origin, at a certain point it branches off into several independent lines, which only later come again into contact with one another.

4. Opinions as to whether something is high or low are, for the most part, judgments of value in which subjectivism plays a great part and consequently scientific objectivity can no longer be sufficiently guaranteed. (10)

This evolutionism in the untenability of its contents and the inadequacy of its methods has been recognized in its true colors for some time; the beginning of this recognition falls around the beginning of the twentieth century. It has most vigorously broken through in Germany, Austria, and North America. Also the more positively inclined northern countries, Denmark, Sweden, and Finland soon turned away from evolutionism. It held out longest in England and France, where it had attained its most brilliant development. (11)

In this rejection of evolutionism we must by all means avoid a misunderstanding: if a person opposes and refuses to accept evolutionism, he does not thereby oppose and reject evolution

—the inner development. He only does not insist that the inner development be always considered as the first choice and, so to speak, be accepted without any positive proof, the external development through historical influence coming into question only when the impossibility of the inner development has been demonstrated. We must insist all the more that both internal as well as the external development need be proven. Since, however, the proofs for the latter are more easily found, method therefore demands that we begin with the latter. This will be explained more in detail later on.

Fr. Graebner in his *Methode der Ethnologie* (p. 92) applied the term "evolutionistic" to this method which we have criticized here; he writes: "The method of applying ideas of mere development without any regard for the particular events of culture history might therefore be best called 'evolutionistic,' " while I (Graebner too refers to this [*op. cit.*, note 1]), in my book, *Die Stellung der Pygmäenvölker, in der Entwicklungsgeschichte der Menschen* (12) was of the opinion that this movement did not make any effort to investigate the real evolution and therefore did not deserve this designation at all. Graebner further remarked that this method is distinctively different from the others in so far as it put forward and thought to explain the development of culture in the sense of mere evolution in the philosophical meaning of the word. That does not seem to me to be very clear, because the evolutionism of modern ethnology was based upon the principles of the natural sciences rather than upon those of philosophy.

However that may be, it is at any rate manifest that evolutionism is unable to give us a clear and trustworthy criterion for the determination of the succession of chronological culture events of those earliest periods of mankind. Who then will supply this urgent need for such a measure of time?

5. THE SCHOOL OF CULTURE HISTORY

It is the school of culture history which purports to meet this deficiency. This school intends to be *historical* with the principles of general history, but with means which go beyond those used by history in general; namely, written documents, and this it does indeed by applying the culture itself and its productions as methodological media. It is just for this reason that the school has been designated the school of culture history, in contradistinction to its sister (or mother), written history. (13)

1. The specific task as well as the real value of ethnology consist in the methodological application of *these* means, not only to understand the conditions existing among the primitive peoples today, but also to recognize in them witnesses and survivals of the oldest development of mankind and thus to reach back over the epochs of written history, far back into those distant millenia of mankind's past history, and with their help to construct the objective succession of events and thereby the actual genesis of culture among the different peoples; in a word, to change juxtaposition of culture circles into succession of culture layers. The other sciences expect this from ethnology because they cannot do it themselves. If ethnology cannot fulfill this expectation, it will cause great disappointment and lose the greater part of its worth and importance. This would inevitably manifest itself in the loss of interest and means which have been given it up till now.

For to concern ourselves only with conditions we find among the primitives today in order to "explain" them on the basis of present-day circumstances is a matter of little interest considering the insignificant role the modern primitives play in the history of mankind. Besides, such an "explanation" on the basis of present-day conditions could not be a true explanation, as it remains too much on the surface; time and again it must be the cause of misinterpretations and could not even satisfy the needs of colonial administrations, for whose "practical" purposes such "explanations" might allegedly be perfectly satisfactory. (14) In this regard also methods such as the "Strukturlehre" (see below, p. 31 ss.) would not change matters essentially, when they declare the culture historical penetration superfluous; for also they, with the means at their disposal, penetrate only to very shallow levels of time.

2. However, the whole picture changes at a stroke, if these primitives, after the manner of Père Lafitau, (14) be taken as precious documents of mankind, as living witnesses representing the oldest phases of development, through which also the most highly developed culture peoples have passed, so that in these primitives we can study the stages of past development in religion, law, custom, morality, and art. If the culture historical school gives us the means to determine the deepest meaning of those ancient times from their correct sequence, then it shall have made ethnology into what its name implies, to ethno*logy*, which is not mere ethno*graphy*, or description of peoples spread out spacially, but rather penetration into the *ratio*, the λόγος, of the elements and events of culture.

Consequently, the first task which is here imposed upon ethnology demands that it search for means through which it can establish objectively and trustworthily: *1*, the exact spatial juxtaposition of the culture elements, inventions, etc., as well as the identity of their possessors, and from this simultaneity of their existence in space and their mutual interreactions in ever wider scope on up to the culture-circles; *2*, the correct temporal succession of culture events and thus their sequence in time in waves and layers of culture.

But this does not complete the task of our ethnology. Should it go no further, then there would be some foundation to the criticisms made, especially by psychologists, to the effect that it proceeds too externally, too schematically. All that has been mentioned up till now is but preliminary work on the way to attain its last and highest goal; namely, the deeper penetration into the meaning of the objects and events of culture that has been given to them by the agent making use of these things, by man as an individual and as a group. Going still further, it must grasp the deepest signification and the causal connection of all the phenomena of culture in their entirety as such, which could not have proceeded from all of mankind alone.

6. HISTORICAL AND ETHNOLOGICAL METHODOLOGY

Graebner (15) has already pointed out the special position history holds among the sciences because of its well-developed method. Hence, ethnology does but profit by this. On the other hand, however, ethnology as a special branch of historical science has peculiarities enough of its own which call for a special treatment from the standpoint of method. Among other matters it will be our aim in the following pages to throw light upon these special characteristics. At the same time we shall endeavor to show how and where ethnology fits into history by reason of its method. Graebner takes too much for granted in this matter. He failed to observe the fact that only a small number of ethnologists, in contrast to himself, are thoroughly trained in the methodics of history. There is no doubt that much of the lack of appreciation and the frequent misunderstandings that arose were due to overlooking this situation. It is true his peculiarities of writing and style contributed much to this as mentioned above (Foreword), but this other factor retains its share of responsibility.

A. Nature, Aim, and Division of the Doctrine of Historico-Ethnological Methodology

Feder defines historical methodology as "that science, which besides corresponding theoretical explanations, offers us a systematical, scientifically founded sum of directions to examine historical facts as to the scope of their testimony, their value and inner association." (16) If we are willing to include in the expression "Historical facts" also ethnological facts (for the latter are historical facts also) then nothing prevents us from using the same definition for ethnological methodology.

Historical methodology falls into three main divisions:

(a) *Study of sources* (heuristic),* treating of the discovery and criticism of sources that come into question.

* The French have adopted this short but convenient term. *Cf.* Ch. V. Langlois and Ch. Seignobos, *Introduction to the Study of History,* translated by G. G. Berry (New York, 1898), p. 18.

(b) *Explanation of sources* (interpretation), treating of ways to find the correct meaning of sources.

(c) *Synthesis* (combination), treating of the correct arrangement of the sources, from which then the genetic succession of the historical events can be read and recognized.

It is sufficient here to point out that the same division can be preserved in the field of ethnology. Particularities of which we shall speak later do not essentially alter this fundamental division.

Historical certainty appears to be the main goal of the historical method; (17) *i.e.,* the certain knowledge of the historical data in question. Obviously, all ethnological research visualizes the same end as its final goal. However, the fact that in general the results of ethnology contain more of the hypothetical than we find in the field of the ordinary historical disciplines can be explained, on the one hand by the great lack of sources and on the other hand by the lack of an absolute chronology, and finally from the lack of, or better unrecognizability of, individual causal factors. Nevertheless, it still holds good what Ratzel in his day already emphasized, that history is not dependent upon the existence of written sources. In another passage above we have treated of the particular tasks that ethnology has to perform outside the history of peoples with writing in the study of the whole human race (p. 11 s.). There, too, it was pointed out that *only ethnology* can perform these tasks.

Hence, if the demand for the historization of ethnology has any meaning at all, then historical methodology above all must be applied in this field also. To do that conclusively, a corresponding knowledge of both fields is necessary; *i.e.,* both of historical methodology and the whole field of ethnology. Furthermore, the work that has been accomplished in this regard by methodizers of historical ethnology in the course of the last thirty years represents an essential enrichment of the whole of historical methodology as such.

B. Special Character of the Historico-Ethnological Methodology

1. Feder (*op. cit.*, p. 38 s.) describes the special character of the historical method with these fitting words: "The peculiarity of the historical method follows from the special character of historical science which in its turn derives its special character from historical knowledge. Now the material objects of historical knowledge are single facts and not general concepts abstracted from individual modifications. Its final aim is to discover the concrete inner connection of those facts. If historical facts are separated from their particular time and place, or from the special character given them as consequences of volitional acts, or if they are separated from their individual relations, their very nature is lost. And just as the single facts (be they of individual persons or of collective masses) are always of a singular character in history, so also the different series of events manifest a singular character throughout their causal sequence. This character of itself could be different, and in most cases we could not have determined its peculiarity before the actual occurrence of the events, because the latter are not subject to firm laws but in their last analysis presuppose the freedom of man."

In 1906 W. Schmidt (18) clearly demonstrated by keen and successful individual research among the so-called primitives that the preliterates, apart from other things, are also historical peoples. Consequently, this special character which Feder points out for the historical method applies four-square to ethnological methodology as well.

2. The special character of historical methodology and knowledge is more clearly illustrated if we compare them with the *natural sciences* and philosophy. "It is not very important for natural scientific knowledge to investigate this or that concrete object. It is sufficient if the individuals it has investigated according to their number and circumstances allow inductive conclusions as to their nature. Once it has determined their peculiarities it can with every right draw conclusions for each

new individual of the same kind. Historical knowledge is a different matter. For in the case of historical knowledge the concrete historical fact with its particular circumstances and its relations to other historical facts is absolutely necessary. Hence, historical knowledge simply cannot neglect these special circumstances and relations. Consequently history of itself will never be able to induce general laws from which it might infer with certainty new facts before they take place. It can at most establish a certain regularity in historical facts which permit probable inferences." (19)

3. Also *philosophy's* mode of approach must be distinguished from both that of history as well as that of the natural sciences. Of course, philosophy also proceeds from the facts of experience in nature and history. It endeavors, however, to understand them not so much from their particular and concrete causes as from the final and general causes. Hence, just as philosophy applies principally the syllogistic method in its mode of argumentation, so historical research prefers proof by means of circumstantial evidence.

There is no doubt then concerning the usefulness and even necessity of historical methodology for the historian as such. If the words of Lord Aston are correct: "The historical method is the doubling of sound human common sense," (20) still it does not mean that the historian can with impunity neglect the rich treasure of methodological directions which arise from the practical experience of thousands of predecessors. *Mutatis mutandis,* the same applies for the ethnologist. (*Cf.* Graebner, p. 5 s.)

c. Preliminary History of the Historico-Ethnological Methodology

For a history of historical methodology we refer to Feder's short but comprehensive survey (pp. 65-82), Herodotus († c. 425), who has been honored with the title, "Father of History," could with the same right be called "Father of Ethnology." (21) However, the first writer of history was really Thucydides († c. 396); later on we have Polybius (c. 210–128). Among the Romans, Sallust (86–35), Livy († 17 A.D.) and

Tacitus (c. 55–119) are well known. The real critical writing of history in the narrower and proper sense of the word began relatively late.

It was only in the eighteenth century (the Maurians at the head) that the new foundations were laid. The specific human, genetical development was more and more recognized as the proper object of all historical research. It was not until the nineteenth and twentieth centuries, however, that historical methodology was fully developed. It might be a consolation for us ethnologists to find that even at present it is not yet considered perfect. (Feder, p. 78.)

Bernheim's *Lehrbuch der historischen Methode und der Geschichtsphilosophie* (20a) is one of the best handbooks or compendia that have appeared. His excellent systematization and his fine sense of justice are universally praised. (Feder, p. 81.) However, it is certainly correct as Feder says: "Only the work, at least in the later editions, manifests a certain verbosity here and there and in the exposition of philosophical concepts a clear and firm position is wanting at times." Being a trained historian, Graebner was well acquainted with Bernheim. Hence, he but naturally based his treatment upon Bernheim. We shall soon return to this matter. Let us here mention only a few of these fundamental rules of Bernheim which can best prepare the way for an historico-*ethnological* methodology and which in this sense, too, were certainly not without influence upon Graebner, who changed over from history as a profession to ethnology.

1, According to Bernheim the preliterates are also the object of history (p. 45 ss., p. 99 s.). "Nonhistorical peoples do not exist." *2,* "The identity of human nature is the *fundamental principle* of historical knowledge. In fact, if there were or ever had been a people or an individual that thought with a logic different from ours, then the history thereof would remain more of a closed book to us than the events in a beehive" (p. 192). *3,* History is not governed by fixed laws, though certain regularities exist (p. 101 ss. p. 159). In the same way the homogeneity of development must be rejected (p. 611). *4,* The historian must always be mindful of the complexity of causal factors (p. 633 ss.). *5,* Naturally on the basis of such ideas and presuppositions the whole tribe of evolutionistic-materialistic orientated ethnologists, sociologists, and culture historians such as Tylor (p. 46), Comte (p. 81), Morgan (p. 610), Lamprecht (p. 81), etc., are rejected in principle and are shelved. He finally characterizes them as a group, thus: "Often data are thrown together without investigating whether they belong to the same time and place and stage of culture; in short, the simplest principles of source criticism do not seem to exist for many ethnological workers of this caliber, whereas they are nowhere more necessary" (p. 610 s.).

Evidently, Graebner could profit from this instruction and receive many inspirations which were decisive for the role he was destined to play in the field of ethnology. As far as the history of our science is concerned, it is very important to keep these connections well in mind. Graebner formally renders account for his borrowing from Bernheim in his introduction (p. 3), where he says: "There is a big gap in the work which is also the cause of the one big seeming incongruency of its methods. It is this that Bernheim, at least in the chapter on combination, emphasizes entirely too much that part of history which rests upon written sources. Even in the history of Europe or better in culture history, many definite conclusions play a great role which entirely or predominantly rest upon the comparison of direct testimony, the so-called 'Survivals' of Bernheim. If we insert into the system those methodical principles which thereby come into use, there follows a perfect coherency. However, a minus remains only for ethnology because the use of contemporary written sources is excluded for the greatest part of its field of research."

That minus, of which Graebner speaks here, confers upon ethnology in comparison with the ordinary historical disciplines, a quite special character, which must eventually find its echo in the method of ethnology as well. Of themselves it is all the same whether the "Survivals" occur among peoples with, or those without, writing. Nevertheless, there is a great and important difference in the matter of method. Dealing with peoples with written documents I can, in general, eventually determine the "Survivals," both chronologically and causally with the help of contemporary written sources. Usually I do not have the same opportunity in the field of ethnology, and that is precisely the minus of which Graebner speaks. In his *Methode der Ethnologie,* Graebner pointed out in detail how and to what extent a reduction of this minus may be effected. He showed that despite this minus, we can with full right speak of an historical ethnology (*i.e.,* grasping of a relative chronology and of causal relations in general on the basis of the elucidation of originally associated culture strata, etc.). The present work, following Graebner, endeavors to demonstrate this fact anew. A complete account of the history of the historico-ethnological method since Graebner, which should be added here, can be found in Chapter I of this work.

(1) *Cf.* W. Schmidt, "Die moderne Ethnologie" *Anthropos;* I (1906), p. 158 ss.; Separataus gabe, p. 158 ss.

(2) *Cf.* H. Ulrich, "Logische Studien zur Methode der Ethnologie" *Anthropos,* XVIII-XIX (1923-1924), p. 454 ss.

(3) See below, p. 33 ss.

(4) W. Schmidt and W. Koppers, *Völker und Kulturen* (Regensburg, 1924), p. 25.

(5) See below, p. 25 s.

(6) See more exhaustive treatment of this below, p. 12 s.

(7) *Cf.* W. Schmidt and W. Koppers, *Völker und Kulturen,* page 20 s.

(8) For the first time in his article, "The Development Hypothesis" in the magazine, *Leader,* May 20, 1852.

(9) Fr. Graebner, *Methode der Ethnologie* (Heidelberg, 1911), page 87 ss.

(10) There is an exhaustive critique of ethnological evolutionism in Graebner, *op. cit.,* p. 88 ss.

(11) In this connection see below, p. 25 ss.

(12) Stuttgart, 1910, p. 283.

(13) H. Pinard had formerly used the term "historico-culturelle," but later makes use of "ethnologico-historique" (*L'Étude comparée des Religions,* third edition, II, p. 250).

(14) P. J. Fr. Lafitau, *Mœurs des sauvages americains compares aux mœurs des premiers temps* (Paris, 1724); *cf.* W. Schmidt and W. Koppers, *Völker und Kulturen,* p. 20; and A. van Gennep, *Religions, Mœurs, et Legendes,* Ve série (Paris, 1914), p. 111-133.

(15) Graebner, *Methode der Ethnologie,* p. 3.

(16) A. Feder, *Lehrbuch der geschichtlichen Methode* (third edition, Regensburg, 1924), p. 19.

(17) Feder treats the concept and possibility of historical certainty very thoroughly and clearly, *op. cit.*, p. 30 ss.

(18) W. Schmidt, "Die moderne Ethnologie," *Anthropos,* I (1906), p. 608 ss., p. 950 ss.; *cf.* also R. Lowie, *Individual Differences and Primitive Culture* (Wien: Schmidt-Festschrift, 1928), p. 495 ss.

(19) Feder, *op. cit.*, p. 39; *cf.* Graebner, p. 3 s.

(20) Not being able to find the original English, I can but give a translation of W. Koppers' version of it.

(20a) Leipzig, 1908.

(21) *Cf.* W. Schmidt and W. Koppers. *Völker und Kulturen* (Regensburg, 1924), p. 6.

Chapter I

OUTLINE HISTORY OF THE GENESIS AND SPREAD OF THE HISTORICAL METHOD IN ETHNOLOGY

1. INSUFFICIENT PRELIMINARY ATTEMPTS

1. WE CAN see from Tylor's attempt to establish objectively both the relations as well as the sequences of culture by means of a statistical method, (1) that the evolutionistic method gradually no longer seemed satisfactory to those very ethnologists who had been such classical exponents of its utility as E. B. Tylor himself (*e.g.,* in the development of the Animistic Theory in his work, *Primitive Culture* [London, 1872]). He demonstrated statistically that certain forms of culture elements appeared relatively often in combination with certain forms of other elements, and from this "*adhesion*" he inferred genetic connection, the direction of which he believed he could likewise determine through further comparison. Graebner has subjected this theory to a detailed criticism in his *Methode der Ethnologie,* (2) to which we can simply refer in this place, since Tylor's theory nowhere gained significant acceptance, and still less did it stimulate its further development. In one part it was mere tautology; in the other part it still adhered to evolutionism, especially in the theory of the unilinear development of the course of evolution. As for the valuable element in it, the establishment of frequent adhesions, Graebner in his *Methode* has already put this in the right context and thus made it productive.

2. The concept of convergence transferred by Thilenius from biology into folklore was especially developed in ethnology by Ehrenreich. (3) It then played for a period a certain role among

those Americanists who, as A. A. Goldenweiser, did not at first take up the historical idea so resolutely as did the great majority of their other colleagues. This convergence designates those cases of similarity which are not to be explained from the common inborn disposition of mankind (elementary idea) nor from historical influence, but from assimilation of originally entirely different elements through the influence exerted by a similar environment. Graebner thinks that this theory "as a supplement to the doctrine of elementary ideas is undoubtedly based upon the evolutionistic method" (p. 95). On the other hand, it stands close to the historical school, because of the methodological consideration of the single case the origin of which must even be checked in the event of a similarity. The theory itself, however, did not have sufficient methodological means at its disposal to establish with objective certainty which of the three putative possibilities fitted the case in question.

3. Graebner cannot designate anyone who at that time occupied himself with this question systematically. The only exception is R. M. Meyer, and he used material from European culture history rather than from ethnology. The most of the criteria proposed by Meyer—agreement by chance, criterion of a great but isolated agreement, agreements on basis of the same causes —Graebner with good reason either rejects or is forced to set them aside as hardly coming into consideration (same causes) for ethnology. And also to the criterion of survival, Graebner concedes but a secondary importance. On the other hand, he admits that the principles of original relationship proposed by Meyer, (4) where a great number of agreements occur, "is actually of decisive importance."(5) We really have here before us the criterion proposed later by Graebner, the so-called criterion of quantity. We shall see later on that in the "criterion of a significant but isolated agreement," we have the criterion of quality conceived in its most extreme form. (6)

4. As H. Pinard has noted, (7) in France A. de Quatrefages (since 1877–1887) has adhered to the principles of the culture historical school in his researches. In the beginning he did not propose the method as such and we cannot see just how far he

was conscious of it. Besides, neither in France nor elsewhere was that of any importance for the further development of ethnology. In France neither the materialism of the leading anthropologists and prehistorians of those days nor the collectivism of the sociological ethnologists were weakened thereby in the least.

2. THE CULTURE HISTORICAL METHOD IN GERMANY AND AUSTRIA

A. Fr. Ratzel and L. Frobenius

1. The first conscious steps toward the formation of a genuine historical method in ethnology were made in Germany and that by Fr. Ratzel of Leipzig, who was in a special way also the founder of anthropogeography. (7a) He declared that all peoples without exception and also the preliterates were "historical" and drew attention to the necessity for research into their history, which to a great extent consisted in migrations. (8) During these migrations peoples and cultures came into contact with each other and thus mutually influenced each other. In his opinion this mutual influence has been exercised to a greater extent than had hitherto been admitted. It has also been the cause of new creations and modifications of culture, and whereever positively established, it makes the assumption of independent origin untenable and superfluous. At any rate, it must be investigated in each single case whether it is a question of external culture contact or inner development.

Graebner (9) well points out how the whole system of unilinear evolution was thereby shaken, and entirely new possibilities of research were disclosed. These possibilities increased still more for this reason, that Ratzel saw no difficulty in admitting external culture contacts also in discontinuous distribution even over the greatest distances. When he found a characteristic likeness between forms, provided that this likeness did not take its origin from the very nature and aim of the object in question, or when material, from the stuff out of which it was made, he postulated an historical and genetic connection of such elements of culture.

Hence, he proposed what is called the *criterion of form or of quality,* which we shall study more closely below (Chapter III). By emphasizing the importance of migration for the history of culture, he became the founder of the Migration Theory, which he applied for the first time in his comparative researches on the (West) African and Melanesian bow. He established characteristic similarities between these bows in the cross section of the bow shaft, in the material and the fastening of the (bow) string and the feathering of the arrow. (10)

It is remarkable, that none of the pupils of Ratzel kept to the new way of the historical method for any length of time, but all sooner or later fell back into the *modus procedendi* of the natural sciences and evolutionism, because none of them was able to carry on the exact painstaking procedure of the master, which the application of this method demands. This first became evident in the case of H. Schurtz and also Fr. Weule, both of whom began their scientific careers with strictly culture historical productions. (11) (12)

2. A third pupil of Ratzel, L. Frobenius, began his work more energetically and on broader lines along the way of the master and in the first impetus he even surpassed him. For he showed that between West Africa and both Indonesia and Melanesia, there were not only agreements between of the bow and arrow, to which Ratzel had drawn attention, but also between masks, houses, drums, clothing, shield form, etc. (13) He thus proved that similarities existed not only between single elements of culture, but also between whole culture complexes and even whole culture circles, so that we have here to reckon not only with migrations of mere individual culture elements but even of entire culture circles. Hence he thereby worked out the second criterion of contact, the *criterion of quantity,* (14) and developed the migration theory of Ratzel to the *theory of culture circles.*

He developed all that in the first part of his method, the "geographical-statistical" part; but in the second part, "the biological" or "developmental and historical," he defends the opinion that each culture with its single elements is determined by nature in its original habitat, so that a dislocation from the native matrix brings with it at least a transformation, often a decomposition. Instead of working out the methodological side of this principle which is correct in itself, Frobenius turns to the contents and thereby falls into matters and modes of thinking of the natural sciences pure and simple. Already in the paper, "Die naturwissenschaftliche Kulturlehre," (15) which appeared between his two practical articles mentioned above (p. 26, note 13), and which he intended to form the theoretical foundation for both of them, he, fully in accord with the title, again abandoned the historical character of ethnology and in plain words openly defended "the application of the doctrine of descent as we have learned it from Darwin and his school." Also in his later works, especially, "Paideuma, Umrisse einer Kultur- und Seelenlehre" (München, 1921), he presents ever more energetically a "biology" of culture, according to which, culture is a thing for itself. Man is the carrier of culture and not the creator. Culture has its own biological phases of development; namely, childhood, youth, maturity, old age, and for these stages the material environment is of the highest importance. And also his endeavor to establish a "morphology of culture" only imperfectly attains its otherwise justified goal because he leans too much upon the natural sciences.

Graebner has pointed out in a lengthy criticism what was lacking in the first theory that Frobenius proposed. (16) We can content ourselves with a reference thereto, as Frobenius himself has regretted these works as a kind of "sins of youth" with a formal *"pater peccavi,"* (see later, note 18). Recently however, with a reiterated opposite *"pater peccavi,"* (17) he has endeavored to join hands again with the culture historical school and to claim his share in its method. We have already shown (p. 26) how far his share is of real worth.

B. Fr. Graebner, B. Ankerman, W. Foy and W. Schmidt

1. A few years went by before any new steps were taken for the further formation of a new method out of the critical synthesis in the preliminary works of Ratzel and Frobenius.

That was done with singular insight and comprehensive method in the two lectures which the two, at that time assistants at the Berlin Ethnological Museum (Museum für Völkerkunde), held at the meeting of the Anthropological Society of Berlin on November 14, 1904. The material for these lectures was taken from the rich stores of this fine museum. These lectures were published in the *Zeitschtift für Ethnologie:* Fr. Graebner, "Kulturkreise und Kulturschichten in Ozeania" ("Circles and Strata of Culture in Oceania") (*op. cit.,* p. 28 s.) and B. Ankerman, "Kulturkreise und Kulturschichten in Afrika" ("Circles and Strata of Culture in Africa") (*op. cit.,* p. 54 ss.). They worked out a number of such circles in both areas mentioned, settled their relative temporal succession as culture strata, and pointed out the historical relations between the appearance of these culture circles and culture strata in Oceania and Africa. All that was accomplished without any recourse to evolutionary theories, and only with the help of those criteria alone which already Ratzel and Frobenius had applied, but here they were used with much more prudence and system. The discussion following upon these two lectures was not at all what their great importance deserved. Frobenius was present at the time, and during the discussion he disowned all his previous productions (18) in every respect, so that Graebner and Ankerman became all the more the legitimate representatives of the new movement.

2. The new movement was soon joined by W. Foy, the Director of the Ethnological Museum in Cologne. Graebner became his assistant later on, and after the death of Foy succeeded him in this position. Foy had collected very extensive material for a series of his own works and had worked out broad plans for the enlistment of new helpers for the *Culture Historical Library (Kulturhistorische Bibliothek)* (printed by the C. Winter Co., Heidelberg) which he had founded, the first ethnological series of which was to have been headed by Graebner's *Methode der Ethnologie.* This series, however, came to an end after the war and the death of Foy. In his museum he had previously founded the magazine *Ethnologica,* in which a series of culture historical investigations by himself and Graebner appeared.

3. About the same time W. Schmidt came in close contact with the new school which he had come to know through the results of work on the languages in Oceania, Australia, and Southeast Asia. In the magazine *Anthropos,* which he had founded in the meantime (1906), he took up a position of positive criticism for the progress of the school and in this magazine Graebner's "Melanesian Bow Culture" ("Melanesische Bogenkultur") also appeared. This article for the first time worked out the culture circle idea over the whole earth. In a critical supplement to the application of the culture circle idea, Schmidt likewise gave a lecture in Berlin in 1913 in the Anthropological Society of Berlin (Berliner Gesellschaft für Anthropologie) entitled, "Culture Circles and Culture Strata in South America" ("Kulturkreise und Kulturschichten in Südamerika"). (19) Through this lecture also this third large territory of the primitives was encompassed by the new movement.

4. In 1911, Graebner published his work, *Die Methode der Ethnologie (The Method of Ethnology)* (20) in which he followed his previous studies, but developed them far beyond their original scope. This work introduced the culture historical method for the first time and explained its fundamental principles and systematically applied it on all sides.

Seldom has a new fundamental work been produced all at once in such a firmly concentrated composite whole. Like Minerva sprung from the head of Jove, so was almost the case with Graebner. Already in 1905 in the introduction to the lecture mentioned above, he writes: "[Frobenius] sought and thought he found a method, through which the problems of ethnology may be solved with exactness, and culture relations may be grasped with clarity and certainty; I am groping after traces of culture relations."(21) Also after the appearance of his book he was certainly not of the opinion that the method proposed therein was definitely settled once and for all. In the polemic that arose concerning the book he emphasizes "that neither I nor any of the others who follow the same way believe they have now found *the* true method! We are fully conscious that the method must develop, and we are therefore grateful for every criticism which does not begin with apriorisms." (22)

That all the studies worked out according to this method contribute in turn to the perfecting of the method itself, I have already pointed out at the end of my review of Graebner's work. (23) As I remarked there I wish to add here: "It shall ever remain the merit of Graebner to have laid the foundation for this method to a great extent by himself and to have for the first time and systematically proposed and demonstrated the method as such. I hardly know of a single event in the history of the last fifty years of ethnology that could be compared with it." We shall see later on that in all the further developments of the culture historical method the foundations laid by Graebner not only remained firm, but also continually gave evidence of inner vitality.

5. The greatest part of the criticisms that have been passed upon the culture historical method and its results were not especially well founded, and so far as they were at all well founded, they would hardly be designated as positively constructive. It was principally attacked by M. Haberlandt in several articles in *Petermann's Mitteilungen,* to which Foy and Graebner replied in the same magazine. The whole discussion came to a climax in the encounter that occurred at the general meeting of the Anthropological Society of Germany and Vienna (Tagung der Deutschen und der Wiener Anthropologischen Gesellschaft) at Heilbronn in August 1918, and where Ankerman, Schmidt, and Czekanowsky (Foy and Graebner were not present) represented the culture historical school, while Ehrenreich, Haberlandt, senior and junior, and Kremer stood in opposition to it, the last group not forming a united front however. (24) At that gathering the culture historical method was criticized by Haberlandt, the others openly acknowledging its excellence, only criticized some of the results of researches that had been undertaken according to the method. Not one of the critics was able to propose some other system which was better or even equal to the one they criticized. In fact, not a single compact system was suggested as a substitute.

c. Exposition and Criticism of Krause's Structure Theory

We must here acknowledge one exception in this respect, where an earnest attempt was really made to oppose the culture historical movement with something original and positive. That is the "theory of structure" ("Strukturlehre") of Fritz Krause. He states that these ideas had occurred to him already in 1912 but were first published in 1921. Since then small publications of from two to four pages have appeared year after year, in which the different parts of the system are treated without a set order. Only in 1929 was the lecture, "Change of Culture and Nationality" ("Kulturwandel und Volkstum") published in the "Mitteilungen" (25) of the Anthropological Society of Vienna, which he had delivered at a meeting of the society. He himself says of it: "The principles of the structure theory are presented *for the first time as a whole* in this sketch, even though it be from a particular standpoint." This has also till now remained the best and the longest exposition, but even as such cannot be compared with the comprehensive and solid exposition in Graebner's *Methode der Ethnologie.* Since then but very small summaries have appeared in Krause's publication, "Völkerkunde–Anthropologie–Ethnobiologie" (26) and in a short article "Ethnology and the Study of Culture Changes." (27)

This whole new system of Krause arose, as he himself says, not so much as a criticism of the culture historical method itself (he hardly mentions it) as of a product of it; namely, the doctrine of culture circles (Kulturkreislehre), but unhappily from a total misunderstanding of it. He writes: "The structure theory grew out of the criticism of the theory of culture circles and in particular of its proposal of the culture circle as a complex of culture elements, *which are not bound together by any inner connection.* (28) If you wish to establish culture circles, you must previously investigate the culture elements critically with regard to their mutual independence. But the culture circle school has failed to supply us with such investigations. Since 1912, in attempting to make up for this neglect, I became gradually more and more convinced of extensive world-wide mutual connections between culture elements." (29)

A more gross misunderstanding could hardly have happened to anyone than that which befell Krause in the passage I have italicized above. He principally criticizes my explanation in "Völker und Kulturen" (p. 70). There I wrote that in order to deduce a conclusive criterion of quantity from the individual similarities of culture, which appear between two or more regions, and thereby be able to demonstrate an earlier historical connection, the necessity of mutual necessary sequence must be excluded. For if the last mentioned were the case, then there would not be a conclusive criterion of quantity deducible, *i.e.,* a sufficiently large number of independent single criteria of form or quality. (30) Still it is clear that we were speaking there of a logical connection, which is not supposed to be the case here; these independent elements are called heterogeneous in so far as a material implement is heterogeneous to a social organization, victuals to a myth, etc. I have expressly said immediately on the following page (p. 71) that "also according to the culture circle school the single elements must belong together organically," as I speak there of "an organic whole comprising all the exigencies of the life of the people, a culture circle," from which "no part can be omitted without harming an essential demand." (31)

It certainly gives one cause to doubt when a whole new system has begun on the basis of a great misunderstanding. In fact, that is essentially the only thing with which Krause has reproached the culture circle school; for when he makes the criticism that it does not consider human beings, the carriers of culture, but only the culture in its single elements; that is, as I have already said above (p. 5), incorrect, or at least applicable to but a few of the representatives of the culture circle school. But even these are not essentially at fault ,because at the beginning of the investigation a great deal of analytical work must be done, which naturally begins with the single elements. Then of course all the ingredients must be synthetically united to restore the living whole again.

However, there is some justification for the criticism which Krause expresses here, not on the nature of the doctrine of culture circles, but rather on certain representatives who make *only* analyses and almost *always* investigate *only* the individual relations and thus often neglect the thing related. Wherever there really is a whole individual people or a culture province, it must be admitted as a totality, together with the inner relations also, which bind the single elements together. Krause has given valuable clues for the discovery of such inner combinations, so that his "theory of structure" forms a welcome complement to the culture historical method. (32)

But for any kind of deeper comprehension of the elements and changes of culture, especially for a better understanding of greater depths of time, the "theory of structure" is incompetent, and in this respect remains far behind the culture historical method, so that the structure theory could not by any means be considered a substitute for the culture historical method. Krause is wise enough to see that and honest enough to say so himself. He writes: "Beginning with the assumption that the present structure is not an invariable given fact, but is the last historical member of an historical series, let us attempt *to grasp it historically* (33) by undertaking an investigation of the processes of change which produced the present form. In so doing we draw upon: *1,* historical sources (34) (if there are any); *2,* investigations of genealogies; *3,* legends and myths, which reflect a more ancient culture; *4,* investigation of the facts of the culture itself, observing carefully single structure elements and separating the native and the alien elements; *5,* lastly prehistoric finds and excavations in so far as these have been undertaken." (35)

One must assume that Krause will sometime further develop these means of his for historical investigation enumerated here, with a more extensive exposition of his structure theory, which until now has been lacking. For otherwise it would have to be said that these historical methods are lacking throughout in quality as well as quantity. They do not offer any methodological means whatsoever for the objective demonstration of historical contacts in space, and they do not say at all how the two-dimensional character of the ethnological facts might be given depth in time, at least that time depth needed to penetrate beyond the peoples which have written history. Krause himself notices this and admits it, for he continues: "And so, through wearisome work we discover perhaps *one* (36) older cultural structure and with it *one* (36) change of culture. . . . I do not believe that we shall succeed in making more than one such discovery perhaps at the most two steps backwards; *i.e.,* we shall be able to discover at the very most one to two more ancient cultures of a people." (37)

By these words Krause himself has passed judgment on the worth of the structure theory for historical investigation. Happily besides Krause the theorist there stands Krause the practical investigator, or better, the latter surpassed the former. And his practical studies on the ancient Californians and the North American prairie Indians is an excellent example of historical investigation, which only for its full completion still requires some culture historical training in a more conscious systematic application of the principles of methodological investigation, in order to penetrate into historical depths of many millenia.

In one of these studies, "Zur Besiedlungsgeschichte der Nordamerikanischen Prärie" (38) he himself says that it was made "with the most cautious utilization of the method of the culture circle school." When, however, he further remarks that "this method draws its conclusions *only* from the geographical distribution of the culture elements," it has done so quantitatively no more than every other reasonable method of procedure, but qualitatively it alone, contrary to the opinion of Krause, offers the methodical means to put forward something certain "concerning the age and the origin of such a culture phenomenon." (39)

In the second study, "Die Kultur der Kalifornischen Indianer in ihrer Bedeutung für die Ethnologie und die Nordamerikanische Völkerkunde," (40) it is very much to be regretted that he became all the more entangled in the misunderstanding of the culture historical method. His whole cloudy conception then manifests itself also when he continues: "I am convinced that both modes of inquiry together with the methods joined to them are justified in their particular field of investigation for the time being"; and he believes he has found the possibility "to unite the two methods of investigation, the historical and the evolutionistic, to a common method of research." Since, however, evolutionism has no method at all to offer, *i.e.,* in the only correct meaning of a proposal of systematical means for objective and assured demonstrations, the combination with it is useless and even more a hindrance. But we can see how far away from a clear formulation of his own "theory of structure" Krause still was in 1921, since he did not once allude to it and instead he recommends a questionable coalition between evolutionism and historicism.

Concerning the practical working out of his work on "Die Kultur der Kalifornischen Indianer," it is gratifying to find that there has been very little influence felt from those theories. And what is more, the evolutionistic mode of inquiry and solution is gradually but progressively set forth as untenable and inadequate. In a fundamental and ever more extensive mode of inquiry of a culture historical kind into "where from," Krause was forced to admit that also for California the question "why" in decisive points is not to be solved from California alone, but that far-reaching historical relations of the ancient Californians with other regions have to be taken into consideration. (41) If he had investigated these relations further, he would have discovered at that time a real culture circle, the North American primeval culture.

Much later, in 1932, (42) he speaks of culture provinces "which cultural-historical and archaeological-prehistorical research have laid bare," and he adds the remark, *"Only far-reaching research of such historical depth* (43) enables us to grasp fully the culture of an individual people." (44) Since Krause here considers "far-reaching research" toward significant historical depths as necessary already for the full understanding of the culture of even *one single* people, he agrees with a fundamental principle of the culture historical method. But since, according to Krause's own confession in 1929, (45) his structure theory was not able to penetrate into such historical depths, there remains nothing else than to take up the culture historical method which does possess a method and means for so doing.

I close the critical review of Krause's structure theory with two conclusions: *1*, the culture historical method does well to make use of the structure theory for the ethnological preliminary work and also further for the establishment of certain culture relations of juxtaposition in space; *2*, however, the structure theory must apply the culture historical method for the solution of the critical question of the attainment of greater historical depths and therewith of deeper causal successions. (46)

3. THE HISTORICAL METHOD OF ETHNOLOGY IN NORTH AMERICA

A. In General

1. Outside of Germany and Austria there is no country in which from a certain point of time so much has been written about the method of ethnology as in America. This period begins, it is true, sometime after the appearance of the culture historical method in Germany and Austria. But after this question as to a method corresponding to the historical character of ethnology had once been raised, it has never since been laid aside. However, there are hardly two authors in the whole country who agree even on fundamental principles. The exceptionally meager end result is that up till now they have not yet perfected a detailed historical method, which might also be generally recognized and applied by even a small group of ethnologists. That is all the more remarkable, since the rejection of evolutionism, if it did not begin earlier, was certainly generally accepted sooner and more energetically than even in Germany and Austria. Consequently, evolutionism can muster hardly a single adherent among the ethnologists of North America, while on the other hand the conversion to historicism took place in a correspondingly decisive and comprehensive manner.

2. I have treated of these events quite exhaustively in my

two studies, "Die kulturhistorische Methode und die nordamerikanische Ethnologie" (47) and "Die Abwendung von Evolutionismus und die Hinwendung zum Historizismus in der Amerikanistik." (48) In the first I refuted the criticism which had been made by two American ethnologists, Fr. Boas (49) and A. L. Kroeber, on the culture historical method, or rather on the culture circles worked out according to it, and pointed out that this criticism rested upon deep-going ignorance of this method and these culture circles. I have also pointed out in the same article that Boas himself does not succeed in formulating a penetrating and comprehensive method for ethnology, and that Kroeber in all frankness confesses this lack in North American ethnology and its consequent negative position and deeply laments its harmful effects.

In the second study I treated of the North American Americanists, R. H. Lowie, A. A. Goldenweiser, and E. Sapir. I will come back to the first and last of these three later (p. 71, p. 38). Goldenweiser, (50) even though he of all the American ethnologists does indeed emphasize psychological points of view most strongly, nevertheless he rejects emphatically both the old and the new evolutionism. He did not, however, propose an historical method of his own. Even if he passes criticism on attempts at solution of Ratzel and Graebner, still his distance from them does not seem to be too great.

3. A short but instructive exposition of the peculiarities and groups of the North American ethnologists is given by R. H. Lowie in his article, "Theoretische Ethnologie in Amerika." (51) Somewhat later P. Radin published his article, "History of Ethnological Theories" (52) in which, of course, America is considered in stepmotherly fashion, only with a strong criticism of Fr. Boas. This article is a precursor to a book of the same author, *The Method and Theory of Ethnology,* (53) in which then this neglect is richly made up for. We shall treat of this exhaustively later on (p. 54 ss.). Mitra Panchanan offers an exposition in his *History of American Anthropology* (54) which goes back to the earliest time of North American ethnology. He gives interesting, little-known

facts from those earlier times and he is also well informed on the rejection of evolutionism by the more recent North American ethnologists and their conversion to historicism, but he was not able to report the attainment of a full historical method outside that of Clark Wissler, whose pupil Mitra Panchanan is. We shall discuss this method further below (p. 47 ss.).

In the following we shall present, in chronological sequence of their appearance, the more important works, in which the earnest struggle of the North American ethnologists for a method corresponding to their science appears.

B. E. Sapir

One of the best attempts, the first in order chronologically (in many respects it has not been equaled by any of the succeeding), was received in silence. This is E. Sapir's "Time Perspective in Aboriginal American Culture, a Study in Method." (55) He declares the previous "psychological" treatment of ethnology unsatisfactory; he is desirous of adopting "a thoroughly historical method of interpretation" and goes straight to the central problem: "How inject a chronology into this confusing mass of purely descriptive facts?"

He divides the proofs for a chronology into two main classes: direct and indirect. He quickly passes over the first "documentary evidence, native testimony, stratified archaeological testimony" (pp. 5-10) in order to be able thus to dwell longer upon the indirect. Of these he treats first those formed by the inner connection of the cultural elements. In this his views are practically identical with Krause's structure theory (pp. 15-25). He dwells longest on the external geographical distribution, which he designates as "in many ways the most powerful." He takes the distribution of the single elements seriatim and then the "culture areas," followed by the culture strata. At first he presents the less difficult case, that of the continuous distribution of the culture elements, where he states and substantiates a number of useful rules, not all of which are found in Graebner. Then he proceeds to discontinuous distribution and openly grants that a considerable number of historical associations have been without doubt established in what is now discontinuous distribution.

Unfortunately he here begins at the same time as the polemic against Graebner the discussion of "culture areas," toward which he takes a very skeptical attitude, leading up to the disappointment which he himself has foreseen: "Our rapid view of the concepts of culture area and culture stratum may seem rather disappointing." In fact, since he always sees but single cultural elements (criterion of quality) and is not acquainted with the application of the criterion of quantity, he does not know how to give certainty to his "culture areas" and entangles himself in fruitless abstract difficulties. Naturally, he now remains all the farther from the establishment of culture strata and thereby loses the proper means for penetrating into greater historical depths.

The disparaging remarks which he makes against Graebner and myself cannot but point to the astounding fact that, five years after the publication of Graebner's *Methode,* such an outstanding ethnologist as Sapir, who so intensively concerns himself with the method of ethnology, had not yet read this important work (which we must certainly assume, if we do not wish to come to even less gratifying conclusions). Consequently, his criticism of Graebner is worthless. It is not to be wondered at that he does not come anywhere near the goal grasped and attained by Graebner, since he himself must confess that he could not even attain to historical depths of but little importance. (56).

c. W. D. Wallis

1. One year after Sapir, an American ethnologist entered the discussion, who thereafter took up his pen frequently: W. D. Wallis. He begins with a short article, "Similarities in Culture." (57) It is not a happy beginning, since at the very opening of his article we find the statement, in which he, starting out from Goldenweiser's rule of "limited possibilities" which lead to convergence, continues (page 42): "Thus convergence is assured, provided we can discover the limiting conditions plus the inevitable choice." Naturally, the correct statement

should be: Neither convergence nor historical contact can objectively be proved under such conditions, provided that not another, independent reason can be adduced for the one or for the other." All considerations which he then advances from the different regions of ethnology suffer from the aforesaid error in logic, entirely apart from the fact that among them a great number of the cases he gives certainly do not admit explanation by convergence.

Together with Sapir, Wallis recognizes also criteria for historical borrowing, and indeed *both* the criterion of quality in the words: "So far as the resemblances rest in nonessential and detachable features they imply borrowing" (p. 50), as well as the criterion of quantity which he calls the criterion "of accumulated accidental features" (p. 51). But then he falls into a skepticism which he only superficially justifies, when he says: "No conclusion with regard to independent origin or borrowing will in the end, where there is absence of historical documentary proof, be more than tentative. The correspondence may be of such kind that independent origin seems precluded and historical continuity must be assumed. But it is, after all, only assumed" (p. 52). Naturally, what is "assumed" remains "assumed"; but when "independent origin" is *really* excluded, then historical contact is not "assumed," but rather logically and legitimately inferred.

2. Still shorter is the author's article, "Diffusion As a Criterion of Age." (58) He recognizes external diffusion as an important factor in the history of culture, but he denies that a criterion of age can be derived from geographic distribution. All the reasons he gives against it are directed against rules set up by Clark Wissler (59) (and A. L. Kroeber), which proceed from the presupposition that the district of the most intensive development of a cultural element is always the place of origin, and that the more distant an element is from this place, the older it is. These criticisms, as we shall see later (p. 42 s.) are justified to a great extent; but these rules are not the only means for the determination of ethnological age. Graebner's *Methode* with the means given therein is still unknown to Wallis in 1925.

Therefore, we need not wonder so much over such sentences as the following: "We cannot infer age from distribution unless wise enough to make the inference at the proper historical moment, and, unless we have history at our service we shall not know the proper moment for making the inference. In the absence of history, then, we can make no such inference for we are as likely to make the wrong one as the right one" (pp. 98-99). The whole criticism is completely negative, if not really destructive, and Wallis makes no attempt at all to give a constructive solution himself.

A third article of Wallis's, "Magnitude of Distribution, Centrifugal Spread, and Centripetal Elaboration of Culture Traits," (60) is not much longer nor better. Besides Clark Wissler, he opposes here also Fr. Boas, whom he thus satirizes: "The principle that the more widely distributed traits are the older is correct if properly used, he says, but it must not be used incorrectly. This seems equivalent to be stating that it is true when it is true and false when it is false, but gives us no inkling of when it is true and when it is false" (p. 758; similarly, p. 763). Furthermore, the article does not bring anything essentially new. Wallis recognizes that himself; for he cites a great number of sentences verbatim from his article of 1925 in the same magazine (thus, [1929] pp. 756-757; [1925] pp. 96, 98, 99; [1929] pp. 764, 765; [1925] pp. 96, 97) without designating them as quotations. This article remains entirely negative.

3. For some time I was under the impression that Wallis would not advance beyond the stage of negative criticism because he presented small articles, which naturally do not for the most part have the deeper and broader foundation required for a positive construction. However, shortly after, Wallis published an extensive work, *Culture and Progress* (61) which unfortunately as a matter of fact I only learned to know in the summer of 1936 through the kind instrumentality of Mr. Clyde Kluckhohn. My eagerness to see how he had treated the problems of ethnological method that interest us here was understandably great. It was actually soon evident that the greater part of the book was not devoted to the research and

exposition of the method of the history of culture, but treated of the history of culture itself and, especially, of an important element of it, progress. Still, several chapters of the first part, "Culture and Culture Change" (pp. 1-200), indicate by their titles that they are meant to be an introduction, with methodics being given serious consideration. The titles of this first part are: "Culture Areas and Culture Traits," "Methods of Inferring Culture Development," "The Diffusion of Culture Traits," "Independent Origins of Similar Culture Traits."

I regret to confess that our hopes have not been fulfilled by a closer examination. The negative attitude is continued here in part in more or less justified criticism of Tylor's Adherence theory (p. 36 ss.), on Sapir's "Time Perspective" (p. 46 ss.), and the theories of Wissler and Kroeber (p. 55 ss.). That no essential advance was attained or aimed at here is seen clearly from the fact that the entire third chapter, "Magnitude of Distribution, Centrifugal Spread, and Centripetal Elaboration of Culture Traits" (pp. 63-76) is nothing else but a word for word copying from the article of the same name in the *American Anthropologist* (1929) with some literary additions and some new examples. This article as already shown above (p. 41) is again partly a copy of an article from 1925. This double origin is not pointed out in this case either. And so also "Chapter VII. Independent Origins of Similar Culture Traits" (pp. 149-166) is only an enlargement of the article "Similarities in Culture," likewise from the *American Anthropologist* (1917). (*Cf.* Wallis, "Culture and Progress," p. 150, and *Amer. Anthrop.* [1917], p. 41 ss.; "Culture and Progress," p. 154 ss., and *Amer. Anthrop.* [1917], p. 45 ss.; "Culture and Progress," p. 160 ss., and *Amer. Anthrop.* [1917], p. 51 ss.)

In Chapter VII Graebner is also briefly mentioned, elsewhere not at all; on page 149 it is falsely stated that "Graebner and his followers ascribe *all* close resemblances between culture traits to diffusion." This is repeated on page 160, where this opinion is also ascribed to Rivers. Although in other cases the references from other authors are given very exactly with all their sources, in Graebner's case that is considered superfluous. Therefore we can well suppose that, although on page 453 Graebner's *Methode der Ethnologie* is also numbered among the "References for Further Reading," Wallis has neither read nor studied it himself. Hence, it is understandable that he lacked the strongest stimulus to take up a position with regard to questions of ethnological methodics both before and after and so also his larger work did not get beyond the stage of negative criticism.

D. F. E. Clements, H. E. Driver and A. L. Kroeber

1. Under the title, "A New Objective Method for Showing Special Relationships" (62) Forest E. Clements (with the co-operation of Sara M. Schenck and T. K. Brown) published a treatise to show the historical relations of elements and groups to each other with the aid of statistics. Therein is calculated that number of correspondences among the uniformities which would be expected according to the law of probabilities. For the details of the complicated procedure we must refer to the essay itself. By its very nature such a statistical undertaking cannot of itself produce anything new, but only brings into strong relief the presence of certain cultural relations of spatial juxtaposition with greater exactness and objectivity. Clements himself well determines, as we shall presently see, the other limits of this method.

W. D. Wallis opposes this venture also with one of his negative critiques in his article, "Probability and the Diffusion of Culture Traits." (63) Clements responded thereto in his article, "Quantitative Method in Ethnography," (64) in which he considers the value and limits of his manner of proceeding more in detail. Moreover, he well defends it against the abstract logical objections of Wallis. He summarizes its applicability in four points (p. 308). *1.* This method is for use only in showing the existence or nonexistence of special relationships between subareas within an area of fairly homogeneous culture. 2. The traits utilized must constitute a representative sample of the culture wholes in each of the subareas which are to be studied; all phases of culture should be equally represented for each subarea. *3.* All traits must be reduced to simplest units, or analyzed into such; by this method complex or generic traits are automatically weighted. *4.* The statistical method will only show positive or negative correlations. For a more definite explanation, especially of the direction of the correlations, we must look for help from other methods. (65)

This statistical procedure can therefore only determine the relations of spatial juxtaposition, and these only within certain limits, but no relations of chronological succession, no time periods. For the first point Clements makes some very good remarks on the significance of the compound criterion of quality which already contains a criterion of quantity (p. 302 s.); on this matter see below (p. 147 s.). In an article, "Plains Indians Tribal Correlations with the Sun Dance Data," (66) Clements makes use of the data given in the well-known study of Spier, "The Sun Dance of the Plains Indians: Its Developments and Diffusion," (67) in order to allow the results already obtained by Spier to appear with still greater clarity and exactness and more in detail.

2. This is the place to add a short review of another statistical attempt at presentation of cultural relations, which H. E. Driver and A. L. Kroeber published in their article, "Quantitative Expression of Cultural Relationships." (68) Here the attempts of Clements (Schenck, Brown) on Linton's data on Polynesia and on Spier's data on the "sun dance" are first checked with the new procedure, then an application of it is carried out with Kroeber's investigation on the southern tribes of northwestern America, and W. Tessmann's investigation of the tribes of northeastern Peru. It is not possible to treat all the particulars of this statistical venture here, as they are too technical. However, it will be of interest to consider the general conclusions, to which the two authors came, which hold good by and large for all these and other similar statistical methods (p. 255): "In culture history studies, statistical treatment by the method of presence and absence of unit traits is ancillary to the nonstatistical methods in use. Statistical results can never be better than the data, whose value depends on the

ethnological competence with which they are collected and analyzed.

"To a large extent trait-count computations merely corroborate the ordinary ethnological findings made by students who know their field comparatively. . . . On the other hand, statistical treatment usually expresses results more precisely and definitely. In all cases examined it also indicates greater or less correctness of the ethnological interpretations."

It might still be doubtful whether these corrections would not have even then been impossible, if the ethnological interpretations had avoided certain methodological mistakes which could have been recognized as such without statistics. Still we must recognize the undoubted advantage of statistical treatment; namely, the more precise and more definite and to some extent more objective manner of exposition. But with this advantage must also be balanced a danger into which it threatens to collapse, because, for the purpose of comparison, it necessitates the dissolution of all the cultural elements into the smallest possible units, which are then no longer of the same value not only for the real cultural life, but also for methodological force of the argument. Driver and Kroeber also recognize (69) this danger here, but know of no way to avoid it. It is the danger that the cultural life be presented in a distorted uniformity, which especially does not allow the differences and transitions which make for individuality to receive their full value.

Hence it follows that a statistical method should not be applied alone. This is but natural since this method only makes assertions concerning the spatial relations, but disregards the chronological and causal conditions, the temporal and causal sequences. This is confirmed by the procedure of Driver and Kroeber in the estimation of the age succession which Tessmann has proposed for the cultures of northeastern Peru. (70)

E. J. H. Steward

In his short article, "Diffusion and Independent Invention: a Critique of Logic," (71) J. H. Steward intends to give only the philosophico-logical bases for deciding the question: Independent origin or borrowing? He formulates the result in the following principles (p. 493 ss.):

1. The probability of independent invention is directly proportionate to the difficulty of communication between the two localities, in which there are identical culture elements, to which the factors: geographical accessibility, means of transportation, intertribal relations, and cultural receptivity must be proportionately reckoned.—This corresponds somewhat with the criterion of quantity of the culture historical method (see later, p. 154 s.).

1a. The probability of independent invention is inversely proportionate to the number of traits shared by the two localities.—Steward himself rightly calls this the "quantitative criterion."

1b. The probability of independent invention is inversely proportionate to the elapsed time since the appearance of the trait in either locality—because the amount of communication between the localities is, other things equal, a function of time.

2. The probability of independent invention is directly proportionate to the "uniqueness of the element." Steward himself grants that this uniqueness is the most difficult problem to determine. There is even the danger that here conversely an element which speaks for borrowing, namely, the criterion of quality, which is nowhere advanced by Steward, is here mistaken for just the opposite and interpreted in the opposite sense.

3. The probability of independent invention is inversely proportionate to the probability of derivation from a common ancestral culture, the latter itself being proportionate to the number of elements shared by the two localities.—This is also a form of the criterion of quantity.

In order to ward off from the very beginning unfavorable criticism which might underestimate the proportion of truth and certainty attained by him in his principles stated in terms of "probability," Steward very fittingly recalls that the most exact scientific laws also are philosophically but statements of high probabilities. (72)

To sum up, we see that also the rules and results of Steward concern themselves only with the establishment of culture relations in spatial juxtaposition. The more important and more difficult undertaking, the establishment of time successions, is only touched in 1b. But all in all, and if we take into consideration that Steward only wanted to give the philosopico-logical foundation for the solution of the problem in question, Steward's study with all its brevity is one of the main methodological achievements in North American ethnology. One should wish that Steward would either develop his article more systematically with the co-operation of an ethnologist or make himself better acquainted with ethnological facts and carry out the further development of it himself.

F. CLARK WISSLER

While the majority of the contributions for the solution of the problem of finding a correct method for ethnology treated up till now consisted of only small articles, which naturally could not therefore completely settle these questions, we now meet an outstanding American ethnologist, who, like Sapir, wrote a special work on this subject. The ethnologist in question is Clark Wissler and his book, *The Relation of Nature to Man in Aboriginal America.* (73) Considering the high position that Wissler holds with regard to American ethnology, or rather ethnography of a long list of North American tribes whose culture he thoroughly investigated and published in exhaustive monographs, we could rightly take up his book with justified expectations. He himself also emphasizes that many readers turn with chagrin and disgust from ethnological literature because everywhere the authors were guessing and pyramiding one guess upon the other; that such a method is no longer defensible and that a method must be found that will bring certitude (p. 45).

It is all the more surprising then that Wissler, when he now advances to the solution of this problem, without further ado and without previous research work into the single facts, more or less a priori, allows the independent invention of so many objects, such as feather mosaics (which are supposed to be copying of birds [p. 57]), lip plug and ear mutilation (p. 66), age classes (p. 102), and all of these merely out of "internal" evidences and "elementary ideas." In the course of his book he increasingly keeps us in suspense until at last he promises us a single means that is to enable us to reconstruct the genesis of a cultural element (p. 177).

He then proceeds to present this law, that ethnological trends tend to diffuse uniformly *in all directions* from their centers while formerly there was a tendency among ethnologists to look upon this diffusion as linear, allowing the diffusion to be carried in but one direction. This is the migration concept and was formerly the only kind of diffusion postulated, but in the last millenia its role has not been of such special importance (pp. 183, 186). He is so convinced of the importance of his new "law" as to affirm "that we have laid our hands upon something fundamental" (p. 187). He himself makes some objections; to wit, that neither the peyote cult nor the diffusion of the horse radiated from the middle of their region of distribution (p. 192 ss.). But he nevertheless continues to assert that "the most promising method in cultural chronology is to work out the detailed distribution mechanically and then, with this hypothetical interpretation before one, critically check it with the available data as to structural relation in the couples and by correlations with other trait-couples" (p. 199). For him the center of maximum achievement is the central area (p. 205); the marginal forms are the most primitive and the original basic forms of which the richer complexes were evolved at the centers of distribution. Furthermore, there is not only a coincidence between distribution centers for culture traits, but also between these and the geographic centers of a faunal area as well (p. 215). Summarizing it all he states: "Centers of distribution for the constituent traits will fall in the heart of the ecological area," and the final causes of a culture and its spatial distribution are in his opinion geography and ecology (p. 216).

It is hardly believable that an ethnologist of such standing as Wissler could ascribe such a universal importance to one single principle; we should have to designate that as onesidedness and poverty, even if the principle were to a certain extent correct, which it certainly is not. An equal radiating diffusion from one center would then only be possible—and merely possible then—if the external conditions of communication and the inner conditions of receptivity and inclination of men were the same in all these radiating circles, which of course is never the case. In fact, the difference of diffusion ability in the different groups of peoples is left entirely unconsidered; this ability is a factor which must undoubtedly be taken seriously into account along with the geography and the ecology of a district.

And so this methodological criterion is practical only in a very limited and conditioned degree. However, with Wissler we do not find any other time measurements but this single one. In this close and absolute dependence upon geographical and ecological factors Wissler stands very near to Frobenius; hence, the same criticism applies to him as well (*cf.* above, p. 27).

G. R. B. DIXON

A good criticism of Wissler's theory is given by Roland B. Dixon in his book, *The Building of Cultures,* (74) which is almost entirely devoted to the methodology of ethnology. The criticism of the ecological part of Wissler's theory is given in detail on page 22 ss. In pages 67-105 he yet more exhaustively treats Wissler's theory of concentric zoned diffusion, the weakness of which he also shows by a very instructive study on the distribution of the kinds of double outrigger canoes. There follows (pp. 105-155) a very penetrating discussion of continuous and discontinuous diffusion of single culture elements, well illustrated by a list of concrete examples (pp. 105-166). After this an entire chapter (V) is given to the diffusion of the trait complexes (pp. 156-181), in which we already find occasional attacks upon the "diffusionist" method.

In Chapter VI, "Culture Parallels," he then begins the decisive discussion of the "diffusionists" and the school opposing them. From the very beginning there can be no doubt as to which side is preferred. He unfavorably characterizes the former to such a degree as to be unjust and distorting while he graciously favors the latter (182): "The one grasping at similarities, tries to establish thereby links in a chain connecting the widely separated areas and insists that, whether or not such links can be found, diffusion alone can explain the facts. In their opinion a trait can only have been invented once; and multiple invention, even of the simplest trait, is 'unthinkable.'" Are there or have there ever been such extreme diffusionists? At any rate, if this criticism is meant for the culture historical school, I must declare this characterization a gross caricature, at it has never set forth such extreme views.

Naturally, we shall now look for the proofs of such an energetic rejection of the diffusionists. For Dixon undertakes to present these proofs, in order "to show the character of the problem and the fallacy of the extreme diffusionists' position." However, in the course of the subsequent discussion he deals simply with the diffusionists. From the works of these authors a number of cases are taken where they maintained far-reaching connections, especially between the old and the new world. In the discussion of these cases Dixon reveals great ethnological erudition, and much can certainly be learned therefrom. But since the names of these diffusionists are not cited anywhere and the culture historical school is not included therein, we shall not consider the matter more closely.

Then Dixon turns to "three final examples of culture parallels which will illustrate perhaps more clearly and from a different angle the dangers of the indiscriminate use of the idea of diffusion" (p. 211). The last of these three examples is the diffusion of the flood myth (p. 202). To solve this world-wide and complicated question on less than one page is a self-complacency unworthy of the usual thoroughness and erudition of Dixon. This example proves absolutely nothing. The second example is the diffusion of mummification which Elliott-Smith and Perry endeavor to trace through the whole world to Egypt (p. 212). No collaborator of the culture historical method attempts that. The culture historian does, however, consider mummification as a uniform phenomenon connected with a certain culture circle, but demonstrating it much more thoroughly and cautiously than do Perry and Elliott-Smith.

As the first of these three cases Dixon advances the one from Graebner where he regards the "crutch paddle" as belonging uniformly to the free mother-right culture (p. 211 s.). Dixon's criticism of this thesis is an extraordinarily weak one: he simply says that all paddles throughout the world either have a crutch (T-shaped grip) or they don't, so that all paddles must necessarily belong to one or the other of these types. Even if that were true, there must always have been some special cause at work to bring about the frequency or exclusive distribution of the one form in a certain territory. But Dixon presents the facts here most unsatisfactorily; *1*, the ends of the handle of the paddle may have at least three different forms: *a*, the handle may be plain (round like a broom handle); *b*, or broadened at the end and carved; or *c*, tipped at the end with a crosspiece like the end of a crutch; *2*, Dixon does not even mention that Graebner postulated a special form of the blade of the paddle for this culture circle (of which there may be at least four different forms), namely, the one broadened at the lower end; *3*, also the attachment of the handle to the shaft of the paddle must be considered, which likewise has several different forms. We have here a good case of the quantitative criterion of quality, which at the same time comprises both the criterion of quality and that of quantity, and therefore is of special argumentative force for historical relations. (75) Dixon's refutation of a single case of a culture historian has not only miscarried, but also, considering the position of an ethnologist like Dixon, it has been astoundingly weak.

I must say almost the same with regard to Dixon's whole attempt to refute my application of the culture historical method to South America (76) (pp. 228-238). First of all, he represents this attempt absolutely falsely when he says that I have all the American cultures to the very youngest, that of the blowgun, come over Bering Strait and along the entire length of America. For I most expressly derive the younger cultures of South America from Indonesia, Melanesia, and Polynesia. (77) And again, when I maintain a relationship between the oldest South American with the oldest (southeastern) Australian culture, I do not espouse the nonsense which Dixon ascribes to me, that the Australian cultures had migrated over Indonesia and all along the east coast of Asia and then crossed over the Bering Strait and finally traversed the entire length of America. Rather, my opinion is that one group of the very old common culture migrated from a place in Northeastern Asia over Further India and Indonesia to South Australia, the other over the Bering Strait to the southernmost part of South America. (78) The Pygmies which Dixon ascribes to me I do not suppose for the whole of America. In his criticism of my expositions of the bow and arrow Dixon uses the same naïve treatment which we have seen in his criticism of the crutch paddle by Graebner (above, p. 51): "The bow must be round or flat" (p. 235) ; he shows that he has not the slightest idea of the problem at hand: (79) There is a great number of other forms besides the flat or round cross section of the bow, to which must be reckoned the difference of the material of the bowstring and the manner of fastening, and then too the manner of feathering the arrow, all elements which can appear in the most different connections and mixtures. Each one of these elements presents questions concerning the culture historical "wherefrom" and "whereto," which also require scientific answers. It is also entirely false that I consider "the shield and the throwing stick as among the most fundamental characteristics belonging to the first three cultures of the Oceanic people" (p. 235) ; only to the youngest of these three does the most primitive form of the shield belong; *i.e.,* the parrying stick, and not the throwing stick but the clubbing stick. (80)

In short, Dixon in this criticism evinces an extraordinarily great lack of his usual thoroughness and carefulness, (81) so that unfortunately I could learn very little from it. I have been conscious of the fact for some time that my lecture, "Kulturkreise und Kulturschichten in Südamerika" has its defects, being the first thorough application of the culture historical method to South America; but exactly these were emphasized the least by Dixon. I have already corrected the greater part of them in my lectures at the University of Vienna on the same theme a few years ago (82): in the near future I hope to be able to present this critical work to my colleagues.

We are highly interested to see what method he himself will use in order to establish spatial relations of cultures and culture elements with certainty. Here an awful disappointment awaits us. Instead of such a method, he gives a lengthy discussion in the last chapter (VIII—pp. 265-305), "The Building of Cultures," in which he brings forward much which is well put and worthy of consideration, but not a syllable do we find with the help of what method and in what sure and reliable way one may attain such fine results.

What he has to say concerning method he already stated at the end of Chapter VI (p. 223 s.), and that is the following: "That diffusion is responsible for a large number of apparently disconnected traits is probable, but there remains a considerable residuum for which independent origin is the only rational explanation. For common sense and the laws of probability must be applied to all cases, and when an explanation by diffusion requires us to assume that the extremely improbable or almost impossible has occurred, the *onus probandi* becomes very heavy. Where the physical difficulties in the way are very serious, we must refuse to be carried away by vague generalities and demand very concrete proofs, and until such is forthcoming the alternative of independent invention or convergence must be preferred." But then he restricts the "considerable residuum for which independent origin is the only rational explanation" still more when he continues (p. 224): "That diffusion has been responsible for cultural development *to a far greater extent than independent invention* (83) cannot, in face of evidence, be denied."

After such a confession Dixon also could be counted among the diffusionists. But if we are tempted to rejoice over this, our joy is soon dampened in the face of the fact that a person of

Dixon's importance at the end of a book covering several hundred pages knows no other answer to the main question about "diffusion" and "independent origin" than simply to refer to "common sense and the laws of probability." Furthermore, he does not undertake to tell us what "laws of probability" are meant and how they ought to be applied in single cases. In fact, he is satisfied with "probabilities" as the final aim of his science and does not strive after certitude. No wonder, since he does not know any way or method to reach such certainties.

To this great deficiency there must still be added that only the cultural relations of spatial juxtaposition have been treated in this whole great work of Dixon. The greatest and most difficult problem of ethnology has as good as not been touched upon; namely, how the juxtaposition which characterizes its material might be changed into chronological time depths and how ethnology with the aid of an objective time measure should unveil those dark times of mankind unilluminated by written documents.

In comparison with this discouraging discovery (of the year 1928!) it is no longer of such great importance, but still it is noteworthy and significant that Dixon in his whole work, in which he cites so many authors, did not give one word to the discussion of the fundamental work of Graebner, *Methode der Ethnologie* of 1911, and that he did not in the least criticize this method itself, but directs all his criticism to several applications of the method by Graebner and myself. I think I have already sufficiently shown above (p. 50 s.) how inadequate this criticism was.

H. P. RADIN

If one may judge from the book of Paul Radin, *The Method and Theory of Ethnology,* (84) which has appeared recently, it would appear that the development of North American ethnology in the quest of a method had reached a stage that by its quite unrestrained criticism of ethnological colleagues of all approaches—not only of North America, but also of Europe—it might be proclaiming something either altogether astonishing and entirely new—or the end, its bankruptcy. We must wait and see which of these two alternatives is to be realized.

In North America, Boas, Wissler, and Kroeber are most sharply and extensively criticized by Radin. Boas is criticized most severely of all, Sapir and Benedict less so (pp. 1-60). However, Swanton, Lowie, Spier, Dixon, and Wallis and even Sapir are praised because they refrained from proposing theories. Certainly, neither Lowie nor Sapir deserved this discrediting praise and above all not Dixon, whose highly theoretical book, *The Building of Cultures,* is not even mentioned. Considerably shorter and more gracious is Radin's criticism on the ethnologists of England and the different countries of Europe (pp. 61-86).

The Graebner-Schmidt school is also left out here. All that he has concerning it are a few lines from my *Handbuch der vergleichenden Religionsgeschichte* (English edition: *Origin and Growth of Religion*). Graebner's book, *Methode der Ethnologie,* is not cited in the book anywhere, apparently because Radin himself has never read it. But that does not prevent him from condemning the ethnology of Graebner as well as the entire ethnology of Germany and Austria, thus (p. 80): "There is something compelling in the effrontery with which Graebner lays down the laws that govern culture growth, and this is probably the reason for his very great influence in Germany and Austria." (85) Outside of this impudent censure, however, Radin advances no other criticism. Neither does he offer other criticisms later on when he presents the method a little more extensively, but still only from the short and correspondingly incomplete summary in my *Handbuch der vergleichenden Religionsgeschichte* (pp. 163-166). He dashes the criticism off with a short rhetorical question in a few lines (p. 167): "What can one possibly say to such schematization that with Graebner and his followers the search for chronology became an obsession and the obsession a dogma?" That he is not troubled in the least by this "obsession" we shall see later on (p. 56), and also how plain and unimportant his words thereby become.

The one constructively good chapter of the book that really

brings something permanent and useful is Chapter IV, "The Factors in the Determination of the Ethnological Record" (pp. 87-129), in which he gives a healthy examination of conscience of field research work and offers good advice for the same.

The following chapter, "The Quantitative Method in Ethnology" (pp. 130-167), under which distorted title he criticizes the schools directed along historical lines and deals with Boas, Goldenweiser, himself, Wissler, Kroeber, Spier, Lowie (in this case of course less than the rest, see note above [p. 55, note 85]), Rivers, Elliott-Smith, Perry, Graebner, and Schmidt. The very fact that he can dispose of such a motley list of authors in one chapter sufficiently shows the superficiality of this criticism. We can illustrate this in the one example where he calls Tylor's rule of adhesions (86) the cornerstone of all theories criticized by him (p. 133) although Graebner had comprehensively criticized and rejected it, (87) and my requirements for the criteria *are entirely* different as well. (88)

Now in the next chapter (VI) Radin has to acknowledge the "quantitative" method is in vogue today. But still he thinks its star is visibly beginning to set by reason of a certain reaction that is rising against it. The "reactionaries" whom he treats in order, Radcliffe-Brown, Malinowski, Margaret Mead, Ruth Benedict, Thurnwald, Fortune, are, as can be seen, in the main representatives of the "functional method" and the "structure theory to which the former is related." (89) But neither do these have any reason to laugh: Insufficient length of sojourn to study the natives, incomplete accounts, dogmatic statements, neoevolutionism, occasional relapses into the older evolutionism, uncritical philosophizing, piling up of one truism upon the other to indulge in belletristic distinctions that have no content: "like Radcliffe-Brown and Malinowski, she [Fortune] too is crying for the moon," "reinvigorate an erroneous and futile method." Those are a few examples of the compliments Radin pays to these "reactionaries." They show at least that Radin is at pains not to be mistaken for them.

After Radin has so unrestrainedly criticized everything and everybody, we could with all right eagerly look forward to what positive method he will proffer on his part. He does this in the following Chapter VII, "Reconstruction from Internal Evidence and the Role of the Individual" (pp. 192-252). After so many grandiloquent promises seldom indeed has so bitter a disappointment been prepared like the one Radin gives us in this chapter. It is nothing less than the expression of veiled despair of attaining to an historical and causal comprehension of primitive cultures over even moderate spans of time. For in what then does the whole "method" of Radin consist? Merely in the advice to write a good monograph of a tribe. And then Radin quotes again and again the monograph he wrote himself, the one on the Winnebagos, certainly a first-rate work, and endeavors to show through extensive examples how historical time depths may be obtained. That should not be underestimated, but in comparison with the whole task that is to be accomplished here, they are but very modest time depths that can thereby be reached. It would never be satisfactory to write a real history of culture of the Winnebago, and remain entirely silent about the history of all the Siouan and Algonkian tribes, which have made great contributions to the building up of the culture of the Winnebagos. But let us not waste any more words over the absolute insufficiency of simply writing monographs. More important problems await us.

Having come to the end of the first part of his exposition, Radin has enough discernment to speak of the possibility (p. 238): "And surely if all I have contended should prove to be completely unacceptable, the document still remains for them who can interpret better and more profoundly." What paltry claims are here advanced by the man who before had made such lofty and exacting demands on all the others! For his sentence states nothing else than: Even if it should turn out that I am not an ethnologist, still I remain an ethnographer! 'Tis true, and nothing more; for where are the methodological rules, where is the carefully worked out and systematized methodology, so that it might be objectively and safely decided whether an interpretation is "completely unacceptable" or whether the document must be "better and more profoundly interpreted"?

Radin, who but shortly before knew how to criticize the others with such caustic eloquence, remains completely mute on this question.

I would consider it an offense to offer to prove to someone that there can be no real investigation of causes without setting up a valid chronology and that without an inquiry into causes there will be no real ethnology; in fact, no science at all, at least no historical science. It should be self-evident that the causal connections of rather large peoples and complexes separated from each other by great distances cannot be established by simple monographs. In fact, anyone who had even the slightest acquaintance with more extensive undertakings of this kind would understand this immediately. But this is unhappily not the case with Radin. He has written monographs exclusively, excellent indeed, but still mere monographs. His other works are, *Religion of North American Indians,* (90) *Monotheism among Primitive People, Primitive Man As Philosopher.* (91) These are of a nonhistorical nature. Had Radin thoroughly and earnestly devoted himself to the discovery of such somewhat larger relationships, he would have soon experienced how wholesome a little bit of "chronological obsession" also would have been for him. For his particular critical judgments would certainly then have been essentially more wise and useful.

I. A. L. Kroeber

There is hardly one of the North American authors who has taken such a lively part in the discussion of questions and method as A. L. Kroeber. This can be seen in his many articles which he has published, especially in the *American Anthropologist.* These articles also allow us to observe a development in his own opinions on these matters. It would take us too far afield to consider this matter here in detail. It will suffice to treat his last three publications in this regard in which a development can also be detected.

1. The first is his article, "The Culture Area and the Age Area Concepts of Clark Wissler." (92) This first of all treats of the "culture area" of the Americanists in general, giving us

a very instructive exposition. We shall give this question a special treatment later on (p. 187 ss.). He points out that this concept has found its latest and best development in the case of Clark Wissler. He is, however, compelled to admit that in North American ethnology the "culture area," which essentially expresses the geographical spatial juxtaposition of cultures and their elements, stands isolated alongside the "age area," which indicates historical succession. But Kroeber thinks that Wissler's stated conception of the center within the "culture area" (93) goes a long way toward bringing about the desired union of the two. (94) For he is to a great extent a follower of Wissler's doctrines. (95) We have already shown (above, p. 47) that these in general present too small a foundation and in many cases no suitable basis whatever for the actual historical succession of culture strata. Consequently, I could not give my assent to the following statement of Kroeber: "A still further logical step, though apparently an inevitable one, is the inference that the present center of culmination is also the presumptive locus of origin" (p. 255). It is true what Kroeber says: "The age area method is accepted in principle by Kroeber, but employed more cautiously" (p. 257), and he also finds several appropriate critcisms of Dixon, though he rejects those of Wallis as "negativistic toward a historical attitude or the recognition of diffusion except within the field of conventional history." He also gives a number of points in which Wissler's method could be improved (p. 261 ss.); but his own criticisms are all too general to be able to meet the basic deficiencies of Wissler's method.

The distinction which he sets up between Wissler and the culture circles of the culture historical school is not exactly to the point (p. 260): "The difference between Wissler and the English diffusionist and the German Kulturkreis schools, which also aim to supply history for undocumented periods and areas, lies in the fact that these make their explanations in terms of a single or few origins, respectively, in place of an indefinite number of variable centers. The limitation of factors yields a simple scheme, but almost inevitably involves an arbitrary or subjective choosing of the original centers." I pass over the "English diffusionists" (Elliott-Smith, Perry). As far as the culture historical school is concerned, it does, of course, recognize but few culture circles for the beginning, which go back to the oldest one; it is also convinced that these few older culture circles still manifest themselves in all the later circles in some way or other. But for later times, it also considers the number of culture circles to be unlimited, and it does not yet find itself in a position to name them all. The number of culture circles will not, however, be as great as that of the "culture areas," because of the essential difference between the culture circle and the culture area, of which we shall speak later on (p. 189).

2. The article, "Historical Reconstruction of Culture Growths and Organic Evolution," is of greater and positive importance. Here Kroeber states his views in a number of programmatic theses (and, hence, here and there unfortunately too short). We shall pass over the comparison of ethnology and biology, which Kroeber chose only because biology has quite a high standing in North America and which he wished to make use of to justify views for ethnology that had long been accepted in biology.

Here we find the full recognition of almost all the methodological criteria which are used by the culture historical school (see below, p. 141 ss.), even though the names for the most part are not expressly given. Thus we find the criterion of quality well described and supplemented by reference to "limited possibilities" of certain sequences of development in theses 5 and 6 (Kroeber, p. 151 s.). The criterion of quantity is treated in theses 7, 8, and 9 (p. 152 s.) and also the criterion of continuity is touched upon in theses 3 and 4 (p. 150). With regard to the recurrent criticism that is given also here on the "six or eight blocks of culture traits associations" (his not entirely happy term for the culture circles of the culture historical school), I refer to what I said before on that question. Below we shall also discuss his demand to "indicate the approximate time and place and peculiar circumstances of these primary blocks and associations." Furthermore, he acknowledges that "Father Schmidt's valiant and brilliant remodeling has done much to deprive the original Graebner scheme of its stark baldness and methodical rigor" (p. 154). I hope that my exposition will convince him of the uncorrectness of his following words: "But the value of his modifications lies in themselves, not in rendering the scheme more demonstrated."

3. The third publication of Kroeber on this subject is his article, "History and Science in Anthropology." (97) This is primarily and principally intended as a critical exposition of the position of Fr. Boas with regard to the historical character of ethnology. He charges that his position is only partly historical, being in part influenced by his educational training in the natural sciences. His resistance to historical interpretations of any sort are due to this also (p. 549): "Such a resistance is most easily understood in the deep-seated distrust of a mind schooled in the approach of the inorganic exact sciences, toward a fundamentally and qualitatively different type of interpretation; although also a mind intelligent enough to realize that in dealing with historical material—as cultural material is, in the wider sense—the methodological safeguards of history must be observed." Boas replied to this exposition with an article with the same title in the same magazine. (98) I will not follow this controversy here any further, neither shall I consider more closely his interesting critical remarks on the position of a number of other ethnologists (Elliott-Smith, Perry, Rivers, Spinden, Radin, Fortune, Mead, Benedict, Durkheim-Mauss, Radcliffe-Brown, Malinowski, Bastian, Ratzel, Frazer, Tylor), from which much can be learned.

Only to his remarks on "the Kulturkreis theory" must I here give brief consideration. Fundamentally, they are not different from what he had said in the article treated before, only that he takes up a more antagonistic position against Graebner. Beginning with the fact that Graebner was a professional historian and that his *Methode der Ethnologie* is largely based upon Bernheim's *Lehrbuch der Historischen Methode* he writes (p. 549): "It may be conjectured that Graebner, finding no veritable outlet in his earlier career, tried to force one by attempting in the unpoliced no-man's land of ethnology what would have been promptly suppressed or ignored in history." That is a very unkind conclusion. Kroeber does not consider that, *1,* Graebner's *Methode der Ethnologie* is represented entirely falsely when he says that it is only "reduced and made over to some extent to allow room for his own scheme" from Bernheim's book. (99) The greatest part of Graebner's book is his own intellectual property, and that applies fully with regard to the important part of how objective chronological and causal successions may be obtained from the superficial material of ethnology. *2,* that Graebner lost several years when he was retained as a war prisoner in Australia, (100) and his life was greatly shortened through a mysterious serious sickness, which prevented him from supporting the practical application of his method everywhere in such a manner as he had in part done in single cases. (101)

It was for these reasons also that I was not so pleased when Kroeber continues (p. 549): "The reformation of the Kulturkreis scheme into the kulturgeschictliche 'Methode' of Schmidt and his collaborators is to be taken more seriously, because Schmidt undoubtedly possesses genuine historical insight, in regard to language as well as culture. The skill with which he has gradually remodeled the stark Graebner scheme out of all semblance to its original form is evidence of his capacity. However, it does remain a scheme, and therefore all Father Schmidt's keenness, immense knowledge and love of argument cannot make it a genuine, empirically derived, historical interpretation." I only repeat and supplement what I said above (p. 61) when I remark thereto: *1,* the culture historical method itself is not mentioned, still less criticized by Kroeber, and it can by no means be supplemented to any degree by Wissler's theories, which Kroeber in great part follows; 2, in the practical application of the method and so also in the setting up of culture circles, we shall endeavor so long as time and strength are given us to do justice more and more to the demands of this method.

The historical method which Kroeber in principle follows entirely is not given closer treatment in detail in this article. He only defines more sharply the more exact character of the real historical approach (p. 545): "I suggest as the distinctive feature of the historical approach, in any field, not the dealing with time sequences, though that almost inevitably crops out where historical impulses are genuine and strong; but an endeavor at descriptive integration. By descriptive integration I mean that phenomena are preserved intact as phenomena, so far as that is possible, in distinction from the approach of the nonhistorical (102) sciences, which set out to decompose phenomena in order to determine processes as such." In these principles it must be criticized that the time factor only "almost inevitably" comes to the "descriptive integration"; it belongs to it "necessarily and inevitably" and in the series of investigations it must be put in the first place, if, as is demanded, the integration of the phenomena should also embrace the causal sequences. Kroeber seems to agree with this in another passage, where he writes (p. 547): "I am not belittling the time factor; I am only taking the stand that it is not the most essential criterion of the historical approach. Space relations can and must sometimes take its place." We will not argue about whether the time factor be the "most essential," it is certainly an "essential" factor; for history ("Geschichte") comes from the "happened" ("geschehen") and the historical event takes place essentially in time. Space relations can take the place of time relations only in so far as the latter are obtained from the former by means of the culture historical method.

J. Clyde Kluckhohn

1. After such utter ignorance and so much prejudiced misunderstanding of the culture historical method which we had to point out with regard to a long list of North American ethnologists, it is a veritable surprise to find an appraisal that offers its criticism with sympathetic understanding and honestly endeavors to obtain this understanding. As a matter of fact, the author even has the courage to oppose its superficial

and often not entirely fair critics among the other Americanists. This is Clyde Kluckhohn's article, "Some Reflections on the Method and Theory of the Kulturkreise." (103)

What we do not like in this paper—to dispose of the point right at the start—is his designation of the culture historical movement as the "Kulturkreislehre" (doctrine of culture circles). As is shown in another passage (p. 175 ss.) the culture circle is not something belonging specifically to the culture historical school. It is an element that every developed ethnology must recognize and work with. It is correct that the culture circle has been fully appreciated in the culture historical school. But also here it is not the foundation for, but a result of, its researches. The "Kulturkreislehre" does not form the essence of the method of our school, but is only one, even though an important one of its auxiliary means. (104) In fact, Kluckhohn also discusses a great number of other important elements of the culture historical method besides the culture circle; but his main attention is given to the culture circle, and that confines the perspective somewhat, which his critique could otherwise have had. But nevertheless it remains even so quite fruitful and is very praiseworthy.

The article is divided into two parts: first, his own criticism of the "Kulturkreislehre"; and second, the refutation of unjustified attacks upon it by others. We shall deal with the second part first, because we shall then obtain a better connection with our own defense against such assaults, which I have presented in the foregoing. For the correct understanding of what I have to say concerning Kluckhohn in this as well as in other respects, let me mention that when I saw this article for the first time, I had not only finished the historical section of my present work on the method of ethnology, but the whole book was already finished in manuscript so that these lines on Kluckhohn's article had to be inserted later.

2. Kluckhohn in his second part first takes up in some detail the exposition and critique of the "Kulturkreislehre" given in Dixon's *Building of Cultures* (pp. 175-179). It is astounding

how many simplifications and misrepresentations he was able to unearth here; here and there one would almost think that he had my criticism of Dixon (above, p. 49 ss.) at hand, since he has so well grasped and refuted Dixon's sophisms and obfuscations. But I can assure you that neither was my critique of Dixon known to him nor his to me in any way whatsoever. He concludes with the words: "I am not interested in purely verbal differences or discrepancies, but I feel that these are such in number and nature as [together with Dixon's biographical omissions] to justify the conclusion that Professor Dixon has approached the 'Kulturkreislehre' not from the point of view of giving his readers a balanced, critical picture of its merits and demerits but rather from the point of view of demolishing it. It is a polemic, not a critique." That is is the same result reached in my critique of Dixon's criticism.

But Kluckhohn believes he must allow a similar condemnation fall upon the attitude of the majority of American ethnologists with regard to the "Kulturkreislehre" (p. 179) : "Now if the *Building of Cultures* were the single American example of this attitude, the matter would have only trifling significance, but it is my impression, after reading with some care, most, I believe, of the pertinent books and papers, that the attitude of the greater number of American anthropologists who have discussed the 'Kulturkreislehre' in print seems similar to Dixon's in that the judgments pronounced or implied hardly ever bear evidence of being fair and detached verdicts which attempt to weight all the evidence." He proves this judgment with a long list of cases which he quotes from different authors. These have for the most part been given already in my exposition (above, p. 36 ss.), in part however they are also new ones (pp. 182-187). Also Kluckhohn points out that "It is notable that no review or discussion of the *Methode* [by Graebner] by an American anthropologist attempts a comprehensive survey of the whole book. Invariably Graebner's controversial ideas are seized upon."

But also with regard to the expositions of the "Kulturkreislehre" on the part of the functionalists Radcliffe-Brown and Malinowski Kluckhohn pronounces judgment thus: "Here also it seems to me we may observe a certain rather inconsistent unfairness" and he also documents this judgment with numerous proofs (pp. 187-195). When in his conclusion he emphasizes the fact that both methods of research belong together as complements of each other in order to support each other mutually, then he will indeed see from what I have written above (pp. 33-36) that I am of the same opinion. From another point of view also I can but agree with Kluckhohn when he writes (p. 194): "The insights afforded by both 'historical' and 'functional' approaches are quite indispensable. It cannot be denied that sound historical reconstruction must be in accord with inferences drawn from the observation of living societies. But this is not to say that the relationship between ethnology and social anthropology is to be conceived, as Radcliffe-Brown has alleged, as a one-sided dependence of ethnology upon social anthropology. On the contrary, their relationship is certainly that of a complex mutual interdependence."

3. If we now take up the first part of Kluckhohn's article, in which he advances his own critique of the "Kulturkreislehre," then we see that he proceeds from the standpoint that it is important also to analyze the background and the general assumptions of a theory and method (p. 157): "It may well be that the chemist can pursue his researches perfectly effectively without regard to philosophy of method, but in such a subject as cultural anthropology method and theory are so intimately and immediately related both to the subject matter itself and to the student's own fundamental attitudes that it is imperative to examine the connections of a particular method and theory with more general systems of thought. Otherwise we are likely to examine a given proposition only in the light of our own premises and sentiments which are usually quite unconsciously treated as absolute. The resultant intolerance of other conceptual schemes leads us to see mutually exclusive alternatives, where actually one scheme of concepts sheds its own illuminations, another another." We can but consider this

postulate as well founded, especially because it ought to be used on both sides; namely, that of the criticized as well as that of the critic.

After Kluckhohn has given a short sketch of the culture historical method according to its latest form up till now in P. van Bulck—which, as I will point out, is not free from all objection —he thinks that, following Herskovitz and Boas, he can propose the following assumptions as basic for the culture historical method (p. 165): "*1,* Poverty of man's ability to devise new means of meeting his environment; *2,* Imitativeness of man and contagiousness of culture; *3,* The essential mental uniformity of mankind; *4,* The stability of the union of culture elements." He thinks "some respectable evidence" has been adduced in favor of all four of these assumptions, and he himself is favorably disposed toward them, but thinks that all four assumptions would seem to merit a systematic investigation, at best by a scholar unidentified with either position. As far as my humble self is concerned, I have never considered these assumptions as necessary for the acceptance and application of the culture historical method. On the contrary, I regard the results of culture historical research in great part as confirmations of those four propositions. In my entire exposition of the culture historical method here, no one, I think, will be able to find a thesis or rule which might have one of the above-mentioned propositions as a necessary assumption.

I must accord more weight to the critique which Kluckhohn devotes to the concept of the culture circle (p. 167 s.) concerning which he thinks that it wavers between historical and biological points of view, with the domination of the latter. He sees no reason to exclude biological concepts from ethnology nor from the culture circle either (p. 167 s., note 24): "On the contrary, on the a priori side, it would seem that since culture has been produced by and distributed by a biological organism, and is conditioned on every hand by biological limitations and considerations, there would be reason to think that some biological schemata would be appliable." This oscillation that was actually here rested more, however, upon the unexplained relation betweeen the culture circle as such and the culture circle as a methodical aid, which was not explained by Graebner either; I think I undertook this explanation satisfactorily (*cf.* later, p. 175 ss.).

Kluckhohn with all right points out that the "Kulturkreislehre" does not exclude the subjective element entirely. That applies especially to the criterion of form and then also to the criterion of quantity, as well as to the arguments cited to prove the presence or absence of a culture circle (p. 170 ss.). But he adds that the representatives of the culture historical method recognize the problems still remaining here as such and endeavor to solve them, and, I think, he will find that confirmed in the present exposition. Also Kluckhohn admits that the very nature of the subject matter makes an "inflexible formula" absurd (p. 171), and it seems to be "a fallacy to demand, as some of the critics of the 'Kulturkreislehre' apparently do, that methodological principles must lead us to the precise uniformities of the physical sciences" (p. 171).

4. In conclusion, Kluckhohn also touches upon the question of presuppositions due to intellectual make-up and world outlook. The delicate and courteous way in which he handles this touchy question is deserving of all respect. Only he could have pointed out that of the founders of the culture historical school Graebner, Foy, Ankerman, and so many of their followers as well probably stood upon the basis of a different "Weltanschauung" than Koppers, Pinard, van Bulck, and myself, of whom he points out the fact that they are (Catholic) priests. Of course, not only their "Weltanschauung" is to be emphasized, but also their formal schooling in theology and philosophy. But then he continues (p. 173 s.): "I do not in the least mean to imply that the scientific worth of their researches is thereby negatived. Kant was surely right in maintaining that cognition is impossible without the application of interpretative principles—and those underlying the metaphysics of the Roman Catholic Church are as intellectually respectable as any others in the present state of our knowledge about man

and universe. We must, I think, rigorously avoid the temptation to dismiss the 'Kulturkreislehre' as founded upon 'bias.' . . . A 'bias' I suppose has what the psychoanalysts call 'affect-content.' But if we are quite honest, how many of the fundamental presuppositions upon which the thinking of any of us are founded are truly free from emotional content? Are not the fundamental operations of science at best little more than consistent arrangement of data in accord with a few dominating concepts?"

When Kluckhohn then thinks that to the "intellectual climate" in which the "Kulturkreislehre" has matured there also belongs the philosophy of Hegel, "with its central proposition 'nicht causae sondern rationes beherrschen die Welt,' " that is quite a surprise for us culture historians; for we do not think we have taken a position with regard to Hegel in any manner whatsoever. When he believes that, in contrast, the theoretical position of Professor Boas and other American anthropologists has very close connections with modern dominant currents of American thought, notably the philosophical thought of Dewey and James, he may well be right, as also when he thinks: "Indeed such a typically American anthropological concept as that of the culture area is more fully comprehended in such a frame of reference. Compare the revival of Morgan in Russia."

5. How positive Kluckhohn stands with regard to the "Kulturkreislehre" in other matters may be made clear by two more quotations (p. 196) : "Perhaps the central reason for careful examination of the 'Kulturkreislehre' is that it attempts to provide a schematization for the archaeological and ethnological facts of the whole world—at a time when the recognition that even very early peoples were no respecters of continents is being forced upon us. The followers of the 'Kulturkreislehre' have at least resolutely devoted themselves to the task of scholars: they have endeavored to ferret out and establish unperceived relationships between facts, and we will be unwise to condemn them too austerely if the relations they think to have discovered are not always approved in detail by their fellow scholars." (105)

Summary

Whoever is acquainted with Radin's position somewhat more closely knows that it will not do to consider his book as typical or representative of North American ethnology. But in one point I still believe he has brought out something peculiar to North American ethnology—it is true, distorted—but for all that genuine: that is the instinctive inner uneasiness of this great and worthy group of ethnologists, who have so early and completely dismissed evolutionism, but yet despite a great number of individual studies to their credit have, nevertheless, not produced a universally accepted method for their science. Kroeber had quite early already given eloquent expression to this uneasiness and deplores especially the absence of a more thorough investigation of causes. (106) But also later, *and quite* recently at that, Kroeber found himself obliged to justify historical reconstructions in ethnology and to overcome the mistrust of them. (107)

Radin is also filled with this spirit even to the point of passion which, not wishing to confess its insufficiency, now violently makes a "virtue" of "necessity," and instead of defending itself turns around to "attack," and since it is not in a position to satisfy the demands which it requires of ethnology, simply argues away the title to these claims.

It is only that this standpoint forgets that it thereby robs ethnology of its unique position which consists in making it possible for all other sciences to gain certain access to the beginning of mankind's history unillustrated by written documents, and thereby offer a deeper comprehension of the history of culture. It is not to be feared that the rest of the American ethnologists take part in this *capitis diminutio* of their science, even if Radin would really stand his ground, which I still permit myself to doubt. They will therefore not give up their honest striving after a solid uniform method and I would be glad if they might obtain some aid from this book as this book has also learned from them. The article of Clyde Kluckhohn gives me the assurance that the way which they shall find will flow into that of the culture historical method somewhere, somehow, in the not too distant future and bring with it valuable confirmations and additions.

As I have pointed out elsewhere, of all American ethnologists R. H. Lowie stands the nearest to the culture historical movement and especially its method, as he does not deny any of its more important principles but recognizes them at least theoretically, even though the practical application of them on a large scale is still to be actualized. (108) He upholds the necessity of historical investigation, preferring indeed investigation of spatially continuous areas, but he also admits cases "where the distribution . . . is rendered plausible by documentary evidence or at least by known ethnographic principles." If he includes among the latter also the methodological principles laid down by Graebner, then the identity in principle is complete.

4. THE HISTORICAL METHOD OF ETHNOLOGY IN ENGLAND AND FRANCE

England and France are the two countries in which evolutionism held on the longest, even to our days. The causes for this are not the same in both countries.

A. England

In England the evolutionistic movement had had its most brilliant representatives in men like Herbert Spencer, Tylor, Robertson Smith, Sydney, Hartland, Frazer, Haddon, Marett, etc.; as far as method is concerned, Andrew Lang must be reckoned with them also. Through their numerous and extensive publications they had made a very deep impression on the whole country, which could not easily be broken down.

1. Through his careful studies, especially in the field of implements and weapons and the exact localization of their distribution, H. Balfour came near to historical ethnology, without, however, taking the final steps in the application of

its method. Seligman, in his valuable ethnographical works, holds himself entirely aloof from evolutionism; he gives an exact and constructive exposition of the facts he has conscientiously investigated, and when his ethnography becomes ethnology, as, for example, in the treatment of North African problems, he proceeds in the spirit of the historical school, without, of course, following any established method. N. W. Thomas comes still nearer to the historical school in his studies on Australian and West African ethnology, but did not grasp the system fully. (109) A. C. Haddon in his short sketch of the culture historical school falls into the mistake that there is no organic connection between single elements of its culture circles. (110) (*Cf.* above, p. 25.)

2. The "conversion" of such an eminent ethnologist as W. H. Rivers to the historical method was of great, so to speak, psychological interest. It took place during the elaboration of his big work, *History of Melanesian Society.* (111) Whereas the first volume still follows the lines of the old evolutionist method, the insight into the necessity of an historical method became even stronger in the second volume, till it finally gained the upper hand. Under such circumstances it is also psychologically understandable that Rivers there speaks of a combination of evolutionistic and historical research in words which, of course, I must say, are not convincing. In his presidential address, "The Ethnological Analysis of Culture," (112) he had programmatically announced the change in his ideas. This is seen also in his article, "The Contact of Peoples," (113) and in his booklet, *History and Ethnology.* (114)

3. His pupil, W. C. Perry, who had also begun in his spirit, soon fell under the influence of the Pan-Egyptianism of Elliott-Smith, with whom also Rivers seemed to be in sympathy; hence, his works suffer under its one-sidedness and bring much discredit upon the historical school. Let us mention here: *The Megalith Culture of Indonesia,* (115) *The Children of the Sun* (116) *The Origin of Magic and Religion,* (117) *The Age of the Gods.* (118)

4. Beginning with the study of the races and cultures of

Egypt, G. Elliott-Smith also investigated the influences of Egypt upon other peoples and cultures. In thus bringing out the importance of migrations for the history of culture, he attached himself to the historical movement. By proving the influences of the high culture of Egypt upon peoples of lower culture, among whom these influences have by far not always retained their original high level, he also gave more credit to the importance of degeneration in the history of culture, which progressive evolutionism had unduly kept in the background. He lessens the effect of his investigations by the one-sided emphasis upon Egypt as the place of origin for cultures and culture elements, whereby, especially in England, the approval of the historical conception in ethnology was hindered not a little. His larger works are: *The Evolution of the Rock-Cut Tomb and the Colmen,* (119) *The Migrations of Early Culture,* (120) *The Evolution of the Dragon,* (121) *Human History.* (122)

5. On the basis of principle, A. W. Hocart takes up the standpoint of historical investigation in his two works, *Kingship* (123) and *Progress of Man* (124) and in a long list of small writings, without thereby attaining a firm method in particulars. E. E. Evans-Pritchard in his two studies, "The Intellectualistic (English) Interpretation of Magic" and "Levy-Bruhl's Theory of Primitive Mentality," (125) gives a decisive and competent criticism on the prominent representatives of the old classical evolutionism, in which also the personal historically disposed point of view of the author is at work.

6. A. Radcliffe-Brown and Br. Malinowski are both representatives of the functional school. (126) The name was coined by the latter and used the first time in his work, *Argonauts of the Western Pacific* (1922) and later in *The Sexual Life of Savages* (1929; 3rd ed., 1932, with an introduction on method). Students of his are R. Firth, A. I. Richards, R. F. Fortune, M. Mead. Radcliffe-Brown had begun almost the same method in his book, *The Andaman Islanders* (Cambridge, 1922, p. 229 s.). At that time he had a very poor opinion of historical research in ethnology: "In the absence of all historical records. the most we could do would be to attempt to make a hypothet-

ical reconstruction of the past, which, in the present state of ethnological science, would be of very doubtful utility. The making of such hypothetical reconstructions of the past has been regarded by a number of writers as the principal if not the sole task of ethnology. My own view is that such studies can never be of any great scientific value." He thinks quite differently today as we may see from his article, "On the Conception of Function in Social Life" (127): "There need not be a conflict, but there is a difference. There is not, and cannot be, any conflict between the functional hypothesis and the view that any culture, any social system is the end result of a unique series of historical accidents. . . . The two kinds of explanation do not conflict, but supplement one another. I see no reason at all why the two kinds of study—the historical and the functional—should not be carried on side by side in perfect harmony," (128) and then he goes on to say that he did just that thing during the fourteen years of his professorship. Since I, on the other hand, have recognized the utility, within its limits, and the necessity of the functional method, (129) the two approaches here join in a profitable co-operation.

7. The principles for this are laid down in an excellent way by A. Lesser in his article, "Functionalism in Social Anthropology." (130) After he has criticized the one-sidedness of the functional method and also several representatives of the historical school, who are too quick in construing historical connections, he comes to the conclusion that the two belong together: "The extremes toward which these apparently divergent doctrines tend point the moral of sound method. On the one hand, the functionalist, insisting upon founding his functional statements upon immediate relations in the present, is too blind to the fact that determining and fundamental relations only too often lie behind the present in the past. And, on the other hand, the historically minded ethnologist is too ready to seek remote historical relationships and overlook others nearer at hand. Obviously, it is true that the first consideration must be of the context of cultural phenomena in the present, and it is also true that for the most part determination of events in the

present lies in the past. In beginning with the present conditions, exact understanding of any particular institution or custom demands not only the calculation of its apparent connections in the past, but calls more a recourse to the past, so far as it is relevant to the particular inquiry, for an understanding of the determining relationships which lie behind the event." (131) Then he offers several useful directions for this co-operation in the same sense as I did above (on pp. 33, 36). For this co-operation he coins the word "functional historicity."

8. If we, in addition to what has been said here, take into consideration the fact that there are hardly any young representatives of evolutionism in England, and further, that the most numerous and important English archaeologists, though they willingly make use of the rich collections of material and occasionally of the brilliant guesses of Frazer and other older evolutionists, if they work ever more earnestly along historical lines, but under the direction of research workers like G. Childe, Myers, etc., then the triumph of the historical idea in England is only a matter of time.

B. France

1. In France A. de Quatrefages had joined the method of historical research already at an early date, without, of course, being always conscious of it in everything and therefore he did not come to a solid method. (132) He was not highly appreciated, because the physical anthropology and prehistory of those days, which in France worked on principles of progressive evolutionism, was in its heyday, with the result that for a time ethnology in general held back. (133)

Later A. van Gennep, in the introduction to his work, *Mythes et legendes d'Australie* (134) took a similar line; but with his later work, *Rites de passage* (135) there is a regression to psychological evolutionism. For the particular area of Africa, M. Delafosse has always worked along strictly exact and historical lines in his detailed researches. This is true also of R. Rivet for South America. Recently going a step further, he has recognized the important results of historical investigation regarding the connection between American cultures of the older and oldest strata and those of Oceania and Australia; these results he tries to supplement by investigations of his own, which, indeed, often neglect more rigorous historical methodology, and therefore he was not able to achieve results which are acceptable in all particulars.

2. With geat clarity and a solid philosophical foundation A. H. Pinard de la Boullaye, in his important work, *L'étude comparée des Religions,* (136) describes the culture historical method and has made many valuable contributions to its inner construction and external diffusion.

3. The critical works of O. Leroy, *Essai d'Introduction critique a l'Étude de l'Économie primitive* (Paris, 1925) and *La Raison Primitive* (Paris, 1927), are also filled with the spirit of the historical school. We only hope that he finds it possible to undertake other positive researches.

4. G. Montandon had quite early taken note of the most significant results of culture historical investigation, of culture circles, and is more or less in accordance therewith. He gives a report of them in his article, "Des Tendences actuelles de l'ethnologie à-propos des armes de l'Afrique." (137) He expounds these again in his study, "La Généalogie des Instruments de musique et les Cycles de civilisation." (138) Recently he has taken up a critical position with regard to these in his larger work, *L'Ologenèse culturelle,* that is supposed to be a "traité d'ethnologie culturelle" and an exposition of the whole of ethnology from the standpoint of the culture circles. (139) On the whole he accepts the culture circles worked out by the culture historical school and tries to bring them into harmony with the doctrine of the origin of man which he had set forth in his work, *L'Ologenèse humaine.* (140) According to this theory, we ought to speak of neither monogenesis nor polygenesis but rather of an "Ologenèse": "l'humanité, dérivée d'une seule souche, a cependant eu une origine quasi panterrestre" (p. 8). By carrying this theory over into the origin of culture he would have the "Primitive cultures" of the culture historical school arise almost simultaneous all over the world.

He assigns an essentially uniform development to these cultures also and believes he can vindicate therewith the validity of the older evolutionistic school with its theory of elementary ideas and unilinear development of culture for this period. He thus believes he has found a synthesis of the evolutionistic and the culture historical schools (pp. 8 ss., 35 ss.).

However well meant this attempt at "reconciliation" of the two schools may be, it does not stand up under a methodological investigation. Certainly the Primitive cultures by their direct dependence upon nature are more similar to one another than the primary cultures in which man begins to dominate more strongly over nature. However, not only the difference of environment in the different parts of the world differentiate these cultures, but also cultural differences of an intellectual and social kind, which do not have anything to do with the external environment. Now precisely these differences allow us to recognize the relationships of these different primitive cultures, which are not separated from the others. Hence, these latter are characterized by special historical relations due to their common origin. But they show that the origin of these cultures also is not ologenetic but monogenetic and point to the one continent of Asia, as I have tried to demonstrate for religion in the sixth volume of my *Ursprung der Gottesidee.* Hence also the Primitive culture, being thoroughly historical, must be studied with the aid of the culture historical method and not by some kind of evolutionistic "method."

The opinions at which Montandon arrived could only have come into existence because he knew the culture historical method insufficiently and applied it too little. That manifests itself already in the astounding fact that in his book of 778 pages not one single page has been devoted to an exposition of the culture historical method. It is significant therefore that the word "method" is missing from the index of subjects; instead, you are referred to "theories." Thus his criticism is also supported almost throughout by mere psychologizing, which in the form of "bon sens" falls back frequently enough into classical evolutionism. A characteristic example of this sort occurs in his treatment of the question of bow and arrow among the pygmies (p. 87): "Le simple bon sens ordonne de concevoir l'arc comme un produit trop compliqué pour être primitive." Here and in other places appear serious regressions into times that ought to have been overcome.

5. THE HISTORICAL METHOD OF ETHNOLOGY IN THE NORTHERN COUNTRIES

In the northern countries evolutionism never held any particular sway and investigation was for the most part dominantly along historical lines.

A. Denmark

In Denmark the historical method had been developed chiefly by the study of the Eskimo region, which is of large extent and presents great variety. This region extends from Northeast Asia over the entire northern coast to Greenland and clearly illustrates the culture historical importance of migrations.

How far-reaching the results of diffusion are appears from the thorough study of W. Thalbitzer, "Die kultischen Gestalten der Eskimos," (141) in which he proves that the ideas of people as far away as the inhabitants of Central Asia have influenced the Eskimo religion.

Knud Rasmussen's expeditions in Thule, which he set up and carried out, were made on a magnificent plan and were inspired wholly by the spirit of geographical and historical investigation. The volumes (142) he and his collaborators, K. Birkett-Smith, Th. Mathiassen, and others, have issued on the basis of the materials thus collected are first-rate examples of historical method well applied.

Especially three short synthesizing works of K. Birkett-Smith are to be mentioned: "Drinking Tube and Tobacco Pipe in North America," (143) "Über die Herkunft der Eskimos und ihre Stellung in der zircumpolaren Kulturentwicklung," (144)

"Folk Wanderings and Culture Drifts in Northern North America." (145) Already at an earlier date, G. Hatt had gone along the same way of historical method in his works: *Artiske Slindragten i Eurasien og Amerika,* (146) "Kyst-og Inlandskulturidet artiske," (147) "Moccasins and Their Relations to Arctic Footwear," (148) "North American and Eurasian Culture Connections." (149)

Outside of this territory of the Eskimos, C. G. Feilberg has furnished the excellent study "Bidrag tie de afrikanske Agerbrugs redskabers Kulturhistorie" *(Geografisk Fidskrift.* Kobenhavn, 1934, p. 228-265).

B. SWEDEN

The historical movement has also been predominant in Sweden. It appears in the works of so eminent an ethnologist as E. von Nordenskiöld, whose researches specialized principally in South America. We quote from his works especially the following, which are more of a synthetic nature: "Eine geographische und ethnologische Analyse der materiellen Kultur zweier Indianerstämme in El Gran Chaco," "The Changes in the Material culture of two Indian Tribes under the Influence of New Surroundings, The Ethnography of South America Seen from Mojos in Bolivia." (150) The geographical-cartographical part of the culture historical method is here developed to a high degree of perfection. However, the full use of the criterion of quantity is still missing, which is necessary to make (151) possible the establishment of the diffusion and migration not only of individual elements of culture, but also of whole cultures.

His pupils are working along the same lines. To mention only a few: S. Linné, *The Technique of South American Ceramics* (Göteborg, 1925); *Darien in the Past* (Göteborg, 1929). G. Montell, *Dress and Ornaments in Ancient Peru* (London, 1929). Also the French-Swiss A. Metraux considers himself a pupil of Nordenskiöld; let me mention his two big works, *La Civilization materielle des Tribus Guarani-Tupi* (Paris, 1928) and *La Religion des Tupinamba* (Paris, 1928).

Along the same lines as Nordenskiöld and his group have done for South America, W. Kaudern has worked in Indonesia, especially Celebes, in a series of valuable monographs. Fruits of his expeditions there have appeared under the general title *Ethnographical Studies on Celebes* (Göteborg, 1925, 1927, 1929).

For Africa G. Lindblom follows almost the same method in his studies on methods of hunting and fishing, stilts, hammocks, cord games, etc., which have been published in the writings of the *Riksmuseets Etnografiska Avdelning* (Stockholm, 1927 ss.).

We shall speak later on the relation of the highly developed Swedish folklore to the historical method. We shall then treat of the relation of ethnology to folklore more in detail.

c. Finland

Finland reached a very high level in historical investigation quite early, especially as a result of favorable circumstances. This resulted from the researches of Finnish scholars seeking for the origin of their national hero epic, the Kalevala.

While the earlier investigators, such as Lönnrot, Castrén, J. Krohn, and others, in their solution of the question assumed the viewpoint of evolutionism and the natural sciences, investigators were already beginning under J. Krohn to make their way, through a process of mapping and studying the geography of their data, to a fully historical method, and this movement has grown stronger under K. Krohn. The result is that the origin of the Kalevala in its present form can be placed in a transitional period between paganism and Christianity and not in a prehistoric pagan time, as is very instructively set forth by K. Krohn in his most interesting lecture, "Kalevala und die finnischen Heldenlieder." (152)

This method has specialized particularly in the field of folklore, in which a whole host of distinguished investigators have applied it. It is explained with exemplary thoroughness also by K. Krohn in his treatise, "Die folkloristische Arbeitsmethode" (Oslo–Leipzig–Paris–London, 1926).

D. Russia

I am here following W. Koppers' useful treatment of Russian ethnology in his instructive article, "Das Schicksal der Ethnologie unter dem Sowjet-Regime." (153) I am also indebted to him for all the particulars of the bibliography given very copiously in that article.

There we see that the older ethnology of Russia had undertaken an exact investigation of the primitive peoples of its great territorial expanse in Northeastern Asia and gave an objective account of them without allowing any evolutionistic or psychological theories to influence them in any way. In fact, they very commendably collected a rich store of trustworthy and critically sifted material on these peoples, which has not been sufficiently utilized and often not even known by ethnologists in Central and Western Europe because of insufficient knowledge of the Russian language. Some names of high repute can be mentioned here: Pallas, Castrén, Radloff, Potanin. (154) This applies also for the earlier years of the *Zivaja Starina,* the ethnographical publication of the old Imperial Russian Geographical Society, while in later years (from 1896 on) evolutionism began to make inroads in the works of Sjeroszeoskij, Haruzin, Czaplicka, Carruthers. (155)

Already in 1911, J. U. Czeckanowski gave a lecture in the same society entitled, "Objective Kriterien in der Ethnologie," (156) which takes a position alongside Ankerman's exposition of the culture circles, and even though this lecture criticized the culture historical method, nevertheless it is favorable to the culture historical method in principle, Nekrasow and Efstifjzew fully approve of the method, while Möller, Sternberg, Rudenko, Lunewoskij and Vitaszewskij assume a more cautious and skeptical attitude. (157)

Koppers gives a detailed treatment of the position of the two important Russian ethnologists, Sternberg and Bogoras. He clearly shows that Sternberg to a great extent thinks and works along historical lines. Evolutionistic and materialistic tendencies break through for the first time in his article, "Die

Ethnologie der Gegenwart; neueste Fortschritte, wissenschaftliche Strömungen und Methoden." (158) Nevertheless, after criticizing the culture historical school he grants justice to its concepts and methods; in fact, in principle considers them fully justified. (159) From the very beginning Bogoras is more evolutionistically inclined than Sternberg. This can be seen especially in his researches on the Chukchee. (160) On the other hand, he advocates a number of postulates of the culture historical method and explains the idea of the culture circle quite well. (161)

W. Jochelson is historical in every respect in his researches on the Koryaks and the Yukaghir. (162) Historical thought and research play a still greater role in the works of Shirokogoroff, who, however, is forced to live as an "emigrant" outside Russia. He lives and publishes his writings in China. (163)

Under these circumstances it is to be all the more regretted that all these hopeful beginnings have been brought to a standstill through the assault of bolshevik politicians in a conference of Russian ethnographers called together in Leningrad, April 5-11, 1929. In this gathering ethnography was ordered to contribute to the building up of the Soviet state and to take up the methodology of dialectic materialism and Marxism. The slogan is: "The classics—E. Tylor, M. Castrén, L. Morgan, L. Sternberg, Fr. Ratzel—are not to be given up, but go from them over to Marxism, from elementary materialism to the conscious application of dialectic materialism." (164)

(1) E. B. Tylor, "On a Method of Investigating the Development of Institutions. Applied to Laws of Marriage and Development," *Journ. Anthrop. Inst.*, XVIII (1899), p. 295 ss.

(2) Graebner, *op. cit.*, pp. 87-91.

(3) P. Ehrenreich, "Zur Frage der Beschreibung und Beantwortung ethnographischer Analogien," *Korr. Blatt deut. Ges. F. Anthr., Ethno., u. Urgeschichte,* XXIV (1903), p. 176 ss.

(4) R. M. Meyer, "Kriterion der Aneigung" *Neues Jahrb, f. d. klass. Alt. Gesch. u. Deutsch. Lit.*, XVII (1906), p. 16 ss.

(5) Graebner, *op. cit.*, p. 97.

(6) *Cf.* later, Chapter III.

(7) H. Pinard de la Boullaye, *L'Étude comparée des Religions,* Vol. II (Paris, 1925), p. 222.

(7a) Therefore it was not surprising, that he—as also his pupil Frobenius—called his new method a "geographical" one (Fr. Ratzel, "Die geographische Methode in der Ethnologie," *Geog. Zeitschr.*, III, p. 268 ss. See in this regard Graebner, *op. cit.*, p. 99, note 2).

(8) Fr. Ratzel, "Geschichte, Völkerkunde und historische Perspektive," *Histor. Zeitschr.* (1893), p. 1 ss.

(9) *Op. cit.*, p. 92 s.

(10) Fr. Ratzel, "Die geographische Verbreitung des Bogens und des Pfeiles in Afrika," *Berichte der Kön. Sächs. Gr. Wiss. Phil. hist. Kl.* (1887); "Die Afrikanischen Bogen," *Abhandl. Kön. Sächs. Gr. Wiss. Phil. hist. Kl.*, Bd. XIII., Nr. III (1891); "Beiträge zur Kenntnis der Verbreitung des Bogens und des Speeres im Indoafrikanischen Völkerkreis," *Ber. K. S. G. W.* (1893).

(11) H. Schurtz, "Die Wurfeisen der Neger," *Internationale Zeitschr. f. Ethnographie* (Leiden, 1889); "Die geogr. Verbreitung der Negertrachten," *op. cit.* (1891).

(12) Fr. Weule, *Der afrikanische Pfeil*, Leipzig, 1899.

(13) L. Frobenius, *Der Ursprung der afrikanischen Kulturen* (1898); "Die Kulturformen Iceaniens," *Petermanns Mitteilungen*, XLVI (1900), p. 204 ss., p. 234 ss.

(14) Which according to Graebner's opinion (p. 99, note 2) was already prepared in Ratzel (Ratzel, *Anthropogeographie*, II, pp. 605, 607 s.)

(15) Allgemeine Verständliche Naturwissenschaft, Vol. 20 (1899).

(16) Graebner, *op. cit.*, pp. 98-104.

(17) Frobenius, "Morphologie des afrikanischen Bogengerätes," *Atlas Africanus*, Heft 4 (Berlin—Leipzig, 1929-1930), p. 18 s.

(18) L. Frobenius, "Now I must confess that today I in part regret these productions. If one recognizes after the publication of an article that it contains many mistakes, the best thing to do, if one has the courage to do so, is to confess: *pater peccavi*." *Zeitschr. f. Ethnol.*, XXXVII (1905), p. 88. Frobenius here regrets not so much the real errors but rather the actual merits in his work.

(19) This appeared with significant enlargements in the *Zeitschr. f. Ethnol.* (1913), pp. 1014-1134. I treated of this again in a series of lectures throughout the scholastic year (1927-1928) at the University of Vienna, making use of all the new material that has appeared since 1913 and hope in the near future to be able to publish this "considerably enlarged and improved edition."

(20) C. Winter: Heidelberg, 1911.

(21) *Zeitschr. f. Ethnol.* (1905), p. 29.

(22) Fr. Graebner, *Petermanns Mitteilungen* (1911), p. 230.

(23) W. Schmidt, "Die Kulturhistorische Methode in der Ethnologie," *Anthropos*, VI (1911), pp. 1010-1036.

(24) See the short summary by W. Schmidt in *Anthropos* (1911), p. 1012 ss.

(25) Vol. LX (1929), pp. 247-265.

(26) *Ethnologische Studien*, I (1931), p. 235 ss. On p. 143 of the same all the works of Krause relating to this new theory are enumerated.

(27) *Africa*, V (1932), pp. 383-392.

(28) Italics mine—W. Schmidt.

(29) Fr. Krause, *Ethnol. Studien*, I, p. 142, note 2. Also Goldenweiser has fallen into almost the same error: *Early Civilization*, p. 312.

(30) See more extensive treatment of this matter, Chapter III.

(31) *Cf.* concerning this whole problem the lengthy treatment of the twofold character of the culture circle, Chapter III.

(32) *Cf.* also W. Koppers, Fr. Krause's, "Strukturlehre"; also "Teil der kulturhistorischen Methode," *Anthropos,* XXV (1927), pp. 614-617.

(33) Italics mine—W. Schmidt.

(34) Should be "written historical sources"—W. Schmidt.

(35) Fr. Krause, *Mitteil. Wiener Anthropol. Gesellschaft.* (1929), p. 264; also "Ethnology and the Study of Culture Change," *Africa,* V (1932), p. 387.

(36) Italics mine—W. Schmidt.

(37) Of course, Krause did not cite this passage when in the article in *Africa* quoted above (p. 28 note, *Africa,* V [1932]) he declared his method the only one capable of studying culture changes.

(38) *Korr. Blatt der Deutsch. Ges. f. Anthr., Ethnn. u. Urgeschichte,* XLIV (1913), pp. 1-6.

(39) Krause, *op. cit.,* p. 5.

(40) Leipzig, 1921.

(41) Krause, *op. cit.,* p. 91 ss.

(42) In the article quoted above, p. 31, "Ethnology and Culture Changes."

(43) Italics mine—W. Schmidt.

(44) Krause, *op. cit.,* p. 389.

(45) See above, p. 34.

(46) Further details may be found in my article, "Die Anwendung von Evolutionismus und die Hinwendung zum Historizismus in der Amerikanistik," *Anthropos,* XVI-XVII (1921-1922), pp. 502-510.

(47) *Anthropos,* XIV-XV (1919-1920), pp. 546, 583 s.

(48) *Op. cit.,* XVI-XVII (1921-1922), pp. 487-519.

(49) Fr. Boas, "The Methods of Ethnology," *Amer. Anthrop.,* N. S. XXII (1920) pp. 311-321.

(50) A. A. Goldenweiser, *Early Civilization, an Introduction to Anthropology* (New York, 1922).

(51) *Jahrbuch für Soziologie,* III (1927).

(52) *Amer. Anthr.,* N. S. XXXI (1929), pp. 9-33.

(53) New York-London (1933).

(54) Calcutta-London (1935).

(55) Canadian Department of Mines, "Geological Survey, Memoirs 90," No. 13, *Anthropological Series* (Ottowa: Government Printing Bureau, 1915).

(56) See also my criticism in *Anthropos,* XVI-XVIII (1921-1922) pp. 510-516.

(57) *American Anthropologist,* N. S. XIX (1917), pp. 41-54.

(58) *American Anthropologist,* N. S. XXVII (1925), pp. 91-99.

(59) See later, p. 42 s.

(60) *American Anthropologist,* N. S. XXXI (1929), pp. 755-769.

(61) New York, 1930.

(62) *American Anthropologist,* N. S. XXVIII (1926), pp. 585-604.

(63) *Op. cit.,* XXX (1928), pp. 94-106.

(64) *Op. cit.,* pp. 275-310.

(65) See also pp. 297, 301, 304.

(66) *Op. cit.,* XXX (1928), pp. 216-227.

(67) *Amer. Mus. Nat. Hist.,* A. P. XXVI.

(68) *Univ. of California Publications in American Archaeology and Ethnology,* Vol. 31 (Berkeley, California), pp. 211-256.

(69) *Op. cit.,* p. 216.

(70) For a criticism of these proposals, see W. Schmidt, *Ursprung der Gottesidee,* VI, p. 105 ss.

(71) *American Anthropologist,* XXXI (1929), pp. 491-495.

(72) *Cf.* in connection with this correct and important remark what is said later on, p. 141.

(73) New York-Oxford, etc., 1926. Wissler had already touched upon questions of method in two earlier works which, unfortunately, I could not obtain: *The American Indian* (1st ed.; New York, 1917—2nd ed.; New York-Oxford, 1922) and *Man and Culture* (New York, 1923). According to Kroeber's article, "The Culture Area and Age Area Concepts of Clark Wissler" in *Methods of Social Science,* ed. by Stuart A. Rice (Chicago, 1931), p. 250 ss., which gives a list of their contents, the first treats of the "Culture Area" concept (*cf.* below, p. 187 ss.), and but lightly touches upon the time problem. This receives more treatment in the second work, but gives rather only culture historical hypotheses than directions for the methodical research of culture history. Kroeber is also of the opinion that the time problem "is made the theme of a book" in Wissler's third work which we treat in the text, *The Relation of Nature to Man in Aboriginal America.* Since we intend only to give a short history of the historical method, this work will suffice.

(74) New York-London, 1928. *Cf.* also the review of Dixon's work by W. Koppers, *Anthropos,* XXIV (1929), pp. 695-699.

(75) *Cf.* later, p. 147 s.

(76) W. Schmidt, "Kulturkreise und Kulturschichten in Südamerika," *Zeitschrift f. Ethnologie* (1913), pp. 1014-1124.

(77) Schmidt, *op. cit.,* p. 1082 ss.

(78) This has been a little more closely considered also in W. Schmidt's, *Ursprung der Gottesidee,* VI, p. 361. *Cf.* also W. Koppers, "Die Frage eventualler alten Kulturbeziehungen zwischen dem südlichen Südamerika und Südaustralien," *Proc. XXIII Internat. Congress. Amer.* (New York, 1928-1930), pp. 678-686.

(79) Concerning which he could have looked up my *Stellung der Pygmäenvölker in der Entwicklungsgeschichte der Menschen* (Stuttgart, 1910), pp. 67-107.

(80) As I then clearly said, W. Schmidt. *Etn.* (1913), pp. 1022-1026.

(81) Thus he cites (p. 237, note) "Marks and Moieties as a Culture Complex" of Kroeber and Holt as "an excellent criticism of the whole Graebnerian theory," but neglects to refer to my comprehensive refutation of this article, "Die kulturhistorische Methode und die nordamerikanische Ethnologie" *Anthropos,* XIV-XV (1919-1920), p. 553 ss., even though this response had been published eight years before the appearance of Dixon's book.

(82) Some of it I have already included in the introduction to my *High Gods in North America,* p. 85.

(83) Italics mine—W. Schmidt.

(84) New York—London, 1933.

(85) With regard to this passage (and also for other reasons), I can only express my regret that Professor Lowie accepted the dedication of this book for his fiftieth birthday.

(86) *Cf.* above, p. 23.

(87) Graebner, *Methode der Ethnologie,* p. 88 ss.

(88) Schmidt and Koppers, *Völker und Kulturen* (Regensburg, 1924), p. 70 s.

(89) See above, p. 31 ss.

(90) *Jour. Amer. Folklore,* XXVII (1914) pp. 335-373.

(91) New York—London, 1927.

(92) *Methods in Social Science. A Case Book,* ed. by Stuart A. Rice (Chicago, 1931), pp. 248-265.

(93) See above, the exposition on Clark Wissler, p. 47 ss.

(94) Kroeber, *op. cit.*, p. 264.

(95) The Wissler point of view as to culture area and age area have apparently been used extensively in only one other general work, Kroeber's *Anthropology* (1923). So Kroeber, *op. cit.*, p. 256.

(96) *Amer. Anthrop.*, XXXIII (1931), pp. 149-156.

(97) *Amer. Anthrop.* N. S. XXXVII (1935), pp. 539-569.

(98) *Op. cit.*, XXXVIII (1936), pp. 137-141.

(99) Kroeber, p. 549. Such misjudgments always give rise to the suspicion that Graebner's *Methode der Ethnologie* has hardly been read, and certainly not studied.

(100) This happened to him, because just before the outbreak of the war he had taken up the official invitation of the government to attend an international congress.

(101) *E. g.*, in his culture historical monograph on the Santa Cruz Islands, *Ethnographica*, I (1909), pp. 71-184.

(102) *I. e.*, the natural sciences—W. Schmidt.

(103) *Amer. Anthrop.*, N. S. XXXVIII (1936), pp. 157-196.

(104) See the extensive exposition later, p. 175 ss.

(105) Of course especially not then, when this lack of recognition of the scientific basis leaves so much to be wished for.

(106) In his review of R. H. Lowie's "Primitive Society" in *Amer. Anthrop.*, N. S. XXII (1920), p. 377.

(107) *Cf.* above (p. 58) in the works of Kroeber we have treated.

(108) W. Schmidt, *Ursprung der Gottesidee*, I 2, pp. 785, 787 s.

(109) N. W. Thomas, "Ueber Kulturkreise in Australien," *Zeitschr. f. Ethn.* (1905), p. 759 ss.; "Australian Canoes and Rafts," *Journ. Anthr. Inst.*, XXXV (1905), p. 56 ss.; "Kinship Organization and Group Marriage in Australia," (Cambridge, 1906); "The Disposal of the Dead," *Folklore*, XIX (1908), p. 388 ss.

(110) A. C. Haddon, *History of Anthropology* (2nd ed.; London, 1934), p. 113 ss.

(111) Cambridge, 1914.

(112) Portsmouth, 1911.

(113) *Essays and Studies presented to W. Ridgeway* (Cambridge, 1913), pp. 474-492.

(114) London, 1922 ("Helps for Students of History, No. 48"); in the bibliography the German literature is not represented.

(115) Manchester, 1918.

(116) London, 1923.

(117) London, 1923.

(118) In "the Frazer Lectures" (London, 1932), pp. 47-65.

(119) *Essays and Studies presented to W. Ridgeway* (Cambridge, 1913).

(120) Manchester, 1915.

(121) Manchester, 1919. A detailed list of his works may be found in Rivers' *History and Ethnology*, p. 32.

(122) New York, 1929.

(123) Oxford, 1927.

(124) London, 1932.

(125) *Le Caire*, 1933 and 1934.

(126) Lately a controversy has broken out between them. See Man XXXV, 1936, p. 74 s.

(127) *American Anthropologist,* N. S. XXXVII (1935), p. 394 ss.

(128) *Op. cit.,* p. 400 s. *Cf.* his lecture, "The Methods of Ethnology and Social Anthropology," *South African Journ. of Science,* XX (1923), pp. 124-147, which indicates a stage of transition.

(129) See above, pp. 33, 35.

(130) *American Anthropologist,* N. S. XXXVII (1935), p. 390 ss.

(131) *Op. cit.,* p. 391 s.

(132) In this regard see A. H. Pinard de la Boullaye, *L'Étude comparée des Religions,* Vol. II (Paris, 1925), pp. 222, 227 s., 235, 241.

(133) W. Schmidt, "Die moderne Ethnologie," *Anthropos,* I (1906), p. 335 s.

(134) Paris, 1905.

(135) Paris, 190; *cf.* to the whole question W. Schmidt, *Anthropos,* VI (1911), p. 101.

(136) Vol. I. (Paris, 1922); Vol. II (1925); 3rd ed., 2 vols. (1929). See in this connection W. Schmidt, *Ursprung der Gottesidee,* I, pp. 83 s. and 790 ss.

(137) *Archives suisses d' Anthropologie générale,* I, (1924), pp. 102-135.

(138) *Op. cit.,* III, pp. 1-120; especially p. 72 ss.; *cf.* also W. Schmidt, *Anthropos,* XIV-XV (1919-1920), pp. 565-570.

(139) Paris, 1934. It was given somewhat earlier in his publication, "L'Ologenèse culturelle et la place de la culture ainau," *L'Ethnologie,* No. 23 (1931).

(140) Paris, 1928.

(141) *Archiv f. Religionwiss.,* XXXVI (1928), pp. 364-430.; *cf.* also W. Schmidt, *Ursprung der Gottesidee,* III, p. 495 ss.

(142) *Reports of the Fifth Thule Expedition,* 1921-1924, Vols. IV, V, VI, VII (Copenhagen, 1927-1931).

(143) *Ethnologische Studien,* I (1929), pp. 29-39.

(144) *Anthropos,* XXV (1930), pp. 3-23.

(145) *Journal des Americanistes de Paris,* N. S. XXII (1930), pp. 1-32.

(146) Copenhagen, 1914.

(147) *Geogr. Tidskr,* XXIII (1916), pp. 284-290.

(148) *Mem. Anthr. Anthrop. Assoc.,* III, No. 3 (1916).

(149) Fifth Pacific Science Congress.

(150) Göteborg, 1918, 1920, 1924.

(151) A detailed criticism of the same is given by W. Schmidt in *Anthropos,* XVI-XVII (1921-1922); *cf.* also W. Koppers, "Methodologisches zur Frage der Kulturbeziehungen zwischen der alten und der neuen Welt, *Mitteil. Anthrop. Ges.,* LXII (Vienna, 1932), pp. 319-327.

(152) *Germanisch. romanische Monatsschrift,* XVI (1928), pp. 337-357.

(153) *Anthropos,* XXVII (1932), pp. 501-523.

(154) Koppers, *op. cit.,* p. 517.

(155) Koppers, *op. cit.,* p. 518.

(156) *Zivaja Starina,* XIX (1911), pp. XXXI-XLIV.

(157) Koppers, p. 518 s.

(158) In the *Ethnografia* (Moscow, 1926), pp. 1 and 2; German translation by A. Byhan in the *Ethnologische Studien,* I, pp. 215-258.

(159) Koppers, p. 519 ss.

(160) Sternberg, *The Chukchee, Jesup Expedition,* Vol. VII (1909), p. 277 ss.

(161) Koppers, *op. cit.,* p. 522.

(162) Koppers, *op. cit.,* p. 518 s.

(163) Koppers, *op. cit.,* pp. 519, 523.

(164) Koppers, *op. cit.,* pp. 501 ss., 509 s.

Chapter II

THE SOURCES OF ETHNOLOGY AND THEIR METHODICAL TREATMENT

1. DISCOVERY AND COLLECTION OF SOURCES

A. Nature and Division of Historical Sources in General

FEDER (1) defines historical sources as "survivals of human life and such products of human activity as were either destined by their orginators or are by their very nature fitted for historical knowledge of facts or conditions." This twofold division is important, particularly for ethnology, because, as we have already seen, it has almost exclusively only the second kind of sources at its disposal.

"The proper object of historical research, however, is not the sources themselves, but the contents of the sources; *i. e.*, all the information given us by the sources concerning the facts or what we infer therefrom. The sources are only the means to historical knowledge. Hence, we can compare the 'search for sources' to the art of mining, for they both have the same task to perform; namely, the discovery of raw material. Niebuhr coined a fitting phrase when he termed it spadework." (2) In the science of ethnology the "field work" done by investigators among the primitives although it does not exclusively correspond to this spadework, still it is a large part of it. The better and more fully rounded the training of an ethnologist is, the more he is able to bring useful material back from his expedition. If he is not so trained, he is more like the unexperienced miner who brings up a lot of stones and waste mixed in with his good coal. We shall take up the discussion of "field work" later on.

The classification of sources is principally grouped under two headings: Origin and Intrinsic Value. (3)

α. *Classification of Sources According to Origin*

1. According to Time:
   a. Contemporary sources (these are contemporaneous with the historical event).
   b. Subsequent sources (these are of later date).
2. According to Place:
   a. Native sources (those which arose at the place where the historical events took place).
   b. Alien sources (where the opposite is the case).
3. According to the manner in which the author of the sources gained his information:
   a. Direct or original (primary) sources (if the communication is directly connected with the historical fact in question).
   b. Indirect or derived (secondary) sources (if the communication comes from an intermediate agent oı otherwise from a second or third hand).

β. *Classification of Sources According to Intrinsic Value.*

Classifying the sources according to their intrinsic value or according to the connection between the source and the historical object we distinguish material and speaking sources. Material sources (intangible, silent sources, *fontes entitativi*) are those which stand in an ontological relation with the object. Speaking sources (cognitive sources, *fontes congnoscitivi*) are those standing in a logical relation to the object. (4)

1. Material (virtual) sources: various culture elements as such come into question here. We may conveniently divide them into:

a. "Survivals" if they are such cultural elements that have some material substratum (implements, weapons, objects of art, burial remains, remains of domestic animals and of cultivated plants, kitchen leavings, debris of dwellings, etc.).

b. "Vestiges" if we are dealing with phenomena of sociological intellectual character (linguistic survivals, religious, moral and legal institutions, notions, corresponding conditions, customs, social and political conditions, etc.).

All these material sources are in the last analysis indices which give testimony of historical events or circumstances. Of themselves they are really silent witnesses. They are, however, made to speak through the conclusions which we are able to draw from them.

2. Speaking (formal) sources. Among such sources may be reckoned all that comes down to us by means of human testimony concerning facts and events. Hence "whatever has passed through human perception and knowledge and been passed on again with the aid of external representations (signs, words, judgments) in order to give testimony to an event (or circumstance in some way or other)." (5) Hence, all those accounts come in consideration here which describe historical events or circumstances. That is done principally by word (tradition) and writing (symbols). The term "written sources" is preferred in this case by some, but speaking sources and written sources are by no means convertible terms.

The sources can be purely historical or not. The first is the case if they have only the character of an historical report. They are not purely historical if they at the same time or even primarily have some other purpose (*e.g.*, text of an imperial proclamation).

Of course, it can also happen that one and the same source comes under both categories, material and speaking (*e.g.*, if a coin shows a picture or inscription from olden times). We have such twofold sources in ethnology; *e.g.*, in the Mexican hieroglyphics. (6)

B. Peculiarity and Classification of the Sources of Ethnology

a. *Speaking Sources*

The preliterates as such do not have the art of writing and therefore it is but natural that they do not in general have a fixed written source of material that might throw some light upon their earlier periods of development. Hence, the preliterates are very poor in speaking sources. If, however, speaking sources should exist in some cases, they should be zealously and carefully made use of. The following are occasional cases of such among the preliterates:

1. Traditions (*e.g.,* those of the Polynesians and of many African tribes, etc.). Of course, they can only claim historical value if their trustworthiness has been demonstrated. (*Cf.* 80 ss.)

2. The speaking sources (possible written reports coming from peoples of higher culture), which afford more or less good historical data of at least single periods of certain preliterates (*e.g.,* accounts from ancient Chinese annals which date back to the first centuries of our era, in which the cultural peculiarities of different primitive peoples of Korea, Manchuria, South China, etc., are described). Naturally, all the reports from earlier times concerning preliterates must also be included here (*e.g.,* Herodotus in antiquity, missionary investigators and others in the Middle Ages and the age of discovery, as well as for later times). When we make use of such sources (and we must do so if they exist) we must, of course, be ever mindful of the chronological sequence of the reports.

β. *Material Sources*

The greater part of the sources of ethnology are of this kind. They cover the whole material and intellectual culture content of the preliterates as the field worker finds it among them at first hand. Of course, the matter is somewhat different in the case of the investigator in the home country. Hence, the (comparative) ethnologist, outside the objects that have been brought back to the home country, which are for the most part assembled in ethnological museums, must resort to reports. Any reports on objects in museums come under the same category of sources (*i.e.,* speaking sources).

We will do well to keep in mind this difference between the field worker and the armchair ethnologist with regard to ethnological source material. Hence the two will utilize a correspondingly more or less strongly differentiated method with regard to criticism of sources. Graebner did not exactly overlook this point, but he gives it only an incidental treatment, perhaps because he himself did not get the opportunity to do field work.

If a field worker has taken inventory of the culture possession of a tribe of the preliterates and has given his results to the world in the form of documentary reports, then we are dealing with written sources, of course. To these written reports the usual critical approach generally applied to written sources is applicable, as follows:

c. Collection of Sources

The literary historian of today finds the documents he needs and uses principally in libraries, archive collections, and museums. Even in case he himself was an eyewitness of the great event he wants to describe (say, for instance, the battle at Gorlice in the World War), his own personal knowledge and experience of the affair is but a relatively small portion of the whole. Consequently, if he wishes to produce a worth-while work he must consult the oral and written reports of many other witnesses. Howsoever the professional historian may go about the details of the task he proposes, he always has to begin by gathering the pertinent source materials. Hence, also the textbooks such as Feder's (7) devote a special chapter to discuss the search for sources.

We intentionally chose the example given above; namely, the report of the battle of Gorlice by one who took part in it. This observer can well be compared to the ethnological field worker in so far as he himself had opportunity to observe. Written history and ethnology only differ in that what happens to be the rule for ethnology is generally only the exception for history as such. The source material at the service of ethnological science remains today still, in great part, in *rerum natura; i.e.,* among the preliterates. Hence, it can and must still be observed and gathered. In literary history such or similar "field investigation" as we have said before only exceptionally plays a role among existing peoples. In lieu of this situation, we would do well, I think, from the very beginning to distinguish the field worker from the ethnologist in the narrower and proper sense of the term. Now this does not mean that the field worker could not be an ethnologist or, conversely, that the ethnologist could not occupy himself with field investigation. In fact, he should do so as much as possible.

a. *Collection of Sources by the Field Worker*

1. Graebner treats field research under the title, *Sammeln und Beobachten; Publikation (Collection and Observation; Publication,* pp. 7-11). The ideal field investigator must in general be a trained specialist, "who must be at home both in the general problems of ethnology as well as those of his own limited field of research. Nothing would be more false than to assume that a person would be able to assemble scientifically sound material merely by an unlimited receptivity and an ever so highly technical routine. He must put in practice all the arts of criticism and that not only upon the material he has gathered, but upon the very observations he made. Such a task, of course, is making demands not only upon the intellectual, but also upon the moral strength of the investigator" (8). At present, and this condition will perhaps always remain to some degree, we find we cannot do without the help of the non-professional investigator. In these cases a critical examination must decide whether and to what degree the proffered material is trustworthy.

The high ideal of a field worker must always be not only to stay for an appreciable time at one place, but also to master the native language. Concerning the field of research in relation to the time at his disposal, it should neither be too small nor too extensive. For special reasons, a reconnaissance expedition may well be in place, such as, for instance, Schebesta carried out in 1928–1929 among the Ituri Pygmies. In this case the object of investigation had first to be studied in order to determine its extension. The deep-going specialized research was carried out by a second expedition (1934–1935), which completed the task.

2. If it is desirable that only a trained ethnologist go out as field worker that does not mean that all of his theoretical opinions must be tested on the spot or be confirmed definitely then and there. On the contrary, a good training in method presupposes not least the clear realization that there may be a danger hidden in personal viewpoints against which he must set himself with all his might. Naturally, on the other hand, nothing is to be said against the desirability of personal conception and opinion in its proper place. On the contrary, Chladenius's words about the historian as such, *mutatis mutandis,* applies here as well: "They have greatly erred who demanded that a writer of history should be a man without religion, without fatherland, without family." (9)

Obviously, the words of Bernheim still hold good both for the historian and the ethnologist: "that he consider his individual prejudices as a [possible] source of error in conception and he must use might and main to eliminate them as much as possible." (10) It is just as evident that the field worker is bound to avoid all attempts at interpretation for which his local material simply does not suffice. In this regard a person might speak of the methodical error of local interpretation. (11) On this point once more opinions differ. The investigator oriented along psychologico-evolutionistic lines does not admit that this local interpretation is a mistake. On the other hand, the ethnologist (and field investigator), trained in and applying historical methods, considers reserve in all these cases as an obvious methodical postulate. Graebner's *Methode* clearly demonstrated that in face of relevant facts the last point of view alone holds water. And we think the present work does but confirm the opinion.

3. If the field investigator must protect himself against the mistake of local interpretation, that does not mean that he should not endeavor to certify all his local data in all possible attainable ways. Graebner very correctly emphasizes that success in collecting material presupposes the critical faculty. We

shall presently show in detail what tasks it has to perform here. We follow Graebner in passing over all purely technical problems here, in the first place because they would lead us too far afield, and in the second place because in this respect matters are quite different in different cases (*e.g.*, research work among roaming hunting tribes or sedentary agriculturists). Consequently, the practical and in general most successful way is in each case best obtained, by and large, from the general circumstances and from the experiences of the past.

It is quite clear that the development of the whole science of ethnology is for better or for worse, dependent upon field research. Consequently, as long as there is still field work to be done, we can hardly give it too much attention. That does not in the least alter the fact that field research and ethnological research are by no means the same thing. For ethnological research has to perform great and necessary tasks for which field investigation as such is simply incompetent.

4. We have already emphasized the importance of the language for the field worker. Not less important is the *trust of the natives,* for this together with the language is an essential requisite for a penetrating investigation into the elements of the intellectual culture. There is no doubt that a missionary as research worker, living among the natives for years on end, has many great advantages in this respect. However, in order to make him a really ideal investigator he must have as thorough as possible acquaintance with general ethnology. That would protect him against the temptation to which even the most excellent and worthy men are subject; namely, of falling into the gross error of local interpretation (*i.e.,* to set up theories and opinions on the basis of data found at that place). Such a procedure sins against the most fundamental principles of sound methodology. Such deviations are clearly all the more deplorable when committed by field workers who went out as trained ethnologists or at least were supposed to be such. It would not be at all difficult to give some examples of this in recent and very recent times.

β. *Collection of Sources by Ethnologists*

We can treat this matter more briefly here because this whole work deals with what we consider to be the task of the ethnologist. If the field investigator can never know too much about the totality of ethnological problems, it is in the very nature of the case that he will not be able to apply directly much of the methodical apparatus. Thus, for example, a criticism of reports hardly ever comes into question for him. At the same time, because of the local character of the material he is collecting, he should avoid all far-reaching interpretation (*i.e.,* not fall into the error of local interpretation). Finally, the whole work of combination lies outside his department; this is part of ethnologico-historical research work that marks the climax of the investigator's activity. In contrast to the field investigator, the ethnologist, if he would proceed correctly, must be practical master of all these activities; and besides, the old saying holds good also here that no expert falls from the sky, and without training and practice one will in general not get far. If that applies to the young historian, then it is certainly true in similar fashion for an ethnologist still in the making.

I have already pointed out that the ethnologist should at least once in his life undertake some practical field research work where this is in any way possible. That is certainly very desirable, though a person cannot and ought not speak of it as a sort of *conditio sine qua non.* Fr. Graebner and W. Schmidt have certainly developed into successful ethnologists, although they had no or very little opportunity for real field work. In written history matters are not much different. Here it cannot be said that only the one who was actually there at the place (*e.g.,* the battle at Gorlice) could write about it. Carrying a principle beyond its logical conclusions renders a comprehensive and successful writing of the history of the past absolutely impossible.

2. THE SEARCH FOR SOURCES: CRITICISM OF SOURCES

A. The Art of Criticizing Sources

Feder (p. 125) defines the criticism of sources as "the systematic sum of principles and rules according to which the actuality and value of historical sources are examined, the sources are restored as far as possible to their original form, their true meaning inferred and judgment is passed upon the certainty of the attested dates." Graebner has so well treated the application of historical methods in ethnology with regard to the question of criticism of sources that his exposition of the matter is in general still valid today. And so nothing essentially new can be added. It has been said—not without reason—that even if one would not accept the following portion of Graebner's work (combination!), one would still have to accept this accomplishment of enduring worth for ethnology which Graebner gave us in this section. Hence neglect or nonobservance of this section on criticism of sources would never be justified under any circumstances. The exposition that follows is essentially based upon Graebner's treatise on the subject. However, I hope it is possible to show that a few new and not insignificant points can be added and a still clearer arrangement can be made.

In his introduction to *Kritik der unmittelbaren Zeugnisse (Criticism of Direct Evidence)*, Graebner first gives a short survey of the peculiarity and classification of historical or ethnological sources. This point has been treated more at length above (p. 88 ss.). Here it seems worth while to put more emphasis on the difference between the view the field investigator has of ethnological source material and that which the ethnologist (working at home) applies. Graebner by no means overlooks this difference, but it seems to me to be a very great advantage to bring this difference in principle more into the foreground and to keep it in mind throughout the subsequent discussion.

For the *investigator in the field* the whole culture of ethnological peoples is treated as direct evidence and source material. Oral traditions are about the only exception to this in so far as they give trustworthy reports on the historical events of the people in question.

The situation is quite different for the *ethnologist* and, indeed, necessarily so from the nature of the case. The material sources are to him the only objects which can be brought home as such. He usually finds these already in our ethnological museums. Among such objects may be reckoned only those that have some sort of material substratum (hence, for instance, objects of the so-called material culture, of art, cult, etc.). In their relationships to this kind of objects the field worker and the ethnologist do not differ, at least not essentially.

The situation is entirely different as soon as the other departments of culture come into question; *i.e.,* those which originally do not have a material substratum and cannot therefore be brought home. This includes then the whole sociological, intellectual, and religious life of a people. In all of these cases only reports, be they oral or written (see above, p. 89 s.) can help. Even with regard to the direct witnesses mentioned above (culture objects originally having a material substratum), all oral and written explanations thereof do but play the role of a report once more; hence, pass for indirect sources. Consequently, when we have to deal with criticism of direct evidence we must first clear up the problem: From what standpoint are we considering the question—that of the field worker or that of the ethnologist?

B. Criticism of Direct Evidence. Question of Authenticity

In the foregoing discussion which we have carried out, we have shown, among other things, what is especially to be understood in the field of ethnology by the expression "direct evidence." It was pointed out, however, that in this regard the situation is somewhat different if we consider the investigator in the field and the ethnologist. It will help to clarify matters if we are mindful of this in the course of this exposition. As for the rest, we can follow Graebner with regard to the main division and the chief points.

a. *General Rules*

1. Graebner explains what is to be understood by the question of authenticity in the following words (p. 12): "Every direct testimony, as mentioned before, is, *per se,* an indisputable, objective proof at least for the existence of the culture phenomenon it represents for the corresponding time and place to which it belongs. There is only the question whether an object which passes for a direct testimony asserts this claim correctly or not. In other words: Is the object genuine or is it an imitation or a counterfeit?" In another connection, Graebner well points out that both from the standpoint of logic and actual fact we have here a peculiar opportunity (besides the matter of determining the place and time). "For, taken logically, the question of authenticity is only a special case of culture historical determination. Every counterfeit is also in the last analysis a culture product. The difference is only that it did not arise from the cultural locale to which it is ascribed" (p. 25). Hence, as soon as an investigation has proven that an article is not genuine, even on the basis of only a single criterion, that object is by that very fact excluded. The case is different if investigation shows that there is no reason to doubt its authenticity. In this case it is not excluded, but rather the research is carried further and the problems of origin, period, etc., are taken up.

2. Since the whole cultural possession of the people in question is of the nature of direct testimony for the field ethnologist, he must apply the criticism of the authenticity to all the departments of the culture. As we mentioned already, in this section Graebner only touches upon the fact that the whole material really has the nature of direct evidence for the field worker. He does this first in the following chapter, where he speaks of the determination of place and time (pp. 22, 30 s.). This is certainly a slip on the part of Graebner, since the

material concerning place is always direct evidence for the field worker, it being all the same whether it be considered under the heading of authenticity or of determination of place and time.

And when Graebner, particularly with regard to this last case, asserts that essentially the same criteria come into consideration here for the field worker as for the ethnologists working at home, then the same applies with regard to the determination of the authenticity (in the case of objects with a material substratum, the material, technique and form come into question; as to objects of intellectual culture, the form and content. We shall say more on this subject presently). As for the rest, Graebner is perfectly correct when he says (p. 24): "Most objects of material culture will always provide the main part of the direct evidence because they alone can be directly studied away from the land of their origin without the aid of a report."

3. Before Graebner begins with his exposition of the question of authenticity, he treats the preliminary question whether ethnology has to deal relatively frequently with counterfeits. He finds he can answer this question in the negative and gives as explanation thereof the small profit that would generally accrue from ethnological counterfeits.

Then Graebner distinguishes in detail: *1*, the real counterfeit; *2*, the mere imitation (where conscious intention to falsify is absent); *3*, production of such at the behest and demand from European quarters.

The first point needs no further explanation.

As an example of the second group, Graebner (p. 13) gives the imitations of nephritic objects from New Zealand, as they are especially manufactured at "Idar in Hunsruck." As far as method is concerned, such or similar imitations belong to the same class as real counterfeits themselves and so must be treated similarly.

For the cases enumerated under point three, Graebner recommends the rule (p. 14): mistrust them. "Even in cases where the European influence does not extend to the form or technique, the degree of genuineness can only be determined by comparison with certified old examples." A corresponding attitude is justified also with regard to the numerous models of boats, houses, etc., even in cases where the manufacture by the natives is not due to their being ordered. For the facts do not leave any doubt that the details of the model do not always perfectly correspond to the original. It is a different case again if the comparison shows that the model is a perfect replica of the original.

β. *The Criteria for Authenticity*

Graebner then discusses the three criteria of authenticity which might be called criteria of material, technique, form.

I. The Material As Criterion of Authenticity

There seems to be a sufficient reason for doubting whether these criteria should really be considered, as the material seems in any case to be so conditioned by nature and the environment. It is true as Graebner also brings out that in this matter nature does indicate certain possibilities. For example, a bow of bamboo would, *a priori,* never be expected in the Arctic. However, through trade and barter, bamboo could certainly come into districts where it does not at present grow. On the other hand, bamboo is not used for making bows (or some other particular objects) everywhere it is found. From these considerations it follows that the material given in nature does limit the possibilities, but that in general it leaves room enough for the choice of man to play a striking role.

In this matter of the specific element's relation to the raw material there is a criterion of quality which, when taken with corresponding carefulness, is able to do good service in the determination of the question of authenticity. Graebner takes an example to demonstrate this from Mexico (p. 15). He says: "It does not, for example, suffice to ask the question whether a kind of stone or clay is found in Mexico, but if it is found there, it must be further asked whether the ancient Mexicans have made use of just this stone for sculpture work and just this clay for pottery. Similarly each category of objects must be compared with others found in the same place and already authenticated." In other words, it is the *other* material that can demonstrate that an object is not genuine in a given case.

The fact that a material has been chosen that can be more easily worked can often indicate whether a material is genuine or not. "A paddle or club from the Marquesas Islands that has been manufactured from a light soft wood gives clear evidence of modern inferior work" (p. 15). "Furthermore, the replacement of difficult material by an easier one is not only a frequent sign of intentional counterfeits, but is also a quite general indication of contemporary native imitations." Such a case would be a glass imitation of the nephrite jade objects from New Zealand.

II. The Technique As Criterion of Authenticity

Genuine objects are characterized among other things by a specific technique. Technique according to its nature is a criterion of form or, as we shall have occasion to discuss later, of quality. However, for the purpose of a better survey, technique will be regarded here without further discussion as a special criterion of authenticity. Graebner (p. 15) sets forth the following as a typical example: "If a nephrite-mere [mere is of jade and the weapon of a chief] from New Zealand has a smooth cylindrical perforation at the grip, it is certainly not genuine. The reason is that the genuine Maori work is ground out from both sides into conical bevelings which meet in the middle. And so every region has certain technical peculiarities even with regard to the technique of chipping and polishing. These peculiarities must be carefully studied in order that one may judge with certainty between genuine and counterfeit objects."

The use of European instruments (saws, steel knives) can often be proven and might soon settle the counterfeit origin of the objects. But here we must make a distinction. If, for instance, the Indians of Tierra del Fuego have recently manufactured boat models at the request of Europeans, and have made more or less use of modern tools to do so, we certainly cannot, on the assumption that nothing else was altered, speak of a complete counterfeit. At most we might reckon it a partial counterfeit; *i.e.*, on the relevant technical side of the object.

III. The Form As Criterion of Authenticity

Under this heading Graebner considers the form in the strict sense. The question of form in this case therefore covers only a part of the ideas we usually designate by the criterion of form or of quality (see below, p. 141). But here, on the other hand, we are dealing with the most important and most characteristic feature, for thence also came the term criterion of form in the first place in Graebner's usage. The fact, however, that if we retain this terminology, we will have to distinguish between the criterion of form in the strict and in the wide sense, is a reason for reserving the term criterion of quality for the latter (criterion of form in wide sense).

Coming back to our present theme, we read in Graebner (p. 17): "The counterfeiter or imitator has practically never really grasped the principles of form or of the style of the original, apart from that purely mechanical, so to speak, galvano-plastic reproduction of objects which is not yet very general in ethnology. Of course, this is only true from the standpoint of an expert." Graebner uses imitations of the nephrite objects of New Zealand here again as an example: the fashioning of certain peculiarities of the curvature of the surface, treatment of the edges, etc., have been produced by the counterfeiter or imitator with the greatest difficulty, if at all.

The formal element, in the strict sense, includes here the *ornament* also. The peculiarities of ornament are still more difficult for the counterfeiter or imitator to reproduce than the form as such. An expert will soon detect the ungenuineness of the article by the uncertainty in the drawing of lines, offenses against the style in the composition, and ornamental outgrowths contrary to the style. In this case also we have naturally to reckon with partial falsifications. As an example, Graebner mentions a Fan knife with cuneiform writing!

Graebner adds a few general rules at the end of this discussion on the determination of the genuineness of objects. These rules are to aid in the quick detection of the counterfeit in the case in question. The genuineness of an article is reasonably, if not necessarily, doubted if spurious signs of antiquity are detected. One intentionally producing counterfeits of this sort will use every means to give his object the appearance of being older. Among other means applied are temporary burial, pouring some muddy solution over them, smoking, polishing, treatment with acids, etc. In general, an expert will detect immediately whether such attempts have been made upon an object and thus declare it ungenuine.

If there are any oral or written reports on the objects in question they must also be consulted in determining the authenticity of the objects. However, such communications fall under the category of reports and consequently are subject to the rules which apply to such.

c. Criticism of Direct Testimony: Question of Time and Place

If the investigation of a piece of direct evidence has proved it to be genuine, then the question arises as to the time and place of the cultural phenomenon. In view of the essentially two-dimensional character of ethnological material the question of place stands in the foreground. The fact that the historico-ethnological method endeavors to change this superficial juxtaposition in space into a chronological and causal sequence does not contradict this in the least. This test indeed demands a special (synthetic) treatment, though here only the first determination and criticism of the material under consideration comes in question.

"The decisive points are classified according to the features of the object itself and the oral and written indications as to its origin and history. These indications are excluded from the category of direct evidence and come under the heading of reports and must consequently be judged from the critiques relevant to this point of view. Hence, we are dealing here only with the characteristic features the object itself presents. Furthermore, in very many cases, especially in cases of objects of material culture, these characteristics offer us the final and most trustworthy rule for deciding the correctness of information as to the objects' origin" (Graebner, p. 21).

a. *Field Worker and Ethnologist*

1. In this section (as mentioned above, pp. 93 ss., 97) Graebner gives special treatment to the situation of the field worker (pp. 22 ss., 30 s.). The whole culture of the natives in question has the nature of direct testimony for him. As the field worker has to try to solve the question of the genuineness of the phenomena, so he must similarly occupy himself with the question of the origin or place. It happens quite often that a person is brought face to face with an object of culture (either of a material or an intellectual kind) that in itself is genuine enough, but which, in the association in which he now finds it, seems to be an alien. In the nature of the case, the critical rules required by a sound search for sources are nevertheless essentially the same for both the field worker and the ethnologist. Following Graebner in this matter, we will treat the criteria concerned together (see below, p. 107 ss.).

2. For the ethnologist generally, only those objects come into consideration as direct testimony which can be brought home and studied there (see above, p. 92). If Graebner, on a theoretical basis, separated the investigation of the two questions of genuineness and place, his division perfectly agrees with the facts. Of course, the two modes of procedure may

overlap in practice, depending upon the circumstances of the situation under investigation. This mutual interdependence makes it impossible to lay down a fixed rule even with regard to the employment of the two main kinds of sources (written and direct testimony). "It is self-evident that this division of the statements into objective and written or oral information has only a theoretical and systematic end; namely, to allow a comprehensive discussion of all matters that are fundamentally relevant. In practice, however, the questions of genuineness and place may frequently and intricately be combined. We are, of course, assuming here a case in which both the genuineness and the place of origin are attested to, for it is a well-known fact that for a great number of objects assembled in our ethnological museums we do not have any information whatsoever about their place of origin. Consequently, in the latter case only the criteria based on the features of the object itself can be applied" (Graebner, p. 22).

β. *The Criteria of Determination of Place*

Fundamentally, the same criteria which are supposed to settle the question of genuineness apply in determining the place. That can, of course, no longer surprise us. In both cases, the question of genuineness and of place, the problem is to determine the products of human culture and consequently of the human mind. The discussion of the authenticity does not take in the question of place or origin in the strict and proper sense of the word. If the question of genuineness can be answered in the affirmative, then the question of the more exact cultural affiliation of the object concerned arises of itself. For the question of place, in the last analysis, means: To what cultural complex or association does the object belong? The place of every cultural event as such is only of secondary importance. The historian interests himself primarily in the carriers, the people who created this particular phenomenon of culture or, as the case may be, are possessors of it. Even though the individual stands in the background somewhat in the field of ethnology, because in general the individual for obvious reasons can only be described with difficulty, still we have the human and cultural community as the carrier of the phenomena. With regard to many so-called culture historical matters, the position of literary history as such is of course no better, or at least not much better.

I. The Material As Criterion for the Determination of Place

The question of material can concern only objects which have a material substratum (p. 92). "The determination of material is that chapter of ethnological methodology in which the natural sciences render the greatest aid as auxiliary sciences of our branch. It seldom happens that some material is used for cultural purposes in such a limited locality that the use of it alone would circumscribe a very exact ethnographical homogeneous district. However, the natural sciences, by determining the material, confine the possibilities of origin to a certain limited area. Other criteria come to our aid and determine it more exactly within this region. Thus, for instance, necklaces and frontlets of kangaroo teeth can have come only from Australia or very limited portions of Melanesia. Conversely the material can decide the case more definitely within a certain region which has been established by other principles. We may have a case in which, as far as the form is concerned, the object may be either from New Britain or from New Ireland; *e.g.*, cassowary feathers. Since the cassowary is found in New Britain and not in New Ireland the origin of this practice is easily settled" (Graebner, p. 25). One may obtain still more exact, often conclusive, results not only by attending to the distribution of the material (established by the natural sciences), but also by studying to what use men put this particular material. "For a material is not used for cultural purposes everywhere it is found, and especially not for every possible purpose" (p. 26). Man makes the *choice* and thereby the material takes on a specifically human character. Assuming certain precautions, this can be used to determine not only the genuineness, but also similarly the place of origin.

II. The Technique As Criterion for the Determination of Place

Graebner already pointed out that the technique could give a more definite answer to the question of place. For "the existence of a technique is naturally much less dependent upon the conditions laid down by nature than the mere use of the material as such. Hence, the technique is more intimately connected with the cultural conditions and it is in a special way determined by culture relationship" (p. 27).

Among other matters Graebner mentions the different technical forms of wickerwork which nowhere shows an irregular diffusion, but rather a characteristic distribution which is in turn "at times unmistakably associated with a great number of other culture phenomena. We could cite many such cases. They clearly show that particular techniques always coincide with culture forms. This in turn gives us many possibilities to determine the objects, which, however, certainly presuppose very extensive investigation of a combinatory nature which goes far beyond mere criticism as such. This is one of those cases in which it is evident that the formal limitation of methodical functions and especially the sequence of treating them is only of relative importance. They also show that in practice criticism and understanding of the matter stand in intimate and fruitful relation and mutually influence each other."

This rather long quotation brings out a point of quite fundamental importance. Criticism of sources and knoweldge of culture relations can only prepare the way for a deeper interpretation and grasp of a single object, but nothing more. It is only after the culture strata have been grasped (which is done with the aid of the criterion of quantity, as Graebner says quite explicitly [12]) that we are able to obtain a comprehensive culture-historical view of the individual objects belonging to these strata. This will also be treated more in detail later.

III. The Form As Criterion for the Determination of Place

It is but natural that the form in the strict sense frequently plays a very decisive role in determining the place of origin. Graebner (p. 27 s.) calls it the most important criterion "because it is absolutely decisive in very many cases, much oftener than the others: A Japanese armor, an ax of the Basonge, a loincloth from Surba, a shield from the Papuan Gulf in New Guinea, a feather headdress from Hawaii, castanets from Northwestern America, a four-edged club from Guiana, and numerous other articles can be recognized at first sight and decisively so in the first instance on the basis of their form." Principally with the help of this criterion, we distinguish not only the different special forms of one and the same group of objects (*e.g.*, the various forms of the shield), but also the groups themselves (*e.g.*, shield, spear, boat, ax, etc.).

Today we know fairly well the regions of diffusion of most ethnological objects of this kind. Once we are assured of the genuineness of objects, we thereby know also the possible places of origin. This determination of the place of origin will, of course, be generally quite vague. Consequently, Graebner does well to emphasize that alongside the more general characteristics of form we must look for more special ones, whereby in some cases the possible regions of diffusion and origin can be quite significantly delimited. He recalls here the results of one of his well-known studies on the diffusion of the "crutch paddle" (Graebner, p. 28): "Excepting certain relatively small districts, there are paddles of some kind all over the world. Those with a crutch handle (T-shaped) however have a pretty well-defined distribution on all continents. These are distinguished by a curved blade that broadens essentially at the lower third section. This curvature develops further on till special forms with a different length-breadth ratio result. Each of these special forms is restricted to a particular limited region, as for instance, the Rio Negro region in South America."

IV. The Ornamentation As Criterion for the Determination of Place

All the formal features discussed up to now are classified by Graebner as characteristic features of the external form. Over against these he sets up the special group of ornamental features. Graebner does not specially mention it, but there can be observed an ascent from elements serving material ends up to those of an intellectual-artistic kind, going from the material over the technique and the external form to ornamentation. An artistic-aesthetic element asserts itself already in the formation of the external form, the "style," but this, of course, only theoretically reaches its completion and perfection in ornament.

In the same sense Graebner (p. 30) points to "the study of the inner formal conditions as that of the decisive criterion of style. The psychical peculiarity and individuality of a people is seen very clearly in these inner form relations and also in the ornament itself when we possess it." Naturally, purely intellectual analysis cannot do this alone, but one must feel himself into it, so to speak. "When one has once acquired the proper feeling by investigating thoroughly the material that has been sufficiently determined, it is not too difficult subsequently to arrive at the real objective features which underlie the impression dictated by one's artistic feeling." This condition must be striven after, "because the subjective feeling of style lacks all the certitude of an objective criterion of truth. Firm decisions on the basis of certified features are and remain absolutely necessary for the foundation of scientific investigations."

V. Rules for the Determination of Extraneous Elements

We have already mentioned that at the end of his chapter II Graebner (p. 30) once more comes back to the special situation of the field worker (p. 91). The whole culture (and that includes also the intellectual culture) has the character of direct evidence for him. "The criteria of raw material and technique are inadequate for this group of phenomena and only those of form and content remain. We must treat the latter in the same way as we do material objects."

Graebner (p. 31) gives particularly two criteria for the recognition of possible culture elements in the department of intellectual culture: First, if an element is unorganic and disharmonious in the whole ensemble. However, the presumption for this is not so easily arrived at. "A greater amount of knowledge of the form and feeling for style is often necessary for such an appreciation than for the determination of the object." The men's ceremony, the "Kina," among the Yamana in Tierra del Fuego could be used as an example of this kind. Already in 1922, during our expedition there, we saw at firsthand that this celebration, when viewed alongside the youths' initiation ceremony (the "Ciéuxaus") seemed like a foreign element in the whole culture make-up. We took it to be a much more recent infiltration from the Selk'nam.

With this we come to Graebner's second rule. It reads: If, on comparing one region with several others, we find an exceptional agreement between them approaching identity, but if in other respects a closer cultural relationship clearly does not exist, we most probably have to reckon with a more recent borrowing or transmission. Going back to the "Kina" celebration of the Yamana, it should be added with regard to this second rule that further research undertaken actually showed such agreements between the Yamana and Selk'nam even as to details (Kloketen!), so that the dependence of the former on the latter was eventually settled beyond all doubt.

And when Graebner further demands the "establishment of the manner and way in which a borrowing was possible" in order to confirm one of the proofs in the rule, we find this example is still applicable: The Yamana border on the Selk'nam along the whole northeast of their country and derive the whole male festival and the myths appertaining to the "Kina" celebration precisely and almost entirely from this district.

γ. *The Criteria for the Determination of Time*

Graebner says: For determining the time of immediate testimonies (of course only material objects come into consideration) a special criterion is to be found only in their possible position determinable geologically or otherwise by reference to various ancient strata. We wish to make two remarks on this passage: First, this is true if, in the meantime, imposing and, on the whole, definitely successful reconstructions of parallels between ethnological and prehistoric finds have been made. We shall return later to this. Second, if Graebner means that with regard to the potential determination of time only objects with a material substratum can come into consideration here and hence not the phenomena of the intellectual culture, then he is indeed right, because here only the direct and local certification of both individual elements as well as whole complexes of culture is in question. In his later methodological expositions (combination!) there are decisive norms which show how it is possible to obtain time determinants for entire complexes (the phenomena of the intellectual side of culture are included, of course).

D. Criticism of Speaking Sources or Reports: External Criticism

First of all we wish to recall here what we understand by speaking sources in the field of ethnology (see above, p. 89 s.):

1. The oral (and under certain considerations also written) traditions of the natives themselves.

2. All written or oral communications on ethnological facts (Graebner speaks here of the main group of reports of travels and research which belong together).

3. "The information given about collections or objects in collections." This is no special group, however, and really belongs under 2.

α. *Lesser Importance of the Question of Authenticity, Place, and Time*

The question of genuineness is less important with regard to reports than it was for direct testimony. "Indeed, one could almost say that a report cannot be falsified as such, but only in its quality as direct evidence. In fact, with regard to the trustworthiness of data given by such phenomena, they are to be treated the same as those of other, unfalsified reports" (Graebner, p. 32). In the last analysis, it depends entirely on the inner value of the report (*cf.* later, p. 116 ss.). On the other hand, it is not decisive to know from whose hand it really originated, even if knowing this does help greatly to clarify the knowledge of the inner worth of the report. Happily the falsification of reports is almost completely lacking in the field of ethnology. There is a certain external relationship here between more or less high-class novels on travel and ethnological data. Naturally, when the storybook character is evident, the whole thing no longer comes into consideration as a source of ethnological material.

"The question of the time and place of the composition as well as the authorship play a small role in ethnological reports. Potential problems of this kind come under the general principles of literary historical research [in the widest sense, including principles of philology, palaeography, and other criteria]. It would take us beyond the scope of a specific ethnological methodology to discuss them." (13) In general, the source of the most decisive material for ethnology, taken from the standpoint of the historian, is the recent past. The methodical operations just mentioned which demand so much attention on the part of the literary historian thus undergo a corresponding simplification in the case of the ethnologist.

β. *Establishment of Mutual Dependence of Sources*

I. The General Importance of Dependence of Sources

Our aim must be to attain the clearest judgment as to the trustworthiness of the reports on hand. Elucidation of possible dependence of the different reports on one another helps not a little. "*Ceteris paribus,* the closer the connection the report has with direct observation, the more certain it is. Further, it is quite evident that a particular date will be more trustworthy if it has been recorded by several reports than if it were reported only by one. This, of course, presupposes that the reports are independent. Hence, it is of the highest importance for culture history if a phenomenon is reported for a particular place in the world at very different times. This again presupposes that the later reports rest upon direct acquaintance with the facts and do not blindly reproduce the oldest report. Such a case is the information given by Ptolemy and the Arabian geographers which found their way unexamined into works of the west in the Middle Ages and even in modern times." (13) Graebner illustrates these rules of criticism and among others proposes the well-known example of modern times from Parkinson and Erdweg. "Parkinson's report ('Die Berlinhafensektion Neu-Guinea,' see *Internationales Archiv für Ethnogeographie. Mitteil. Anthrop. Ges. Wien,* XIII, p. 18 ss.) appeared two years sooner than Erdweg's 'Arbeit über die Insel Tumleo,' M.A.G.W., XXXII, pp. 274 ss., 317 ss. They both show long passages which agree verbatim, with the difference that what Parkinson generally asserts for the whole ethnographical district is restricted to Tumleo by Erdweg. The general situation and, above all, the careful comparison of the two shows that despite the priority in appearance of Parkinson's work, the study of Erdweg is the original source. Parkinson says in general that he received information of all sorts from the missionaries, but does not mention that he received a finished manuscript from them and that he used it to some extent verbatim."

Graebner's warning still holds good today; namely, that, as the given example and many others show, this branch of criticism merits closer observation and study in order to give ethnology a better foundation. The same rule applies also for the axiom that the specialist of a particular region can be the most competent critic of the source of material in question. The whole science of ethnology can but gain from his estimate and classification of the sources. Of course, one hindrance does remain; namely, the circumstance that those who supply us with ethnological source material are very often still among the living. It is much easier and less painful to subject authors to a heartless criticism as to their trustworthiness who lived hundreds or thousands of years ago than our present-day colleagues! However, this, of course, in no way denies that the latter operation is nevertheless often necessary.

II. Criteria of Mutual Dependence of Sources

In a methodology for general history, we naturally expect a detailed treatment of the criteria of dependence and relationship of sources. Graebner here gives a few of them that come into consideration for ethnology.

1. Identity of content, characteristic limitation of material. "However, we must be careful to see if perhaps this limitation is not caused by the matter itself, for instance, when Europeans are spectators at the initiation ceremonies of Australia, since they are looked upon as *uninitiated* by the natives, they usually get to see only certain less secret parts of the rite." (14)

2. Identical grouping of the material and identical description of details.

3. "The connection between sources is still more certain if words or mistakes and errors can be proven to *agree* verbatim, in so far as these are not necessary or probable consequences of the cultural views of the authors."

4. The relation of time, in which the sources stand to one another. Graebner cites the example of the Parkinson-Erdweg case (see above, p. 114) to show that this is not always infallible. "Neither can the dependence of the two from a common source be recognized from this aspect alone."

5. The organical association is one of the most important criteria. "The data in question are organically connected to one another or with the rest of the contents of the source."

The question of recensions and editions is of less importance for ethnology. "This includes different wording of one and the same work, or, in a wider sense, several works of the same author with related contents." In general, the essential and decisive material for us comes from more recent authors, where such circumstances can be more clearly observed. But cases of this kind are not entirely wanting even in ethnology. W. Schmidt has shown this with regard to the well-known meritorious Australian scholar, A. W. Howitt. His earlier publications on Southeastern Australia present the observed facts much more unprejudicially and objectively than the more recent ones, the last mentioned having been written after he had come under the influence of evolutionistic theories. (15)

In conclusion, Graebner remarks that the fact of dependence of the sources is not restricted to derivation from other known written sources. We have to reckon still with the following two possibilities, particularly in ethnological literature:

1. The fact that great or small parts of reports do not go back to personal observations, but are based on some sort of information from others.

2. That the person who brought the ethnological collection back to Europe often did not gather the whole collection personally on the very spot. Thus the accompanying reports go back to a second or third hand. The investigator in question should, of course, render a very exact account of the circumstances of this matter. If he does not do so, an attempt should be made to work out the required information from the biographical data in the report of his expedition.

E. Criticism of Speaking Sources or Reports: Internal Criticism

The importance of internal criticism, when all is said and done, is still greater than that of external criticism of reports. As Graebner pointed out, the former has been neglected in the field of ethnology. "If there is a lack of independent studies of source criticism anywhere, it is certainly here in our science. One cannot only find sources of the best and of the poorest quality often rated as equal in ethnological studies, but also still more serious is the fact that criticism has been exercised upon sources which is unmethodical and merely irrelevant, because it is supported by the subjective opinions of the user or upon plausible but untested inaccuracies. (16) Sound criticism requires a thorough schooling in the art of criticism, which is conspicuous by its absence in ethnology up till now" (Graebner, p. 39).

α. *Rules for Establishing the Sources of Error in Reports*

Graebner offers a number of norms and rules for judging the intrinsic worth of a report.

1. If one error turns up, we must, of course, reckon with other mistakes. However, a single mistake of itself does not say anything decisive as to the value of the whole source, for the best of us can make a mistake.

2. If quite a large number of inaccuracies can be detected, then the value of the whole source becomes somewhat doubtful. The sources of error that come into consideration here are either general or special.

a. The general sources of error are due to faulty power of observation, poor memory, carelessness in checking observations, etc. As an example we have the writings of Parkinson mentioned above (p. 114). Such reports can be used only for scientific studies when and in so far as they can be supported by other material.

b. The special sources of error originate from special causes and consequently affect only certain parts of the data. Thus, an otherwise trustworthy reporter can be perhaps a poor drawer or a poor musician. Even though, in such a case, data resulting from his weak side must be regarded with caution, all the rest of his report may be dependable.

These special sources of error are the most frequent. The different ones that may come into consideration are:

α. For some reason or other the author may try to have the people and land appear rich in culture goods of a high standard. With this aim in view he *exaggerates* and misrepresents matters and when the opportunity presents itself resorts to fabrications.

β. The author (and this case is frequently had in our ethnological literature) tries to have the natives *appear in as bad a light as possible.* He does this to exonerate the shameful deeds perpetrated upon the natives by his countrymen or even to paint them as being justified and forced to such actions.

γ. Yet another special source of error can result from *disposition, education, or habit of the author.* Graebner here mentions the magician or shaman as a capital object for different representations. The visionary takes everything for gospel truth while the "realist" considers it all falsehood and imposture.

δ. There can also be a special source of error due to the *spirit of the time* in which the report was written. The well-known tendency of Rousseau to find the ancient paradise among the Primitives gave the tone and color to a lot of travelogues of the time (eighteenth century). Later on, the materialism of the nineteenth century was unable to discover anything spiritual and more elevated among the natives.

ε. The *profession* of the informant can affect his trustworthiness either positively or negatively: *positively* with regard to the parts of the culture with which his profession brings him into intimate association. "The seaman will be able, *ceteris paribus,* to give us the best information on shipbuilding and navigation, the jurist on law and society, the theologian and missionary on the religious conditions" (Graebner, p. 43). A professional background can affect reports *negatively,* in so far as under certain circumstances there is a danger that such an observer sees matters too one-sided. Graebner thinks that jurists can relatively easily fall into this error, due to their habit of thinking in categories. Occasionally, there is another danger arising from one's profession from the difficulty a reporter finds in his endeavor to do justice to all the native circumstances. Graebner is of the opinion that it is not very easy for the missionary to judge religious conditions correctly and, consequently, neither the social institutions connected therewith. I do not think anyone will deny that at times a missionary investigator is exposed to such a danger. But, on the average, it is very doubtful whether the missionary has greater disadvantages in this regard than lay investigators.

ζ. Another special source of error can come from *bias through scientific theories or convictions.* A field worker thoroughly trained in methodology will keep all these possible sources of error in mind and, above all, he will be careful lest his suggestive questions give rise to something in the native culture that is not its own. Consequently, one must especially guard against this source of error in the reports of lay investigators (or superficially trained ethnologists!).

η. Finally, it is also important to have it clear in a given case just what information of the author has a claim to more credibility and what part less. It is particularly important in this regard to know what was the spatial and temporal relation of the informant (witness) to the facts he reports. Did the author see the happenings himself? live through them? How long was he at the place? Did he go there repeatedly? Did he have ample opportunity to come into close contact with the natives (knowledge of the language!)? Did he have good opportunities to investigate? Did the natives trust him enough so that he could investigate the phenomena of their intellectual culture, etc.? Graebner recalls the case of Parkinson here. The parts of his work which are based on his permanent sojourn along the coast district of the Gazelle peninsula are more credible than those based on incidental information acquired on his journeys or upon reports of others (see above, p. 114).

β. *Critical Comparison of Several Sources*

In the following, Graebner (p. 45 ss.) analyzes the critical possibilities that result from comparison of different sources.

1. A demonstrably trustworthy report confirms a doubtful one. *a,* "In case of perfect coincidence then there is no need of the doubtful source." *b,* If they only agree partially or in essentials the case is not exactly the same though it is quite similar. "For if there are no other grounds to doubt, then there is no reason to mistrust the sections of the doubtful source not checked by the better one. It is more probable that these sec-

tions also correspond to the facts." Of course, such or similar proofs made on the basis of better testimonies might allow the doubtful sources to appear in a new and better light.

2. Mutual confirmation of several reports which are not of themselves absolutely certain. "This possibility follows from the great improbability that several informants would falsely represent the same happening or the same event in exactly the same way. For that, of course, as for every such confirmation of one source by another, it is presupposed that the two descriptions are independent of each other; *i.e.,* that neither is the one dependent on the other, nor are both dependent on a mutual source. Further, it is certainly necessary to see to it that the two similar sources do not arise from the same subjective background which I numbered among the sources of error." The reference to "the same subjective background" is objected to by W. Schmidt with regard to the example adduced here by Graebner; namely, the case of Howitt and Mathews. (17) W. Schmidt is certainly right in this matter, because the same or similar effects need not always have the same causes.

3. Confirmation of reports by direct testimony. In ethnology, especially, the following cases appear possible: *a,* An isolated report is confirmed by a demonstration from the object itself later on at the place concerned, "as, for instance, the absolutely isolated reports of Powell on shields with figures of faces and battle maces on the morning star clubs of Great Bay [southern coast of New Pomerania] have been meanwhile confirmed in full through collections from this region." *b,* Confirmation of phenomena of intellectual culture (rites, shamanistic and magical practices, etc.) through objects which are used for them (masks, shaman dress, bullroarers, etc.). "They all support the report on the ceremony at which they are used. They at least testify to the existence and particular details of these ceremonies."

γ. *Critical Examination of Data Reported Only Once*

When we have data that have been reported only once and the trustworthiness of this report seems not yet fully settled, we then find ourselves in a less favorable position. However, different norms and rules can come into consideration here also. These are given by Graebner (p. 47 ss.):

1. "If an author is absolutely trustworthy in parts we can control, we run no or very little danger by granting him credence in those of his reports we cannot control."

2. "The same applies to such sources as are only partially doubtful with regard to all the data that do not come directly under the influence of this source of error."

3. "No author will easily fabricate reports on matters that lie outside the range of his ideas and knowledge. Such information therefore can, as a rule, be taken as trustworthy." We can have examples of this thus: when an author describes certain characteristic mother-right phenomena for some region, or penis-sheath as an article of dress, or nose plugs as bodily decoration.

4. "Reports give an especial guarantee for their correctness if they cannot be explained from the sources of error that come into consideration for the informant concerned and even contradict these sources." Thus, a report of a European, specifically of a European jurist, to the effect that among this or that group of natives fruit trees belong to other people than the owners of the land is especially credible.

5. "A final criterion for single data is had in the *agreement with the whole body of our knowledge*. This principle, however, must be applied with the greatest reserve." This caution recommended so highly by Graebner is very understandable, as our knowledge of single data remains still fragmentary at present. Hence, it must be well considered whether it can be said in a given case: This or that report does not fit in with the stage of our knowledge.

This is all the more so, because exactly the opposite criterion, which was just treated above (3), can also be applied. It reads: "An observation creates all the less mistrust the less the author who made it had reason to presume something similar to that at the place in question" (p. 50). We must agree with Graebner that very great tact is necessary to balance the two principles evenly in a given case. It often happens that only the more objective criteria proposed above can give the decision. "That applies almost to a greater extent for the cases in which the degree of probability is not given simply by the distribution actually established, but by the possibility of diffusion which has been inferred scientifically. Neither is this principle to be rejected. The observation of Surville [mentioned above (Graebner, p. 48)] becomes more certain after it has been established that the cultural complex to which the penis-sheath belongs is more strongly represented in the southeastern part of the Solomon Islands." As can well be seen, we have here another of those criteria of source criticism that presuppose some work of a combinatory nature. Graebner rightly warns against a too confident use of this, especially as a more thorough culture historical working out of the single regions has not yet been undertaken, which is certainly necessary for the use of this principle. We hope it will gain more importance in the future.

There is a great danger clearly recognized by Graebner to which every one is exposed who attempts to apply the principles set up here. The culture complexes of Graebner which he himself proposed for the first time are, as is well known, based essentially upon conditions in the South Seas. The danger in applying them comes in when the form and arrangement of these complexes are taken too strictly and dogmatically and considered absolutely settled quantities. And there is also the danger to try to fit mechanically circumstances found elsewhere into this scheme, as a matter of course.

δ. *Critical Examination of Disagreeing Sources*

Graebner gives the following possibilities and rules (p. 51) for reports which disagree.

1. The discordance is merely apparent. We have such a case if the sources in question seem to refer to different places, but which, upon closer examination, prove to treat of the same locality.

2. Seemingly disagreeing reports mutually supplement one

another. Thus, for instance, if on further examination of the reports it turns out that the same tribe or people is concerned, but specifically different localities or subgroups are handled by the different reports respectively. Such an elucidation at the same time leads also to the recognition of local differences. The older reports on matrimonial conditions among the Yamana in Tierra del Fuego give us a good example of this rule. Some emphasize monogamy, others polygamy. A closer examination shows that the latter must have referred more to the eastern part of the Yamana tribe. Graebner mentions the different cases possible (p. 51). "If two observers have seen two different parts of one and the same ceremony, or if two authors describe two different proceedings as initiation ceremonies of the same tribe, which not only celebrates one ceremony at different times, but even several different ones." Contradictions of this kind or similar ones can occur, of course, in the writings of the same author.

3. Whenever efforts to reconcile these discordances are not successful, the single reports must be judged with the aid of the principles given above: "the one that is trustworthy being preferred to the untrustworthy one." Graebner, however, warns against setting up a scale of trustworthiness in such or similar cases without sufficient foundation. He also condemns the use of the principle of the majority here.

4. Of itself, a good source is, *eo ipso,* preferred to several poor ones. But if it cannot be ascertained why different sources which, as such, are inferior with regard to one and the same matter, do not agree with the good one, then the suspicion becomes quite strong that nevertheless the good source just missed fire in this particular case.

5. Finally, Graebner emphasizes that under certain circumstances the stage of our general knowledge can be applied as a criterion to examine contradictory sources. However, the greatest reserve should be observed in this respect. Good building material is of the very first importance (*cf.* above, p. 121 s.).

F. Miscellaneous

1. Oral traditions of the natives. We have already seen above (p. 91) that these, in so far as they report past happenings or conditions very faithfully, are to be classified under reports. Graebner devotes several special brief explanations to the paradigm of these traditions; namely, those of the Polynesians. These and other similar traditions of other natives (*e.g.*, of the Sudan negroes) are sometimes overrated, then again underestimated. Hence, they must be investigated carefully in each case. We can but agree with Graebner's conclusion (p. 53): "The agreement of different traditions is one of the main criteria, in so far as they do not rest upon a common basis. Another criterion is the agreement with the events to be deduced from the cultural conditions."

2. At the end of his chapter IIb, Graebner briefly mentions phonographic records and photographic views. In both of these cases we are dealing with "reports," even though the objectivity of the reproduction comes very near to direct testimonies. Even here sources of error are not wanting. These may arise from different causes. Even at the present day a drawing often renders better service than a photograph. In the meantime the photographic apparatus has been enriched by the film camera. The film has not yet been able to contribute much to ethnology as a science. It is questionable whether we can expect much from it. The drawings, which are almost impossible without making the people "pose," are numerous and large enough, to say nothing of the disturbances which filming causes under certain circumstances both in the normal life of the natives as well as in the quiet and earnest study of the field worker.

3. MEANING OF SOURCES: INTERPRETATION

A. The Special Character of Ethnological Sources

Graebner treats this matter from pages 55-70 under the title "Interpretation": *1*, "Allgemeines" ("In General"); *2*, "Ferninterpretation" ("Distant Interpretation"). He has some things to say here which are of quite fundamental importance for ethnology.

1. It is proper to try to determine the real meaning of the sources after their authenticity has been put beyond all doubt. In view of the special character of ethnological research, Graebner very felicitously distinguishes between direct and indirect or distant interpretation. Under direct interpretation, Graebner understands the meaning and significance which are peculiar to cultural elements here and now. Naturally, all our research must start from this significance. On the other hand, however, it is quite clear that the present meaning of a cultural phenomenon need not be the original one. Migrations, mixtures, or other historical events can bring about important changes. This is what induced Graebner to emphasize the necessity of distant interpretation. He generally means by this the interpretation by comparative research. In this comparative investigation, however, certain methodological rules must be observed; *i.e.,* it has to be based upon a culture historical investigation (combination!). This is also the intention of Graebner when he consequentially demands that distant interpretation be an interpretation of the second degree; *i.e.,* that it presupposes a culture historical investigation.

2. Speaking of the method applied by the older ethnology and of the science of comparative religion, in so far as a person can speak of a real method there at all, Graebner very correctly says (p. 67): "It is very clear to me that this demand, in the face of the almost exclusively customary direct interpretation in vogue up till now, causes a great portion of ethnological work accomplished especially in the history of religion to depreciate in value, if not to be entirely worthless. Of course, this is no reason to depart from what has been recognized as correct and necessary. Perhaps the damage in the end will not be as great as it seems at first sight; for a part of those older investigations, either consciously or unconsciously, have put the main emphasis upon the comparison of districts of culture for

which a closer cultural association was already proven or very easily demonstrable."

The very nature of our sources in ethnology justify and necessitate this demand made by Graebner. The whole matter becomes clear and more convincing if we endeavor to bring out in relief, so to say, the diverse associations and peculiarities of culture that exist here.

3. Once the literary historian has worked through the sources in a given case, *i.e.,* particularly proven them to be trustworthy beyond doubt, then generally his subsequent work consists in arranging them chronologically. In the case of sources authenticated by writing (perhaps contemporaneous!), he gains that chronologico-historical element for his work, which of itself best prepares the way to ascertain the causes of history or often already contains them.

In the case of survivals or vestiges, the task is indeed more difficult. However, even then it does not ordinarily seem an overcomplicated matter for the literary historian. For, besides his survivals and vestiges, he also has sources established by writing. Hence, he can always check the former by resorting to the last mentioned sources, which have been arranged chronologically. If, for example, archaeological excavations, made somewhere by an expert archaeologist, have been proven to belong to ancient Roman culture (by means of the various criteria of relation), then the essentials for the chronological and causal sequence have been established (consequently, in the sense of true history).

4. The situation in the field of ethnology with regard to these matters is entirely different. As we have seen, the first task here is also the search for and examination of sources. But once this has been done, in contrast to written history, one is no further advanced with regard to a chronological arrangement. In general, the material in ethnology is only given in two dimensions. Besides, the ethnologist lacks the great advantage which the literary historian usually has; namely, the possibility of checking his survivals and vestiges by written dates. In fact, as we shall see later (chapter on "Combination"), the ethnologist

is only able to attain the chronological and (causal) moment by means of extensive culture historical investigations. We would only remark here that, in this matter, the culture unities and complexes that have been obtained with the aid of the criteria of culture relationship (p. 141 ss.) are of fundamental and decisive importance. The chronological and causal radication of formerly associated individual elements may eventually be recognized and determined, on the one hand from the whole peculiarity and spirit of such complexes, and on the other hand from the accessible chronological relationship (matter of position, etc., p. 154 ss.) of the complexes to one another. It is evident that only then can we speak of a trustworthy causo-historical interpretation (that is the point in question here) of the phenomena.

Thus, it has been shown clearly enough that the present association is actually based upon the peculiarity of the material for sources of history in general when Graebner demands that the legitimate interpretation must be a distant interpretation. Such an interpretation, however, must be of second degree. This will be treated more extensively later (below, p. 131 ss.). Taken purely externally, the fact that Graebner handles the whole question of "interpretation" in only sixteen pages gives some idea of reciprocal connection between interpretation and combination for ethnology.

B. Direct Interpretation. Interpretation of the First Degree

α. *General Rules for Interpretation*

Let us now consider the main ideas and the rules according to Graebner's detailed treatment (p. 61): "Critical precaution is highly recommended in every interpretation. Naturally, the testimony on the basis of which the interpretation is made must be certified by a critical investigation. Secondly, the fact attested thereby must be formally or conceptually so similar to the one to be interpreted that no error can creep in or is at least improbable. Above all, the points of comparison must be clear."

Further, Graebner is very emphatic in stating that the sequence of the procedure often has only a theoretical value. He also points out, as we just heard, that often the final and conclusive interpretation can only be undertaken at the end of the whole investigation. Graebner proposes these ideas thus:

1. A criticism of the data on the purpose and significance of a phenomenon often presupposes much work of an interpretative kind.

2. Use of the general cultural conditions as a criterion presupposes that all the facts known to date have been synthesized.

3. "Moreover, even these two functions of apprehension exist in a much narrower interdependence. It is evident that an answer to the questions concerning the primary significance of many phenomena can only be attempted at the end of the complete methodical process. Hence, the treatment of important problems of interpretation even with regard to one and the same object follows after the synthetic work" (Graebner, p. 55). Graebner calls this species of interpretation "indirect interpretation" or "interpretation of the second degree, over against interpretation of the first degree (or direct interpretation), which does not require such preliminary work."

If the source itself gives an unobjectionable interpretation of the fact, then all further methodical interpretation is superfluous. Evidently Graebner had only the direct or local interpretation in mind here, the sort which the field worker, above all, ought to and can apply. It has already been clearly shown that thereby the final interpretation is not yet obtained and that it can only be attained by comprehensive investigation. But apart from this, there are many opportunities in the field of ethnology to practice the art of interpretation.

β. *Interpretation on the Basis of Form and Peculiarities of Object*

Often the general significance of objects (that applies especially to objects of material culture) is seen more or less clearly from the form and peculiarities of the objects themselves.

It is self-evident what an ax, a bow, a spear, or a basket, etc., is and what they are intended for. But even here ambiguities are by no means excluded. Thus it cannot be seen at once whether one has to do with a tool or ceremonial ax, with a bow for hunting or trapping, with an ordinary basket or one of a shaman, etc. Similarly, skull decoration points to some kind of skull cult, but it is not yet clear whether it also means head-hunting. The fact that some natives do not eat the meat of certain animals does not give us of itself the least hint for the motive of their abstinence. The same applies to the practice of not uttering or of changing the names of different members of the tribe, as, for instance, the changing of names is known for China and Tierra del Fuego (Yamana tribe). But how different the motives in these cases! The Yamana change the name of a tribal member when a person with the same name dies. They do this lest the mention of this name would recall the deceased one and cause them sorrow. The Chinese sometimes change the names of their children, or they call them nicknames. The purpose of this is to deceive the evil spirits and thus protect the child against harm.

Even though ethnology has a long enough list of difficult problems entailing interpretative work, prehistory in the frequent fragmentary character of its materials has to contend with still greater difficulties, some of which are partially or wholly insoluble. Of course, it is but natural that ethnology can give its sister science much help in this regard. But whereas in ethnology it is possible in general to attain the desired goal in ascertaining the meaning, in the field of prehistory this seems not seldom to be an end which is simply unattainable. To give an example: Where is there a certain criterion for determining whether we have arrow- or spearheads in many given cases? There are many cases of this kind.

γ. *Interpretation from the Comparison of Several Objects*

If the meaning and purpose cannot be ascertained from the form and peculiarities of an object, the methodological tool of comparison must also be applied here to reach this end. Graebner is correct, however, when he says that this function of comparison also has its place in cases like the foregoing. What determines that an object with a particular form and other special features is a spear and not something else? In the last analysis, I make that decision, even if unconsciously so, by excluding all other objects through a process of critical comparison and hold on to the idea of the spear.

Besides, to make a comparison, in general and also in this case, presupposes that the one source lacks what the other source has. We can also distinguish two kinds of interpretation, unilateral and reciprocal. Note that this division is also in part an artificial one and is therefore primarily of schematic value. In practice the two are often commingled. "Quite often interpretation is essentially based upon but one source of testimony, but for single points it takes in the one or the other source" (Graebner, p. 59).

1. Unilateral interpretation (Graebner, p. 58 ss.): We have to deal with this kind of interpretation if the meaning and significance of one of the phenomena to be compared is known "and from the identity proven to exist with another phenomenon the meaning of the second unknown member is also firmly deduced." It is applied:

a. In general, "when we wish to determine more exactly unknown objects in a collection by help of those objects whose significance and purpose are established on the basis of written testimony.

b. Moreover, those cases in which an incomplete complex (consequently not determinable out of itself) is identified with a relatively complete (and therefore easily interpretable) complex. Thus, if comparison shows that a certain woodcarving is identical with the decoration of a boat or a boat model or, for instance, if the meaning of a part of a legend is made clear by the use of a complete tradition."

c. Conversely, if the whole phenomenon to be compared is identical with a part of the complex. Graebner says that this case occurs less often and is not so important, "because, *ceteris paribus* [especially with regard to critical trustworthiness], the scientific evaluation of a phenomenon will naturally be based upon the more complete formulation."

2. Reciprocal interpretation. We have to deal with this kind of interpretation whenever "the meaning of neither of the complexes to be compared is solidly established by the study of each, but only becomes possible by a recapitulation of all the features of all the components in the comparison" (p. 59). Information on the food prohibitions among some people does not of itself reveal anything definite. If I find out from another source that this people practices group (clan) exogamy, then I could, by combining both reports, infer the existence of pure group totemism. Take another case, "this time from the department where interpretation plays the greatest role; namely, mythology. Hardly one of the many different figures of gods of the earth will be perfectly recognizable in terms of their mythic character from one single myth that refers to them. Most of such attempts would only give a one-sided picture, which would have to be corrected with the aid of all the other relevant myths."

We obtain special kinds of reciprocal interpretation by comparing different groups of sources; namely: *a*, Direct testimony through direct testimony; *b*, Reports by reports; *c*, Direct testimony by reports and vice versa. The kind of interpretation mentioned under *c* is of special importance. It occurs, for instance, in the "significance of the Mexican hieroglyphics on the basis of the description of religious conditions in Mexico given by Spanish informants, such as Sahagun and others" (p. 60). Of course, the opposite circumstance is valid here also: "the elucidation of written sources by means of direct testimony, in this case hieroglyphics and sculptures."

C. Distant Interpretation (Interpretation of the Second Degree)

a. *Nature and Importance of Distant Interpretation*

1. "Various data can be treated in the most intensive sort of mutually interpretative activity only when they belong to the

same geographical and chronological culture entity." (18) These words are the kernel of Graebner's transition to the treatment of true distant interpretation. By the expression, "a geographically and chronologically closed culture unit," Graebner (the whole context leaves no doubt about it) does not mean culture circles (below, p. 175 ss.) or something similar, but refers to locally circumscribed and specially defined cultures in the case of which the time element generally does not play any special role. The elements which prove themselves to be characteristic of such a particular culture (culture unity) I cannot interpret from the particular culture itself. Graebner says in the same sense: "If I can prove that the whole culture of a region did not change essentially in a certain space of time or only in accidental matters, then I come nearer to interpreting the data in this space of time by considering them as if they were contemporaneous."

The more or less unstable element which must be taken into account here is the admittedly slow development which we generally find among the primitives. Since the locally and, generally, also the temporally limited culture unities stand in question here, the source of error will mostly not be very great. Graebner (p. 63) points out the limitations of these possibilities of interpretation and cautiously warns: "Possible neglect of this temporal element would have its revenge not only in questions concerning the high cultures of Asia, but also probably in attempts at interpreting the old Mexican monuments from the culture of today of which we just spoke a moment ago."

2. Having laid down these principles, Graebner proceeds to discuss distant interpretation as such. First, he remarks that the danger of falling into a false interpretation in the cases of arbitrary hurdling of great distances is, of course, incomparably greater. But, nevertheless, to limit interpretation exclusively to data of one and the same culture unity would rob interpretation of the best part of its importance; consequently, we could not subscribe to such a restriction. The whole of comparative history of religion, comparative history of law, in short,

all comparative treatments of culture historical problems, stand or fall upon the possibility of interpreting phenomena of one geographical region by analogies from another.

The justification for this rests not only in the often incomplete transmission of data, but above all in the well-known historical tendency to degenerate and to decay. Due to this tendency, myths become legends and fables, meaningful institutions degenerate to formal habits, parts of an important association disappear, etc. Hence, in all of these cases the meaning of the phenomenon cannot be derived from this single region alone, but a comparison must be instituted with similar phenomena in other regions. Consequently, the question can only be: What precautions must be observed to limit the sources of error in such attempts at interpretation—if not with certainty at least with a very great degree of probability?

β. *Possibilities of Error in Distant Interpretation*

Graebner enumerates as coming into consideration here the following possibilities of error in interpretation:

1. To apply reciprocal interpretation to phenomena on the basis of their greater or less similarity in form or content. "No one is justified in concluding that the same meaning must underlie identical appearances." Hence, I cannot simply and promiscuously interpret cultural phenomena which appear at different places in the world on the basis of purely external similarity. For the similarity can be purely external and accidental; hence, the phenomena in question do not really have anything to do with one another, and it would be a wholly gratuitous assumption to conclude from identity of known phenomena the identity of as yet unknown phenomena.

2. Likewise, the assumption of a general similarity of the human psyche does not afford any sufficient basis for an unlimited interpretative comparison. For the question as to how far this very similarity (which was itself assumed to start with) is expressed in the details of cultural evidence must indeed itself be answered out of the conception of these data—the solu-

tion cannot, therefore, in its turn be the criterion for the comparison of the data.

3. "Furthermore, it is at least theoretically thinkable that originally altogether heterogeneous phenomena undergo a process of approximation to a high degree through convergence and combination with similar phenomena. In such a case an interpretative comparison based upon this apparent similarity would lead more or less to false conclusions."

γ. *How to Insure Distant Interpretation Against Error*

"The surest and, in my opinion, the only means to prevent false conclusions in the field of distant interpretation, or at least to reduce them to a minimum, is the greatest possible approach to *local interpretation.*" (19) The connection in which he mentions local interpretation here shows that Graebner speaks of culture historical conditions which are already well known and locally determined. Of course, the term "local interpretation" can be understood differently; for instance, if taken in the sense of *purely* local interpretation of phenomena in the strict sense, as the field worker, above all, has to apply it. But this meaning is excluded here. For the local interpretation of which Graebner speaks in this passage he gives the following important rule: "Two or more phenomena are comparable and may be interpreted through one another when it can be demonstrated that they belong, if not to the same local culture unity, at least to one and the same culture complex." We have shown above already what kind of distinction there is, particularly in this connection, between culture unity and culture association (p. 132). Just how Graebner understands interpretability of phenomena from the same cultural association can be seen in his own words which follow: "This demonstration should be carried out not only for this or that part, but rather for the whole basic complex or complexes of the data and, wherever possible, down through the very individual elements dealt with." To give an example: I am thoroughly justified in interpreting the Quato (20) Saga of the New Hebrides from the Polynesian Maui myth, for I can not only prove that the northern New Hebrides to which the Saga belongs stand in close linguistic and general cultural relationship to Polynesian culture, but I can also point out the particular relations of the two saga complexes in their essential content. However, it would be an error to include in the interpretation also those elements of the Quato Saga for which such connection is not demonstrable. Thus, the Taso-Episode, which as a typical cannibalistic twin saga belongs to the older complex of the two-class culture.

δ. *Unilateral and Multilateral Distant Interpretation*

As in direct interpretation (p. 130), so also in distant inferential interpretation we have to distinguish between unilateral and multilateral interpretation. The last example given above might be taken as typical of the first kind of interpretation. Almost the same assumptions apply for the other kind also.

"Neither am I justified here to subsume several apparently similar complexes of data under the same interpretation, if I cannot make it appear probable that they belong to the same culture unity (or same cultural relationship). And once again I can bring only those elements into the interpretation which can be shown definitely to have such an affiliation." As an example, Graebner chooses the prevalent phenomena known under the term "totemism." It is not permissible to try to interpret these facts in one sense as long as their cultural relationship cannot be demonstrated. Graebner would find this condition fulfilled for the "special type of father-right, local-exogamous group totemism." (21)

Here Graebner (p. 67 ss.) concludes his demonstration with the following theses: that *a*, distant interpretation is necessary; *b*, that "if it wishes to lay claim to objectivity it must still remain interpretation of the second degree"—*i.e.*, that such an undertaking sometimes (only sometimes!—W.K.) presupposes far-reaching culture historical investigations. Then Graebner adds those weighty principles already quoted above (p. 125). The examples he gives are taken from several of the known attempts at interpretation by Frazer. Where his interpretations (consciously or unconsciously!) remain within certain cultural relationships, his results can be more or less trusted. Wherever this is not the case, since "Frazer's proposals in this regard lack the cogency of a firmly scientific demonstration, they present an overbalance of the artistic element."

This short but fundamental and important chapter on interpretation by Graebner is concluded with the following words: "Interpretation of the second degree is a turning point of the historical method in ethnology, upon which the future of our science rests to a great extent. It stands very close to the real work of combination, to the treatment of which I now proceed."

(1) *Op. cit.*, p. 84.
(2) Feder, *op. cit.*, p. 84.
(3) Feder, *op. cit.*, p. 85 ss.
(4) Feder, *op. cit.*, p. 87.
(5) Feder, *op. cit.*, p. 88.
(6) With regard to material, completeness and clarity, let us quote Bernheim, *Lehrbuch der historischen Methode* (5th and 6th ed.; Leipzig, 1908), p. 466. He says very correctly: "Every source that belongs to tradition can always be considered a 'survival' in so far as we look upon it as a product of the human mind."
(7) Feder, *op. cit.*, p. 105 ss.
(8) Graebner, p. 8 s.
(9) Quoted by Bernheim, *op. cit.*, p. 762 s.
(10) Bernheim, *op. cit.*, p. 763.
(11) On the use of the term "local interpretation" by Graebner see below (p. 124 ss.).
(12) Graebner, *op. cit.*, p. 27.
(13) Graebner, p. 33; *cf.*, Bernheim, p. 391 ss.; Feder, p. 168 ss. (Ch. V. Langlois and Ch. Seignobos, *Introduction to the Study of History* [New York], p. 199 ss.—Translator's note.)
(14) Graebner, p. 36 s.
(15) *Cf.* W. Schmidt, *Ursprung der Gottesidee,* Vol. III (Münster, I. W., 1931), pp. 577 ss., 589 s., 591 ss., 639 ss.
(16) Graebner, p. 38 s.—In this connection Graebner in a note accused W. Schmidt that in his book, *Die Stellung der Pygmäenvölker in der Entwicklungsgeschichte des Menschen,* "he had no right to designate as false the report that single isolated Bushman tribes do not know of impediments to marriage between parents and children, brother and sister." In the meantime, thorough investigations (let me here mention Dornan and Lebzelter) have proven Schmidt to be right. But even apart from this, considering all that had been known of Pygmies and Pygmoids at the time already, Schmidt had not only the right but the duty to doubt strongly such a report.
(17) *Anthropos,* VI (1911), p. 1024.
(18) Graebner, p. 62 s.
(19) Graebner, p. 164 ss.

(20) Here and in the following, Graebner continually uses "Quatu," but it is a question of the labioguttural consonant, for which H. Codrington uses the orthographic *o* (without *u*); see Codrington, *Melanesian Languages* (London, 1885), pp. 198, 211 s.—W. Schmidt.

(21) *Cf.* W. Koppers, "Der Totemismus als menschheitsgeschichtliches Problem," *Anthropos,* XXXI (1936), pp. 159-176.

Chapter III

CRITERIA FOR THE ESTABLISHMENT OF CULTURE RELATIONS

1. GENERAL CONCEPTS DEFINED

A. Active and Passive Culture Relations

1. CULTURE from its deepest nature consists in the inner formation of the human mind; in the external formation of the body and nature only in so far as this is directed by the mind. Thus, culture, as everything intellectual, is something immanent, something entirely internal and as such not directly subject to external observation. However, it is observable, not only through the influences exercised upon the mind from without to which the mind is exposed, but also by those influences which radiate from the mind itself out upon the body, other human beings and external environment. It is through these that the soul manifests both its own culturally molded nature in some way or other, as well as the inner development itself that has matured in these transformations.

We unite these two, both the internal and the external under the title, "Culture Relations" ("Kulturbeziehungen") and name the first passive, the second active, culture relations. Only if we keep the active as well as the passive culture relations in mind is the following statement of Graebner correct (p. 107): "For the first and fundamental problem of ethnology and also of the whole history of culture is and remains the working out of culture relations."

It is clear that the distinction between active and passive

culture relations is identical with that of cultural causes and effects. It is easily understandable then that historically aligned ethnology, which first of all aims at the restoration of the correct chronology, with which it might establish the ethnological age of the culture elements in an objective way, devoted itself at the start more to the passive culture contacts, the cultural effects. For ethnology could draw conclusions from the latter back to the cultural causes which, historically, always preceded the effects, and thus could take a step backward into unknown time depths. It is true, at any rate, that through the accumulation of inferences upon a cultural cause, we eventually come so far as to be able to grasp its nature and character, and we are satisfied therewith.

But it was not sufficiently taken into consideration that the nature and peculiarity of this cause is not an additive sum of individual features, but rather an organic, living whole. The task of attaining this whole and, after it has been grasped, of once more passing over in review the effects it produced has been overlooked. Then also these effects would be still better known as proceeding from this peculiar cause. In fact, in this new light many influences would have been recognized which had not even been previously observed at all. We must thus take the active culture relations into consideration as a prerequisite to the full discovery and evaluation of the time problem, the objective time succession. But it is also indispensable for this reason; namely, that the active culture relations are very important themselves especially with regard to the establishment of the complete uniqueness of a cultural cause, since the other phase of a development of culture is thereby placed in its true light. With this aid many effects would have been discovered which formerly were not considered to be such.

2. The consideration of both of these, the active as well as the passive culture relations, refutes the objection that culture historical ethnology which opposes evolutionism concerns itself only with external relations, migrations, and other such culture contacts and opposes and gainsays evolution, the inner development. Those who speak thus seem to identify evolution

and evolutionism, since evolutionism, according to usage in the German language, indicated a one-sided and exaggerated emphasis of evolution; compare, *e.g.*, nation and nationalism, reason (ratio) and rationalism. This has already been sufficiently treated above (p. 10). Since we here require the consideration of both the active and passive culture relations, it is clear that we recognize both in principle, the external and the internal development. For every single case there is no *a priori* determinant as to which of the two must be taken up first; each of them equally demands positive proofs before it can be accepted.

3. Also the other objection can easily be answered; namely, that culture historical ethnology gives too much attention to relations which have been exerted upon an object and neglect the referent, the (passive) subject of the relations. That is by no means the case, for culture historical ethnology considers not only the (passive) object of external influences, but also the active agent producing the different effects that proceed from it.

The objections which the representatives of the structure theory (1) and the functional method especially advance in this regard apply with a certain justification, at most, to several representatives of the culture historical idea, who at times are so preoccupied with relations that they no longer see the thing related. The representatives of the structure theory and the functional method, on the other hand, make a much greater mistake of taking up culture relations insufficiently or too late and already pass judgments on the nature and age of a culture before they have sufficiently established its geographical and chronological relations! A human being with his culture exists in space and time. But all that exists in space and time is interrelated. The relations going forth from the subject form a part of this spiritual self and without these relations we would never be able to know this "self." And the stimuli which reach the "self" from outside are in process of becoming manifestations of the "self." Consequently if we do not know the relationships of the person or tribe in question, we do not grasp the innermost self of the person, the tribe, or, at least, do so but inadequately.

4. Even though the study of culture relations has, in fine, human beings, the carriers of culture, as its object (who, as the subject of culture not only receive culture relations passively, but also actively exercise them), nevertheless the study of external objects and elements, and also those of the so-called material culture, should not be forgotten. For upon all of them the human mind has in some way impressed its mark and has taken them into its service.

Besides, the differences of objects of material culture can, for the most part, be more easily and more sharply grasped. Hence, it is good that the methodological study of a tribe begins with these. And also, whoever would wish to make principally the intellectual and social culture the object of his studies should also take care to study at least some part of the material culture.

B. Logical Demonstrative Value of the Methodological Criteria

Precisely then, when we maintain that culture always and everywhere, also in the so-called material culture, is nothing else than either a passive manifestation of the spirit (which the spirit itself experiences and in which it itself is formed), or an active manifestation (which, by activating and confirming the spirit's own inner disposition, molds it anew and influences other persons or things), can we give epistemologico-theoretical proof for the demonstrative value of the criteria which we shall presently put forward. Graebner did not concern himself with this epistemologico-theoretical basis. It appears that he did not feel the philosophical and logical necessity for this. It was different with H. Pinard de la Boullaye, who came to ethnology from philosophy. He offered this proof for the first time in his two articles: "Quelques précisions sur la méthode comparative" (2) and "Essai sur la convergence des probabilités, (3) both now included (with additions and slight alterations) in his work, *L'Étude comparée des Religions* (Vol. II [3rd ed., Paris, 1929], pp. 1-80, 381-423). A short summary of the sequence of his ideas now follows.

1. The human individual as such exists only once, and the same is the case with an historical happening, which is an event in which one or several individuals actively or passively take part. Hence, such an event can only be represented idiographically and not as a (indifferent) part of a series or a fixed course of events. It is true every natural occurrence happens but once, if we consider the exact spatial and temporal conditions in which an event takes place. But an historical event is unique to a higher degree and in another way, because here an individual existing but once carries something out with the absolute unforeseeable freedom of a decision made but once.

This individual, existing but once, is then recognizable as such only through the union of certain characteristics (as we have seen above [p. 138], of active influences which he exercises outward, or passive influences which he experiences within) which are found in this quality and quantity only in his case: it seldom happens that an individual can be known from merely *one* of such characteristic peculiarities which can be found with this individual alone. Wherever, therefore, we meet *this* union of characteristics, entire or with sufficient clues, or this one characteristic distinguishing mark, we can be convinced of the historical presence of this individual or this group of individuals, or of a culture group, of its active or passive existence there.

Conversely, if we wish to prove this presence for a particular place and at a particular time, then we must establish this union of characteristics or a singularly characteristic distinguishing mark exactly at that place and time. Further, when we demonstrate this union or this distinguishing mark for two or more places, we have then proven that this particular individual was present or active there at different times. In other words, we have shown that the two places and events stand in historical connection with each other. If it be a case of a group of individuals, then it can be present and operating at different places simultaneously or at different times; in the first case, we would be dealing with geographical relations and in the second, similarly, with historical relations.

2. This whole demonstration is of a strictly scientific nature, not based on mere theoretical grounds. In history, any other procedure is impossible, but nevertheless it is altogether sufficient if it is applied with all the restraint which it demands and together with the criteria and auxillary criteria which we shall soon learn to know. For that matter, calculus in mathematics rests upon the same logical and philosophical basis. J. H. Steward justly recalls here that even the most exact natural laws are, philosophically speaking, but statements of very high probability. (4) This fact is also generally recognized by modern higher mathematics and by the theory of the natural sciences. (5)

As I said before, the individual and the historical relation as well are recognizable in the union of certain characteristics, which are found in *this* quality and quantity only in this one case. From this it follows that on the whole there are two criteria with which the presence of culture historical relations can be established: criterion of quality (or form) and criterion of quantity. In comparison with these, all the others are auxiliary criteria and belong according to their nature to the one or the other or to both together. First we shall deal with the criterion of quality (or form).

2. THE CRITERION OF QUALITY (OR FORM)

A. The Positive Criterion of Quality

1. The criterion of quality was already proposed and used by Ratzel (6). When he found characteristic similarities between two culture elements, provided that this likeness did not take its origin from the nature of the object in question or (when material) from the stuff out of which it was made, he postulated an historical connection, even though the particular culture elements were distributed over wide and discontinuous

regions. Graebner (p. 98) gave this criterion the name "criterion of form." In parallelism to the name of the other criterion (criterion of quantity), I would rather prefer to call it criterion of quality. And also because, as Graebner (p. 106) points out, it makes its appearance not independently as an object, but together *with* an object, the quality of which it characterizes.

Graebner justly maintains that exactly because of the last-mentioned reason this criterion of the comparison of single elements also makes it possible to take their nuances into account and thus puts in our hands a means "to carry out that study so important for the question of genetic relations; namely, the study of the transitions, modifications and crossings of culture" (p. 108). From this it follows that a certain flexibility *(souplesse)* must be reserved for this criterion, in order that it be able to do justice to all the nuances of the traits. Among these criteria of quality there are also, of course, fixed points of very decided, to some extent, psychical precision, which Graebner would designate "formal elements in a stricter sense." They are particularly perceptible in cases of borrowing through changes of form, whereby the borrowing people express the predilections corresponding to its own psyche in modifications of the borrowed element.

2. That the criterion of quality does not appear independently, but is only present together with an object, is not, however, to be stressed too much. There can be cases where the mere appearance of a certain implement or of a certain social form or other culture elements can be used as a criterion of quality; namely, if it is considered in a greater organic unity, to which it in some way belongs, to some extent, because of its quality. Thus, the fact that two tribes make use of lances and daggers only; *i.e.,* of pointed weapons alone, and that others, as the Pygmies originally, use only the bow and arrow. This fact, I say, can pass for a criterion of quality, because this limited and characteristic manner of arming is understood as the quality of the armament equipment in general. In a similar way the fact that a culture knows only moon mythology can

be a criterion of quality, since this fact refers indeeed to mythology as a whole.

3. The explanation of the criterion of quality given by van Bulck (p. 179) has been unnecessarily complicated. It is also incorrectly curtailed and consequently his formulation is not convincing, for he restricted the "culture relationship," which should be proven through the criterion of quality, to the inner relationship, which is caused by the migrations of peoples. Graebner is partially responsible for this; *e.g.*, when, without further ado, he uses the two terms "culture relationship" ("Kulturverwandtschaft") and "culture relation" ("Kulturbeziehung") as synonyms. (7) But first Graebner uses the more general word "culture association"(8) ("Kulturzusammenhang") and secondly he then expressly distinguishes between "the categories of original relationship" and those of "borrowing" within "culture relationship," (9) as he also places "the questions of culture relations, migrations, and borrowing" alongside one another. (10) Finally, Graebner in that statement, ostensibly regarded by him as fundamental, designates as "the first and fundamental problem of ethnology as well as of the whole history of culture the working out of *culture* relations." (11) Here he uses a more unambiguous statement to the effect that he included *all* culture relations, be they those of external or those of internal relationship. And the criterion of quality is destined and able to establish both of them and not merely the latter (internal relationship), as van Bulck thinks. The criterion of quality alone cannot establish which of the two relationships is concerned. Hence, in discussing this latter question there is no reason to bring in the criterion of quality again.

B. The Negative Criterion of Quality

In the examples we just offered, it was obvious that there are also negative criteria of quality, which can consist in the negation of qualities as well as of objects, when the latter are considered as parts or qualities of a greater whole, as was discussed above (p. 144).

1. From the standpoint of method, a twofold negative criterion of quantity must be distinguished according to whether it is a question of contrary or contradictory negation.

> We are dealing with the first case if a tribe does without stick and pointed weapons, but has cutting and striking weapons in their stead; or where sun myths do not occur, but we find moon myths. The second case is in question, if the presence of a particular culture element is merely denied, without considering whether something positive is present to supplement the missing element; thus, if the existence of astral myths is denied without asking or saying whether or not animal myths are to be found in that region. The evidence of this case is still more clear if the negation knowingly excludes all the rest; for instance, if it is said by a tribe that they lack every kind of means of protection (shield, cuirass).

The value for demonstration of a contrary-negative criterion of quality lies not in its negative but in its positive part, to which it more or less clearly points by means of its contrary negation. The contradictory-negative criterion of quality cannot demonstrate cultural relations as long as and in so far as it remains purely negative; but it attains this demonstrative value when the lack of a culture trait expresses a certain positive feature; *e.g.,* the lack of armor, which indicates the use of weapons only or primarily against animals and not against men.

A demonstrative force restricted in space and time can then and there also retain a contradictory-negative criterion of quality wherever and whenever the occurrence of an absent culture element is elsewhere actually frequent, so that its very absence in this spatial and temporal setting becomes something striking and characteristic.

> That can be so, for instance, in the case of the nonoccurrence of rectangular houses in Polynesia or certain districts

in the Congo region; on the other hand, hardly for certain parts of Sudan.

2. Thus in certain statistical procedures in which the nonoccurrence of an object is expressly noted (12) this nonoccurrence cannot be everywhere regarded as a negative criterion of quality, but only within the framework of the rules laid down above. In other cases, the express testimony of the nonoccurrence of a culture element has only the more practical function of excluding with some certainty the possibility that it might still be found through a more diligent search.

Through these rules, I think, the indecision which, for example, Driver and Kroeber (13) showed toward negative criteria can be remedied to some degree.

c. The Negative Conditions for the Criterion of Quality

We must still examine more closely the negative conditions of the criterion of quality. There are two: the characteristic similarities, in which the essence of the criterion of quality consists, should not arise (*a*) from the purpose and nature of the characteristic of the object or, in material objects (*b*), from the material from which they are made.

1. That two cultures use a lance or an ax can furnish two criteria of quality; for there are cultures which know neither the one nor the other or know only one of them. But now, to set up the fact that the lance has a point and the ax a cutting edge as a new criterion of quality is invalid: for the former belongs to the essence of the lance and the latter to the essence of the ax. However, a new criterion of quality can well enough be furnished if the point of the lance and the form of the ax edge show special characteristics.

2. Each material out of which an implement or a weapon is manufactured has its peculiar laws of fabrication; these are

different for wood, different for stone, and different again for metals. Similarities in two culture elements, which follow from the nature of the material, cannot be used as criteria of quality. A criterion of quality, however, is furnished if the work on the two culture elements goes against the law of manufacture of this particular material.

> Thus, if the earlier method of wood manufacture is applied to a metal implement or, vice versa, if in the manufacture of wooden or stone weapons the old iron technique is imitated. Likewise, neither can the same succession of motives in two lunar myths be taken as a criterion of quality if this is identical with the natural course of the phases of the moon: new moon, crescent moon, full moon, waning moon. However, a criterion of quality is deducible if the same characteristic disturbance of the natural succession can be found in two or more different tribes or peoples.

3. In all these cases in which the two conditions given above have not been fulfilled, we are not dealing with a real criterion of quality that might fulfill the methodological function of giving us trustworthy information as to the former historical connection that once existed between two culture elements or culture complexes, which connection would be the cause of the characteristic similarity existing at present. For the latter does not owe its existence in these cases to an historical contact or historical relationship; it arose independently at the two separated places, following from the nature of the object or from the peculiarity of the material used for it.

4. Another factor must be pointed out here which can greatly diminish or even entirely nullify the demonstrative force of a similarity for historical relations. This factor is, namely, the *limited possibilities* in the development of certain cultural elements. Kroeber emphasizes this also and proposes as examples the few possible types of arrow releases and the "sacred" numbers, all of which must almost of necessity be chosen from the numbers between three and twelve. (14) Pre-

cisely because the possibilities are so few in number, the similarities that occur are, therefore, no longer characteristic enough, since they have come about, so to say, of necessity. This determinism could also have brought it about that elements of entirely different historical origin were constricted externally along the same lines in the further course of their development, and thus a kind of convergence occurred. Consequently, the more the possibilities of development are limited the less will be the evidential force of these homologies in any given case.

D. The Compound or Quantitative Criterion of Quality

1. If, then, a similarity between two culture elements does not proceed from either of these two sources, then it speaks for an historical association of the two elements, and that the stronger, the more seldom and the more characteristic it is, and the less it could be expected (then and there). The less frequent ("more unusual," "more strange") certain peculiarities are, according to all laws of probabilities, it is less probable that they arose independently. (15)

The same is valid for the unexpected. It can be due especially to this: that, as we have explained above (p. 139), similarities exist which are against the nature and purpose of the object, hence impractical, but are still retained.

> Thus when the Tungus, who according to the researches of S. M. Shirokogoroff sprung from Central China, retain much of their old style of clothing, which is less practical for them at present in the North, where they now live. (16)

2. The high degree of unusualness of a criterion of quality can, however, be due to the combination of several and precisely these particular features. In this case we have a *compound* criterion of quality. We can call it also a *quantitative* criterion of quality, as it has something of the nature of a criterion of quantity, of which we are about to speak, because of the great number of these single features present. The more single features it manifests, the greater its value as evidence will be.

Such a criterion of quality is at hand when the bows of two tribes not only agree in the cross section, but also in the mechanism at the ends of the bow for fastening the bowstring and, finally, in the material of the bowstring. In addition to that, since the bow and arrow together form one instrument, the arrow adds other peculiarities to the compound criterion of quality in its manner of feathering, its length, and its placement. Ratzel began his investigations on the bows of Melanesia and West Africa with such a compound criterion of quality, which consequently has that much greater demonstrative force. (17)

3. THE CRITERION OF QUANTITY

A. The Criterion of Quantity Considered in Itself

The criterion of quantity consists in a multiplicity of criteria of quality which, however, are independent of one another.

1. Its methodological function is the certification and the confirmation of the criterion of quality. A certification because, in the evaluation of a characteristic trait as such and, consequently, the avowal of a criterion of quality, some subjective element might still play a part. Through the multiplicity of these similarities this subjectivity will be ruled out. A confirmation because several similarities prove more than a single one. We might also add that in the multiplicity of these similarities strong enough ones will easily be found to compensate for any possible weak ones.

But the criterion of quantity can perform this methodological function only if the several or many similarities are independent of one another and do not follow necessarily from one another, for, in that case, it would cease to be a criterion of quantity.

Hence, we cannot take the occurrence of bow and arrow as a criterion of quantity (*i.e.,* as two criteria of quality), since they both form one weapon.

On the other hand, there is no objection to the assumption of a criterion of quantity, if the association of two similarities is not necessary, but only more or less useful or suitable.

> Thus, the cuirass as defense armor corresponds to the lance and dagger as weapons of attack; the shield as defense armor against other weapons of attack, the club and sword. But since there are tribes with those weapons of attack without the corresponding defense armor and, furthermore, since through later displacements the shield comes together with the thrust and pointed weapons as defense armor, the cuirass as defense armor for cut and striking weapons, it is evident that the association between the offensive and defensive weapons in question is by no means intrinsically necessary. Therefore, the occurrence of one of these in association with the other can, in the fullest sense, be regarded as a criterion of quantity. Thus, also the saddle, halter, and spurs are part and parcel of the riding gear for horses. However, likewise these paraphernalia are not necessary, but only useful, since there are equestrian tribes among whom these "accessories" are more or less missing. Also they can serve as criteria of quantity. (18)

2. Thus, in the second place, the criterion of quantity attains a special kind of evidential value because it reveals hints of culture complexes and, particularly, of those culture entities which are not logically but organically bound together. These we call "Kulturkreise" ("Culture Circles") * and they consist of associations not simply of discrete culture traits but rather of total culture complexes of such. They are, in part, the associations of single culture elements which Tylor called "adhesions." (19)

* The many and various translations of this term (horizons, planes, cycles, etc.) have not helped to make it more comprehensible to English-speaking readers. It is hoped that from now on, and it will certainly make for greater clarity, "Kulturkreise" will always be translated by the term "Culture Circles."—Translator's note.

Thus the criterion of quantity by establishing culture complexes and culture circles also prepares the way for the establishment of culture strata as we shall show more in detail below (p. 191 ss.) and consequently it alone makes the real historical research into temporal and causal sequences possible. For the latter the criterion of quantity is of special importance, in fact it is absolutely indispensable.

B. The Qualitative Criterion of Quantity

1. We must accord a still stronger demonstrative force in this direction to those criteria of quantity in which the single similarities are not restricted to one department of culture alone, for example, that of material culture, but also reach into economics, society, the arts, mythology, and religion. The more such spheres are represented, the more *evident* the culture complex becomes, which satisfies *all* human wants, and is, therefore, named culture circle. We call this criterion of quantity *qualitative,* because the distribution of the single traits in the several spheres has something of the nature of a criterion of quality.

Of course, we must note carefully here whether the association of the various spheres of life is an inevitable one, because in this case the criterion of quantity would cease to be such. So, for example, the fixed extended family belongs to breeders of large animals, because without this greater and more solid social foundation the actualization of the type of economic life in question would not be possible. In such a case, coexistence of the family type and economic form would not give us a criterion of quantity. (20) But if the association is not essential but only probable, there remains at least something of the nature of the criterion of quantity. Thus, if the breeders of large cattle are forced to live in the tundra and steppes and, hence, more under the open sky, the limitless vault of heaven, this, probably, though not necessarily, has its effect in a stronger emphasis of their relations of the Supreme Being to the sky. Compare, for instance, the Samoyeds, among whom the name of the Supreme Being, "Num," also means "sky." (21)

2. It seems also that what we read in Driver–Kroeber must be restricted: "We believe that culture traits are in the main, if not in absolutely all cases, independent. This is because so many of them have been shown over and over again in all domains of culture and in all parts of the world to occur at times dissociated even if at other times or places they are frequently or even preponderantly associated, that it becomes a fair inference, until contrary cases are demonstrated that all traits can occur independently of one another," even though they cite also Graebner and Schmidt in support of this opinion. Driver–Kroeber (22) themselves make an exception in a note (four): "essential parts of a trait cannot, of course, be counted as separate traits." But this reservation is hardly enough. My remarks above are but an attempt at the "general inquiring on this point" (p. 213) which Driver–Kroeber consider necessary.

3. As was the case with the criterion of quality, so also with regard to the criterion of quantity the exposition of van Bulck suffers from his identification of "culture relationship" with "inner culture relationship," which is caused by migrations of peoples (23) and by granting an importance to the criterion of quantity principally for this inner relationship. I say principally, for he here in some way betrays the view that that is an inadmissible restriction, since he writes: "The criteria of form (in order to produce a good criterion of quantity) must, *above all,* (24) be based upon traits of the fundamental categories of a culture." (25) The distinction that he introduces between "fundamental elements" and "secondary elements," which he made before (26) and repeats here, really does not pertain to the question whether we have a case of internal or external culture relationship. Hence, this distinction is not of essential importance for the formal methodological function of the criterion of quantity, since "fundamental elements" are also carried and taken over externally and "secondary elements" can belong to the inner development of a culture as well.

c. The Concurrence of the Criterion of Quality with the Criterion of Quantity

1. As already stated above (p. 150), the methodological function of the criterion of quantity is in so far not of independent importance, since a criterion of quantity cannot exist without a criterion of quality. The criterion of quantity consists essentially in a plurality of criteria of quality, and the function of this plurality consists in the certification and confirmation of the discrete criteria of quality. We might rather ascribe such an independent importance to the criterion of quality. Theoretically, at least, a single similarity can be so characteristic that it would of itself be sufficient to demonstrate the historical association of the two culture elements, both of which exhibit this similarity. As such I consider for instance the diving motif of the creation myths of so many North American and North Asiatic peoples. (27) These cases are not any too frequent, and here I cannot agree with Graebner when he says (p. 118): "Indeed, there are a countless number of cases in which the striking coincidence of form does not leave any doubt." It may well be that he had in mind the quantitative criterion of quality.

On closer investigation, we shall also discover in most cases that, wherever such a criterion of quality was believed to exist, it was a compound or quantitative criterion that already contains something of the nature of the criterion of quantity.

As such a case I consider the belief of the Samoyeds that the rainbow is the hem of the mantle of the Supreme Being, and the belief of the Yuki in north central California that white and red, the colors of the rainbow, are also the colors of the Supreme Being. That man in a tribe who represents the Supreme Being is decked out in these colors. This supposition is supported by the fact that of all the North American peoples, as well as those of North Asia, the Yuki have preserved the close relationship of the Supreme Being with thunder, which is his voice there, and also that among the Samoyeds the last trace of this belief has been preserved in this: the thunder bird to whom the function of the thunder has been transferred also has the rainbow as hem of the mantle, which is not the case with any other of their more exalted beings. (28)

2. In most of the cases we do well to look around for a weighty criterion of quantity. At the same time, the rule applies that the criterion of quantity must be the stronger, the weaker (*i.e.*, the less characteristic) the criterion of quality is. It may be less strong the more characteristic and, consequently, the stronger the criterion of quality is. Moreover, we must firmly hold that a doubtful criterion of quality cannot be improved by any criterion of quantity be it ever so strong. Furthermore, if the single similarities in the criterion of quantity remain doubtful, the piling up of them does not give any authority to the single ones nor, by the same token, to the whole. It is indeed admissible that among the single elements of the criterion of quantity several weaker ones may so be included. These do not indeed become strengthened by association with the rest, but in the totality they may nevertheless add a certain confirmation.

In the endeavor to gain a criterion of quantity as strong as possible, we should not allow ourselves to be led astray by making a parade of as many trivial single features as possible. Such an accumulation comes about naturally in the statistical method by the analysis of similarities into their smallest features, in order to be able to compare them with one another in the different tribes. We need not allow ourselves to be too greatly impressed by the astounding great number of points of comparison which is often attained in this process. They are only too often the *disjecta membra poetae*. They are occasioned (*1*) by the dissection of all quantitative criteria of quality; (2) by the dissolution of all qualitative criteria of quantity; and (*3*), hence, by the exclusion of the organic culture complex from the comparison, which (*4*) is identical with the atomization of the comparison of culture, in which the real culture life can only with difficulty be grasped in its fullness and truth.

In concluding, it is quite in place to refer again to the "great advantage" of the universal application, which Graebner praises in both of the great criteria (p. 109). "While all the criteria of independent origin continually presuppose the knowledge of the causal series won through tiresome work, the criteria of form and of quantity may be applied, without any previous subjective construction, to that situation still so two dimensional, a circumstance which is not without meaning for the objective worth of the criteria themselves." With the aid of these two principles, we can set to work immediately with all method upon all material that has been reliably collected, critically sifted and arranged, in order to find culture relations.

4. THE AUXILIARYY CRITERIA (29)

The application of the two criteria of quality and quantity make it possible to establish with scientific certitude historical relations between two culture elements or culture groups at a distance from each other, as soon as the existence of these criteria has actually been demonstrated in the two (or several) elements or groups. From the standpoint of principle, it does not matter how great the spatial separation existing in between the two elements or groups may be. In order to be exact and honest we must, of course, grant that the greater this distance is, the longer the time (for migration) it presupposes during which the two groups have been separated. Therewith greater possibilities for changes in the character of the culture present themselves. This becomes still stronger through the increased possibility of thus coming into contact with alien cultures, which exert their influences for changes. But if the criterion of quality and that of quantity are actually present, we then have a proof that all these possibilities which from the very start were only possibilities, in this particular case, did *not* become realities or only partly so and, therefore, did not extinguish the old culture affiliations.

A. The Criterion of Continuity

1. Still some methodic prescriptions must be laid down in the case of these great intervening distances, in order to make the former culture historical associations somewhat more credible. First, *the possibility of a continuous migration* from one place to the other must be demonstrated, for no culture acts where it is not present, but operates only from person to person, from tribe to tribe. Therefore, the possibility must be proven that these persons and tribes could come into connection with each other in their migrations (by land or sea). If we have the proof for this possibility, then, of course, only the *possibility* of a culture connection is demonstrated and not the reality, which on its part still needs positive proofs. However, if the culture connection has been proven impossible, then the reality is without further ceremony excluded.

In this whole process of demonstration we must consider that the possibilities of culture relations over certain areas are smaller for the oldest times of mankind. This is so, first of all, because of the slight knowledge of the earth and, secondly, because of the small development of means of travel; especially of seagoing vessels, as those which they had in the beginning were only floats and bark canoes which could attempt only trips along the shore or journeys from one island to another one near by.

The last mentioned reason alone suffices to render the theory of Dr. Rivet impossible. His theory is that the Australian languages are related to some of those of Tierra del Fuego, supposedly as a result of direct contact between the two. This cannot be accepted, as neither the Australians nor the Fuegians had seagoing vessels at their disposal nor had knowledge of the sea for making the journey over the immense distance of the Pacific Ocean. Furthermore, the criterion of quality and that of quantity are both missing here, (30) since the comparison was carried out between languages of Tierra del Fuego and the most heterogeneous languages of Australia, which do not have any relations to one another.

2. In case of greater distances, the criterion of quality as well as that of quantity are strengthened in proportion to the culture elements and culture groups which are found along the intervening distance in which the same criterion of quality is repeated. These cases are characterized as the last remains of former continuous connections, which have remained even after the partial obliterations of these connections through alien cultures. They function, so to speak, as bridge pillars, which guarantee greater firmness and awaken greater confidence in the assumption of culture historical connection of two or more widely separated cultures over such an extensive region.

We call this criterion after Graebner (p. 120) "criterion of continuity." It is not a criterion different from that of quantity or quality, but is a special form of the criterion of quantity, which we could likewise designate as qualitative criterion of quantity, for it joins to the criterion of quantity a peculiar spatial localization as of quality.

In many cases where the life of the peoples no longer at present offers these bridges, they are restored in a surprising way as witnesses of the past by prehistory. Hence, here we see the great worth of prehistory as an auxiliary science of ethnology to aid in establishing geographical continuity. We shall see in the course of this work what still more important services it can render for the discovery of temporal culture relations.

3. It is hardly to be wondered at any more that also here van Bulck's exposition of the criterion of continuity suffers, for he restricts its function to the establishment of only the inner relationships. (31) Still it is his merit to have pointed out the lack of sufficient formulation of this criterion by Graebner. (32) There are, in fact, cases in which the occurrence of elements or complexes in the intervening territory, which separates two culture regions bound together by criteria of quality and quantity, which cannot be explained as survivals of a previous

migration through this intervening region by the culture in question. There is no reason to assert with van Bulck the occurrence of the superposition of a conquering tribe rather than survivals of a migration. It would be only a special case of cross-migration, for example, that of nomad herders. On the other hand, van Bulck is correct when he rejects cases of radiation of high culture and infiltration through trade as criteria of continuity, since they only came into this intervening region subsequently. But we might doubt whether these two cases are ever to be found alone, without the presence of genuine criteria of continuity. Both can exist side by side. That can be distinguished by the more recent and, therefore, unadjusted character of high culture influences and trade infiltrations. But van Bulck is right in his demand that both kinds are to be kept apart and the forms following upon high culture influences and trade infiltrations are not to be added to the genuine criteria of continuity which would then be increased by the addition of the former.

B. The Criterion of Degree of Relationship

1. If two or more discontinuous regions have been proven to stand in historically related similarity to one another by means of the criterion of quality and the criterion of quantity, the proof for the same is strengthened if the regions lying closer to one another show a more pronounced criterion of quality and a greater number of criteria of quantity than the regions farther apart. The only reason for such an arrangement of the criteria of quality and quantity is that the districts lying closer together have remained joined for a longer period than the more distant ones, the latter coming more easily into contact with foreign agencies and thus being longer exposed to their influence. If the similarity arose independently in the single regions, there would be no reason why they were not equally divided everywhere, and it would be incomprehensible why precisely the more adjacent regions should manifest a great accumulation of such similarities.

Graebner (p. 121) calls this auxiliary criterion the criterion of degree of relationship. The demonstrative value lies in the differentiation of the "degree of relationship" of the different regions according to their proximity to or their distance from one another and in the greater "degree of relationship" found in more adjacent regions. Graebner rightly remarks that the converse conclusion is not acceptable; namely, to infer the complete absence of historical relations in case such a gradation of relationship were not present. For there are plenty of factors which could have disturbed the original stratification. It must always be kept in mind that we are dealing here with an auxiliary criterion that supports and strengthens historical similarities already repeatedly established.

2. In his exposition of this criterion, van Bulck did not allow the restriction upon inner relationship to apply in this case, but rather seems to have accepted fully Graebner's explanation. But damage has been done thereby, because he here in one stroke treats the general function of this criterion together with its special function with regard to the establishment of the direction of the distribution. He writes (p. 192): "This criterion is extraordinarily valuable if it is present, but the application is difficult. Graebner himself points out that this criterion for the establishment of the direction of the distribution is susceptible to serious errors." Graebner himself, however, treats the general function of this criterion (p. 120 s.) and there in no way lessens its worth and validity. He did this only with regard to the problem of establishing the direction of the diffusion which he, however, treats much later in an entirely different connection. (33)

It is also unfortunate that van Bulck here already treats of the establishment of the inner development and causal associations which Graebner quite correctly proposes much later in a special section, (34) while van Bulck himself, when he treats the "causal arrangement of cultures" *ex professo* (35) really remains rather sterile.

c. The Concurrence of the Criterion of Continuity with the Criterion of Degree of Relationship

There are cases in which the criterion of continuity on its part is made doubly strong by the criterion of the degree of relationship simply as such and, thereby, also in its function as auxiliary criterion.

If we can call the criterion of continuity a bridge pillar, which aids in bridging the wide expanse between two (or more) culture regions which are bound together by means of historical relations of similarity, the weight of this bridge for the argument appears all the stronger the greater the frequency (criterion of quantity) and the more pronounced the character (criterion of quality) of these relations of similarity are to be found at the two farthest starting points of the whole bridge, which at the same time lie nearest the termini of the two separated culture regions. Here also the greater frequency and characterization of the similarities precisely at both termini would be incomprehensible if they arose independently. On the other hand, the historical relation explains them immediately: the greater proximity of the two main regions has here exercised a conserving influence.

Consequently, we must also keep van Bulck's critical check in mind here; namely, to examine whether the spreading influence of a high culture or trade infiltrations did not cause the greater frequency and more pronounced character of the similarities existing at the present only later and secondarily, or at least contributed thereto.

5. THE CO-ORDINATION OF ALL CRITERIA

a. The Establishment of Spatial Relations Between Cultures

With the help of the criteria just proposed here, we are in a position to establish objectively first of all the spatial culture relations, and even such relations the bearers of which are separated from one another by great distances. With regard to the practical application of these criteria, Graebner thinks (*op. cit.*, p. 125) that we can hardly set up general rules for it; that it is "to a great extent a matter of tact and delicacy and, above all, one of self-criticism." It seems to me that all this ought not to be emphasized too much, because in that case one could hardly refute the objection that subjectivism, after all, is let in again here through a back door.

Such rules have actually been given already, for the most part, in the explanation of those criteria, and Graebner himself has added others in the course of his book. I shall give a few directions myself for cases of relations between regions separated by intrusive alien cultures. These are, in fact, the most difficult. My approach to the matter consists in considering the different possibilities in which this separation between the carriers of the culture came about. First of all, we get two groups here, depending upon whether the bearers of these culture relations have been separated from one another by foreign cultures or whether they have gone apart themselves—in other words, whether the separation was an active or a passive one.

I. The separation of two sets of culture carriers is effected through the penetration of foreign cultures:

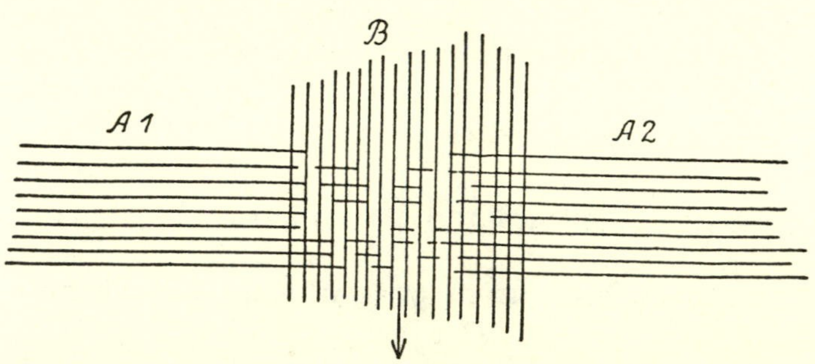

In this case, the criteria of quality are found on both sides, A_1 and A_2, and with a suitable number of criteria of quantity; and in the middle, in B, criteria of continuity will indicate survivals of the former existence of A.

II. The separation of the two sets of culture carriers is effected by themselves (active separation); for the sake of simplicity, let us assume that one had separated itself from the other by migrating. Then the following three cases are possible:

1. A large part of a complex, *i.e.,* a *large* group of individuals, separated itself together with its culture content and wandered through foreign cultures; coming to the end of the migration, the group is still strong enough either (*a*) to supplant the foreign culture settled in that place or (*b*) to mix with it in approximately equal proportions.

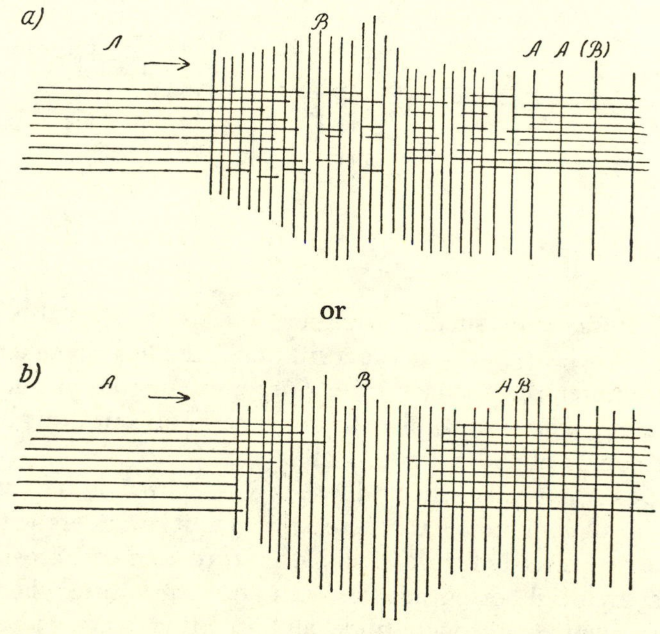

In the first case, many criteria of quality acting as a criterion of quantity will show the historical association between A and AA (B); in the second case, a smaller but still sufficient number of criteria of quality will point to the historical association between A and AB. In both cases, the criteria of continuity (simple and qualified) in the intervening section B show the passage of A through B. They will be the more numerous and the more pronounced the smaller the time is since the passage took place.

2. There is a second possibility, if a *smaller* group of individuals with its culture possession broke away and migrated. At the end of the migration through regions of alien cultures it will be the weaker, the stronger were the alien cultures through which it passed and accordingly it will make up a lesser portion in the resultant mixture.

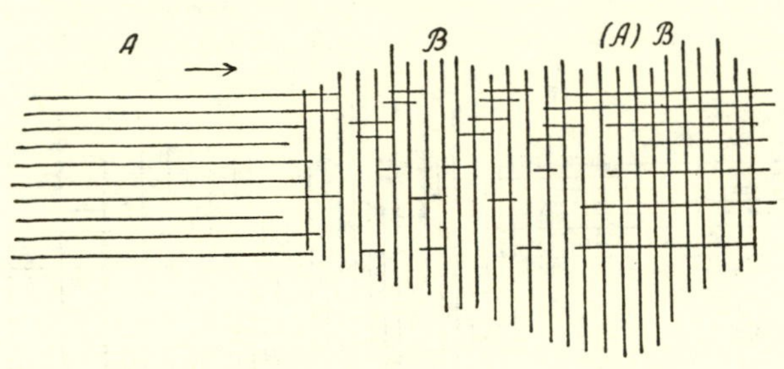

Here a much smaller number of criteria of quality will bind A with (A) B, and they will be all the less characteristic the greater the span of time since the emigration and the crossing. The same applies to the criteria of continuity along the course of the migration of B.

3. A third possibility will then be realized if it is not a group of individuals that breaks away and wanders with its culture possession, but if single culture elements are taken over by neighboring peoples with another culture who then pass them on through trade and in other ways. Here the criteria of quality will be the weaker, the greater the distance and the number of transmitters, since each alien culture exercises an influence for change upon it. The final

result at the end of the migration will not be a crossing any more, but rather only a borrowing.

I have set forth these different possibilities of migration, which could be differentiated still further, in order to give an idea of the multiplicity of the function of the criteria of quality and quantity and the auxiliary criteria from the very start.

The real practical undertaking before which we stand is, of course, an entirely different one; in fact, just the reverse of the foregoing. It is only with the aid of those criteria that we are to establish the fact and the manner of those migrations and, proceeding backward, come again to the former condition that existed before the migrations took place. After the circumstances and result of the migrations have been objectively established, then each time we must proceed backward again and subtract in order to attain to the older state of affairs. With the aid of these criteria, the latter must again be investigated as to whether older and younger components may be discovered therein. The younger ones must then likewise be subtracted from the older. Graebner expresses the same in the following words (p. 125) : "The greater part of human history included in ethnology must be reconstructed by working backward, and that in great part through a kind of subtraction process: After the determination and deduction of the youngest and further of the relatively younger cultural movements and changes, one arrives at even older, more original events and complexes which often were more widely distributed."

Here already the distinction between the older and the younger elements and complexes comes in, which should be gained from the establishment of their spatial position. We shall now undertake to show how this historical sequence in time can be determined objectively. In general, we are already certain that we can here go back to considerable time depths, since we can with certainty ascertain culture relations back over great and very great distances. But the greater the distance is, the greater must the span of time be, in which this distance was covered by the migration of the culture under consideration.

However, we shall now proceed to examine how these time depths may be established, also in particular concrete cases and with objective certainty.

B. The Establishment of the Temporal Relations Between Cultures

a. *The Limitations of the "Structure Theory" in Establishing Temporal Sequences*

Fr. Krause reproached especially the culture historical school, because it did not consider the culture unities of the present, but forthwith took up the comparison often of the most widely separated elements (see above, p. 32 s.). That this objection does not apply to Graebner, at any rate, comes from his following words (p. 125 s.), in which he already gives essentially all the directions of which Krause is later so proud: "The starting point of the whole investigation must in every case always be the study of the culture unities which are now or were present and which can be established by a study of original sources. They offer not only the matter for comparison in the permanency of their elements, but also the changing operations of their elements within the system give a piece of internal culture history, their former antitheses not fully of a piece with the general culture [survivals] afford a diagnostic of heterogeneity, a proof that the culture unity of today is a composite from several originally different culture complexes." In his reference to the words, "The changing interactions of the culture elements," Graebner shows the positive "functional" associations of the parts of a culture whole, while he correctly designates foreign disturbances of this organic association as former antitheses not fully of a piece with the general culture.

More important depths of time may be gained, to be sure, merely by investigating these original culture unities. This is admitted by Krause himself. Here, however, broader and more deeply penetrating investigations must be made, to which we shall now proceed.

β. *Methodical Rules for the Establishment of the Ethnological Age*

1. After the principal and auxiliary criteria have enabled us to establish the historical and spatial relations of a culture, we, also, thereby obtain, even in the case of homologous relations of but one single cultural element, still two or several interrelated surfaces of distribution. For a single isolated occurrence in one or even two instances would not offer a broad and sure enough basis of comparison. It is always a case of distribution within at least a tribe or one of its groups. These planes of distribution become still more extensive when not one only, but several relations of different culture elements have been established, which then represent more or less large culture complexes.

These planes of distribution then form the foundation for working out the temporal sequence of these relations. Their demarcation is nowhere sharp nor ever the same in two cases; now this, now that culture trait, now single, now several culture elements spread over the boundary of their original culture region and thereby come into contact with alien culture traits. In fact, even the entire cultural complex in its full extension can thus come into contact with another culture complex. This contact, be it of single elements or of whole complexes, can take place in two ways. If the contact occurs essentially only on the boundaries of the two culture regions, then we have "contact action." The time depths in this case are naturally smaller, since the contact on the narrow border regions is more quickly accomplished. It is also quite possible that we are dealing with local forms which have quite recently originated in the peripheral region and found their way across the boundary into the region of the alien culture.

2. But if a culture has displaced a seemingly great part of the alien culture region and stays there, we then have "mixture," which is nothing else than a more or less mutual blending between culture elements of the two cultures covering a large district. Exactly this circumstance enables us to gain

greater time depths here, since such an overlay and mixing require a longer time.

The terms "contact action" and "mixture" are not altogether felicitously chosen from the point of view of technical delimitation, for "contact action" also grades into "mixture." The degree of extension of the mixture is the differentia between the two. Consequently, for "contact action" I, therefore, use the term "marginal mixture" and for mixture itself the term "planitional mixture." Or when in the following sections I take "acculturation" as the genus for these two species of mixture, I will refer to "contact action" as "marginal acculturation" and to "mixture" as "planitional acculturation."

3. For *both* occurrences of this sort, both "contact action" and "mixture," Graebner (p. 16) uses the term "acculturation," which was coined by Holmes. (36) Hence the two regions concerned are called "acculturation regions." (37) This term was introduced by Ehrenreich. (38) Graebner himself had thus adopted the practice of subsuming contact and mixture under "acculturation" and I have followed him in this. One cannot, therefore, avoid speaking of either "acculturation" or "acculturation region" as van Bulck (p. 50) does (appealing to Graebner and me) "in order to escape misunderstandings."

In fact, since he here again confuses the culture itself and the method of its research, he unfortunately gives a definition both of contact and of mixing entirely different from that of Graebner and myself. Besides, he inserts still another, the "overlay" between the two. He did not see here that Graebner, in his strictly formal methodological undertaking, only intends to obtain a means for the establishment of time depths and, thereby, distinguish between the lesser and the greater time depths. Graebner, in the first place, does not consider whether the two events came about through movements of population or borrowing or in some other way. It is, therefore, also misleading on the part of van Bulck, when he identifies "mixing" with "migration of peoples without displacement or splitting up of the older culture strata" and under "contact" understands the diffusion of individual isolated culture elements and does not include the mingling of the culture bearers.

These restrictions of the term "contact" are methodologically invalid. Therefore, it is also still more incorrect to speak as van Bulck (*op. cit.,* p. 56) does of only "phenomena of contact" as the borrowing of single elements of culture and not recognize "contact cultures," even though it might be admitted that the former is frequent. It is also unnecessary (or, from the standpoint of logic and method, really impossible) to insert the "overlay" of a dominating stratum on another culture between mixture and contact, as van Bulck also does. For in the dichotomy "mixing" and "contact," "broad region" and "small border" are mutually exclusive categories of classification. Hence, there is no longer any place between them for "overlay."

γ. *Criteria for the Establishment of the Chronological Sequence*

1. Here also the first time criterion is attained: each new form resulting from acculturation is younger than the two (or more) cultures which entered into the acculturation. This is a rule of method of the utmost "simplicity" and apparent obviousness which is thus established—almost an "egg of Columbus." But that does not lessen in the least its objective trustworthiness.

This time criterion also contains in itself a still further gradation of time, according to the greater or lesser degree of identity of the acculturation form with the original. A trait, the style of which is already in harmony with the style of the new provenience, is to be placed in the more distant past, is ethnologically older than another in which this assimilation has not yet taken place (*cf.,* Graebner, p. 127 s.).

2. A second time criterion may be deduced therefrom. The discrete culture regions, whose boundaries must be here determined, are very different in size, now embracing only a single tribe, and a small one at that, then again greater groups of tribes and still greater confederacies of several tribes. Quite

great culture regions, in which the mutual acculturation of the single elements has been more or less completed, postulate a longer span of time than that necessary for the mutual acculturation of a small region. Here, of course, we must reckon with the possibilities of communication within the region in question: easier and more abundant possibilities of communication promote and accelerate acculturation, more difficult and rarer ones retard it.

Of course, rather large culture regions will very seldom be fully homogeneous, but in them partial sections of special forms will make themselves felt. Whether these then go back to influences which lie within the region itself or to such that come from without can only be determined through such extensive culture comparisons which carry the research still several degrees further.

6. THE RELATION OF CRITERIOLOGY TO TYPOLOGY

1. "Types" are rational summaries of individual forms or objects. In these summaries certain traits which seem to the one who summarized them as particularly characteristic or important for these objects or forms are placed in the foreground, and the arrangement of the group is made principally according to these. As a natural consequence of this, the other traits (in comparison with those emphasized) retreat into the background. That is the general process of human thought as it proceeds in the formulation of general concepts.

Among the three sciences of man, ethnology, anthropology and prehistory, it was especially and primarily prehistory in which typology was developed and applied to material implements and other objects with which it deals. This formulation was dictated by the fragmentary character, the broken condition, and the general deterioration of the original form of prehistorical objects. By reason of this deficiency and scarcity and the consequent (apparent or real) incoherence of these pieces it was, as it were, forced to create logically constructed groupings, which were intended at the same time to represent so-called inner associations.

Precisely through this close connection between ethnology and prehistory, which has fortunately been brought about through the investigations of Menghin, Heine-Geldern, etc., typology has begun to find more acceptance also in ethnology, even though we do not have to deal with fragmentary and damaged elements, but always rather with living wholes. Nevertheless, typology also has its uses for ethnology and therewith likewise its justification. To be more specific, it makes it easier to discover the dominant groupings amid the oft (for us) bewildering fullness of individual elements and, thus, performs preparatory work for the establishment of criteria of quality, especially the compound, "quantitative criteria of quality."

2. What typology does here is only preparatory work, and a warning must be given not to take these types as criteria of quality without further ado; *i.e.,* to identify types and criteria. In the past, prehistory has not always avoided this danger, and it threatens also in ethnology. We must always keep in mind that the types are primarily rational constructions, so that the similarity of certain types does not necessarily indicate a genetic association. That is often enough not the case, because when a type is established, traits are put in the foreground which were (historically) not of such importance for the actual genetic association as other traits which were neglected and pushed into the background when the artificial classifications were drawn up.

We are more easily protected against the danger of identification of types and historical groups if the list of types is as extensive and as penetrating as possible, because then the greatest number of peculiarities in the many types appear. It is for this reason, too, that the North American ethnologists have not come to a correct understanding of the genesis of the bow and arrow. Neither have they come to the correct evaluation of the task that lies before us here, because they did not know the full typology of the bow and arrow and in their narrow field of operation (North America) could not attain it.

And, hence, they were never able to find the correct criteria of quality for the bow and arrow.

The actual genetic unity and the knowledge of the historical chain which lead to this unity are gained from the multiplicity of the types and never by typology alone, but always through historical research work with the help of criteria, as we shall explain in the following. It enables us to establish genetic relations also between the types which, at first, appear without any historical connection, because in the setting up of types certain traits had been pushed too far into the background and their historical value is only now being recognized. It also makes it possible to find the common point of origin even in a complicated mass of other types in comparison to which the other forms are either individual modifications or influences of forms which date back to other points of origin.

3. Thus E. Doerr in his otherwise valuable investigation, "Bestattungsformen in Ozeanien" (39) essentially offered only a "Typology of Burial Forms" ("Typologie der Bestattungsformen") in pp. 382-420, 727-755 (*i.e.*, 66 pages), whereas the "results" of an investigation of the "living corpse" and the question of "fear or love of the dead" are given in a two-and-a-half-page discussion of the relations of the burial forms to the culture circles. This lack of historical investigation also explains why the author came to the following conclusion: "Actually, it seems impossible to ascribe either each burial form itself or all the single elements of a burial complex to a particular culture circle."

The reason he gives for this opinion clearly shows that he did not grasp one of the main tasks of the culture historical method in order to penetrate into those times without writings. He said: "For the origin of every one of the burial forms goes so far back that both the place on which they arose as well as the culture to which they originally belonged cannot any longer be unequivocally determined" (p. 764). First, the origin of a great number of culture elements does not lie so far back as Doerr seems to assume here.

Second, for the culture historical method there are almost no lengths of spatial distance nor any spans of temporal duration which it cannot bridge with the means at its disposal.

(1) *Cf.* above, pp. 32 s., 73 s.

(2) *Anthropos,* V (1910), pp. 534-558.

(3) *Revue néoscolastique,* XXI (1914-1919), pp. 394-418; XXII (1926), pp. 5-36.

(4) *Amer. Anthropology,* N. S. XXXI (1929), p. 495.

(5) *Cf.* B. Bavink, *Ergebnisse und Probleme der Naturwissenschaft* (4th ed.; Leipzig, 1930) and also W. Moock, "Weltanschauung und Naturerkenntnis," *Hochland,* XXXI (1933-1934), pp. 537 ss.

(6) See above, p. 26; *cf.* also Wallis, above, p. 40; Kroeber, p. 60.

(7) Thus, *e. g.,* Graebner, pp. 95 s., 98, 104 s., 117.

(8) *Op. cit.,* pp. 97, 98, 107.

(9) *Op. cit.,* p. 96, but especially p. 121: "Logically, we can distinguish two forms of culture relationships, the original primary relationship and borrowing." *Cf.* also further statements, p. 122 s.

(10) *Op. cit.,* p. 92.

(11) *Op. cit.,* p. 107. Italics mine—W. Schmidt.

(12) *Cf.* above, p. 42 ss.

(13) H. E. Driver and A. L. Kroeber, "Quantitative Expression of Cultural Relationship," *Amer. Anthrop.,* N. S. XXXI (1932), pp. 215, 256.

(14) Kroeber, "Historical Reconstructions of Culture Growth and Organic Evolution," *Amer. Anthropol.,* N. S. XXXIII (1931), p. 152.

(15) *Cf.* above, p. 45, Steward's explanation.

(16) *Cf.* W. Koppers, "Tungusen und Miao," *Mitteil. Anthrop. Ges. Wien,* IX (1930), pp. 306-319.

(17) *Cf.* above, p. 26.

(18) Also explained by van Bulck, p. 183.

(19) See above, p. 23, and Graebner, p. 119.

(20) Also proposed by van Bulck, p. 183.

(21) W. Schmidt, *Ursprung der Gottesidee,* III, p. 357 s.

(22) Driver—Kroeber, *op. cit.,* p. 212 s.

(23) See above, p. 13 s.

(24) Italics mine—W. Schmidt.

(25) Van Bulck, p. 184.

(26) *Op. cit.,* p. 46 s.

(27) W. Schmidt, *Ursprung der Gottesidee,* VI, p. 32 ss.

(28) W. Schmidt, *op. cit.,* p. 54 s.; also, "Donner und Regenbogen beim Höchsten Wesen der Yuki," *Festschrift* (A. L. Kroeber, 1936), pp. 299-308.

(29) *Cf.* Graebner, p. 120 ss.

(30) *Cf.* W. Schmidt, *High Gods in North America* (Oxford, 1933), p. 14 s.

(31) *Cf.* above, pp. 13 s. and 152 s.

(32) Van Bulck, *op. cit.,* p. 189 ss.

(33) Graebner, p. 143. We shall treat this more in detail below (p. 200 ss.).

(34) Graebner, pp. 159, 160 ss.; *cf.* later, pp. 226 ss., 245 ss.

(35) Van Bulck, pp. 234-238.

(36) Holmes, "Pottery of the Ancient Pueblos," *4th Ann. Rep. of Bur. of Ethnol.*, p. 266.

(37) Graebner, *op. cit.*, p. 126 s.

(38) P. Ehrenreich, *Mythen und Legenden der südamerikan. Indianer*, p. 61.

(39) *Anthropos*, XXX (1935), pp. 369-420, 727-765.

Chapter IV

MEANS OF ESTABLISHING THE CULTURE CIRCLES AND THE CULTURE STRATA

1. THE CULTURE CIRCLE AS THE REAL GREAT SPATIAL UNITY

The culture circle certainly plays a great role in the theory of the culture historical school, but by no means such an important role to justify calling the culture historical school simply the "Doctrine of Culture Circles" ("Kulturkreislehre"), as has been done by several authors. It is regrettable, however, that in the beginning neither Graebner nor I recognized clearly enough nor described the double character of the culture circle. (1) This alone can account for such an unbelievable misunderstanding as that of Krause, who reproaches the culture historical school with having the culture circle consist of mere dissociated parts (see above, p. 31 s.).

We must distinguish the culture circle in its existential order, as it exists and acts in the order of nature, and the culture circle, as it is first formulated in methodic research and then worked out in progressively clearer detail and used as a methodological tool. (2)

Graebner, for the most part, treats of it only in the latter sense and speaks of the "subsidiary concept of the culture circle" (p. 132). Only at the end, without further explanation or basis, he incidentally adds (p. 134): "It must further be mentioned that a culture complex, which is considered as independent, must naturally embrace all the departments of the life of culture." But that is the culture circle considered in its existential order, and we shall treat of it first.

A. The Culture Circle in the Existential Order

a. *The Importance of the Culture Circle As to Content and Method*

1. One of the facts which has been established by culture history beyond all peradventure of doubt is that not only discrete culture elements or small groups of elements migrate and exert an influence, but also whole compact culture complexes. If such a culture complex embraces all the essential and necessary categories of human culture, material culture, economic life, social life, custom, religion, then we call it a "culture circle," because returning into itself, like a circle, it is sufficient unto itself and, hence, also assures its independent existence. Should it neglect or fail to satisfy one of the more important human needs, then a substitute for this must be called from another culture—the greater the number of such substitutes that are required, the more it would cease to be an independent culture circle.

Taken geographically, such a culture circle must comprise at least a rather large group of tribes and peoples, but mostly an incorporation of several groups of peoples. Only such a foundation affords sufficient stability and power to perpetuate itself through generations against all the external influences and inner differentiations. This latter factor introduces another characteristic of a culture circle; namely, the enduring satisfaction of all human needs.

It is clear that such culture circles are very important for the facts of culture history and that, therefore, no kind of ethnology can carelessly disregard them if it does not want to become defective and deficient in essential matters. The older evolutionistic school hardly saw them at all, for the very reason that it was not historically orientated and with its unilinear progressive evolution made the entire course of cultures uniform. North American ethnology, despite its markedly historical orientation, did not grasp these facts, because for a long time their (North American) field of investigation was too small for that and they got no further than "culture areas," which are too closely bound to a geographical region and are in general too small both chronologically as well as spatially. (3)

Culture historical ethnology had to meet with the culture circles in its historical researches. They stand out so significantly and effectively in culture history that they could not be overlooked. Hand in hand with the rather large geographical extension which is taken in by the culture circle and, hence, also mostly the inclusion of a rather great number of individuals, whom the culture circle encompasses and molds, there goes also the increase of influence which it exerts upon the surrounding tribes of different culture, whether it remains at rest in its fixed position or wanders about in its totality or in separated groups.

2. Besides this importance as to content, the culture circle has also a pre-eminently formal and methodological importance as a time measure.

First, being a rather large culture complex, it requires more time to come into existence than smaller complexes or single elements; consequently, a longer period of time is its second essential characteristic (see above, p. 176). If we are indeed able to arrive at its first beginnings, we then come upon much greater time depths than in the research of the age of single elements. (4)

Second, a culture circle offers the means for methodic research in the greater extension of its boundaries, which bring out more contactual effects, and in the greater compass (see above, p. 168) of its territory, which offers more possibilities for planitial mixing.

Third, the greater surface of its spatial extension also presents more possibilities for new means of research when a foreign culture invades this region and splits it into two halves, encircles, or surrounds it (see below, p. 201 ss.).

There is still a useful fourth means to be added, originating from the special character of the culture circle, which we must briefly point out. A culture circle, which satisfies the whole life in all its essential demands, is by definition a living organism like the life itself which it serves. That means that its individual spheres, economics, material culture, social life, custom, religion, do not stand disconnected alongside one another in a merely accidental connection, but rather that they are organically connected with one another, so that one can often infer from the nature of one sphere to that of another. This process is also still further reinforced by the fact that, ordinarily, one of these parts stands out productive and dominating—either the (religious) view ("Weltanschauung") of the world, or the economic life, or the social life—and then affixes a certain seal upon all the other parts and their single elements. This mark is then a new comprehensive criterion of quality, which the single elements take with them when they migrate and attach themselves to alien cultures and which then makes it possible for us to recognize the historical association with the mother-culture circle.

That applies, *e.g.*, to the mother-right-agrarian culture with regard to their emphasis upon mother and woman and earth, which are prominent everywhere, whereas almost the opposite is the case in the patriarchal culture circle of animal breeders, in which the relation to breeding animals and to the patriarchal-hierarchical management of the economic and social life appears everywhere.

β. *The Two Main Types of Culture Circle*

Graebner distinguishes two main types of culture circle (p. 130). Their fundamental difference consists in the manner of their distribution; the one has continuous, the other discontinuous, distribution.

I. The Culture Circle With Continuous Distribution

He describes the first type in the following words: "First there is a group of such unities which in essentials are related to one another as the branches of a tree trunk and in one way or another present variations of the same theme."

He takes the culture of the Polynesians as an example. Identity of language is also a fundamental characteristic of such culture unities, and this, like the relatively undisturbed uniformity of the culture, allows us to conclude "that the spreading of the complex is a relatively recent event, the results of which were only slightly disturbed and disintegrated through later historical happenings." If the distribution is like that of the branches of a tree trunk, then we have here also continuous diffusion, and if the whole to a certain extent presents variations of a fundamental theme, then groups of people have migrated here, who carried the whole of a culture with them, planted it in its essentials everywhere and added only individual variations.

In itself the Polynesian archipelago as such would have been favorable to the dispersion and alteration of culture, especially if they had found a peculiar culture before them on each island with which they would have then fused to produce different kinds of mixtures. Either there was no such earlier culture present or it was only insignificantly represented with the exception of the somewhat larger island of New Zealand, and here, in fact, great variations of the general Polynesian culture appear. Those cases in which the culture remained stable and unchanged, despite the insular character of this region, can only be explained through the fact that the sojourn had not lasted long and, also, that a highly developed navigation well preserved the connection with one another, whereby the isolating effect of the dispersion was hindered.

II. The Culture Circle With Discontinuous Diffusion

Graebner characterizes the second type thus (p. 130): "Its characteristic is, first of all, negative; namely, that no groups of culture unities can be found which, according to the greater part of their content, might be considered as derivations of a basic prototype. They point rather much, on the one hand, to slow transitions in different directions, on the other hand, to seemingly irregular and arbitrary relations; in many cases, indeed, the last mentioned exclusively."

1. Graebner gives two forms of this second type, a more simple one and a more difficult one (p. 131): "A *very simple* case is at hand when the identities so good as exhaust themselves entirely in relations to two or three neighboring territories." To illustrate this he takes the Kwakiutl, (5) who were studied by Boas. Boas has shown that there was an imposition and mixing of adjacent culture complexes, which provoked a highly intensive process of acculturation and that of a marginal kind (above, p. 177). But in order to be able to speak of the example of a culture circle, there has to be a principal culture; in fact, a culture circle that mixes with various other cultures and is preservd in *all* the regions of mixture.

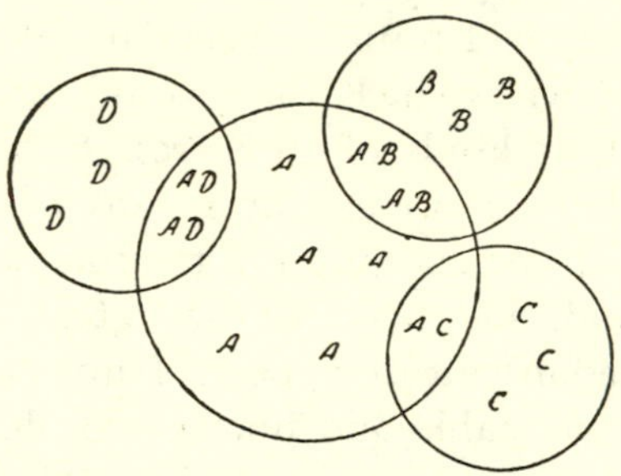

Here the subtraction of the mixed regions, "AB," "AC," "AD," must be carried out in order to get "A" unmixed. This process is facilitated in the present case by the presence of a still unmixed "A" region. The task would be more difficult if this "A" region has also been taken up entirely by mixed cultures.

2. The second difficult form of the second type of culture circles is that of seemingly chaotic relations. As an example, he gives the culture unity of the Papuan Gulf in Southern New Guinea. He also thinks that great continental territories like Africa and America favor the formation of *greater* unities, and that these practically present the type of relations where no rules seem to apply. This "irregularity" is not more clearly

defined by Graebner: it can consist in this, that in the single alien cultures now these, now those elements are found united which do not belong to those cultures, but that, taken on a large scale, particular groupings always reappear which can, of course, appear stronger in the one alien culture and weaker in the other.

Graebner now says of this second type (p. 132): "Methodological difficulties and questions stand out especially in this type. To all appearances the different culture elements could have arisen independently at different places of the region and have been thus combined in many ways through their diffusion, somewhat like stones falling into the water create circles of the most different kind." Then he puts the question: "The question is whether we have a means to control, as it were, and, if occasion should arise, to justify this coarse-grained impression." That is, do we have a means whereby, despite this apparent nonuniformity of the culture relations, we may determine that we have a case of historical relations of a more or less closed culture circle?

To this question Graebner gives the following answer: "Here the subsidiary concept of the culture circle comes into activity." More exactly we say the culture circle, which is a real, complete fact of culture history, functions also as the aim and means of culture historical research; *i.e.,* as "subsidiary concept." In the same sense we now wish to speak of the culture circle.

B. The Culture Circle As the Means and Goal of Research

a. *The Methodological Process of Research in the Establishment of the Culture Circle*

1. The culture circle, like every other group, as also the smaller culture complex, is established with the help of the criteria of quality and quantity and of the auxiliary criteria. But especially the criterion of quantity is active here and, in particular, the qualitative criterion of quantity, because a cul-

ture circle consists of the multitude of associated culture elements and of such that penetrate into all the vitally necessary departments of the culture (see above, p. 176). If these single elements also belong to one another organically, that does not mean that they depend one upon the other logically, so that if the one were proven the others could be inferred therefrom with logical inevitability. In such a case there would be no criterion of quantity there, which really presupposes a majority of elements independent of one another (see above, pp. 150, 152).

Research must then seek out *every* one of these criteria of quality and investigate their relations of distribution and strive to increase them and thus strengthen them into a criterion of quantity. Of course, there can be stages in this research, especially at the beginning, where not all the elements of the culture circle have as yet been established. In fact, under certain circumstances, it may be possible that the requirement has not yet been fulfilled that these criteria of quality must enter into all the departments of the culture. In these stages of the investigation, the culture circle is primarily the goal toward which research is striving, but which it has not yet fully attained. But from a certain point on, even in the case of incompleteness of the single elements, because of the great extension of the (qualitative) criterion of quantity, our research has reason for an inner conviction that this is really a case of a culture circle. If this culture circle seems still fragmentary at this stage and the single elements as well do not yet manifest that organic association to one another, the cause for this is that the research is not yet concluded, has not yet come so far as to be able to expose all the connecting links, and among them exactly such as might allow the organic association to be seen clearly.

This incomplete stage, however, cannot be a mere passing one, but something lasting and permanent, in case the documents from the life of the people in question are lacking because they have disappeared in the course of the centuries and have been supplanted by analagous elements of younger cultures. That can happen, of course, especially in very old cultures, which were exposed for the longest time to the influence of younger cultures, except the cases which in their marginal position or dwelling in mountains, woods, or on islands, could better insure the peculiar elements of their culture possession by reason of their actual isolation.

2. We have now to determine the second and more difficult form of the second type of culture circle, in order that, by answering the question proposed above (see p. 176), we may prepare the way for its methodic establishment.

With reference to the stability and diffusion of the older culture circles with written history—namely, the Greco-Roman, the Hellenistic-Byzantine, the Hindu, to which for the later centuries may also be added the Spanish and then the French cultures in Europe—Graebner first points out, negatively, that the concept of a culture circle does not postulate

a. Absolute uniformity of culture conditions, since the (younger) culture circle can overlay even several subregions with very heterogeneous culture (*cf.* the different Indo-Germanic peoples);

b. Absolute continuity of the single elements, since the (younger) culture circle hardly ever suppresses the old cultures entirely; hence the latter remain in certain subregions as islands and break up the continuous connection of the new culture.

Positively, the elements required and sufficient for a culture circle are:

a. "A determined complex of culture elements is characteristic for a certain region and is in the main restricted to it" (p. 133). This restriction to a certain region is valid in relation to a rather large expanse; *e.g.,* a continent. But nothing prevents the same restriction to a certain region from occurring again in another continent.

b. That in the single regions not only the position of the typical forms be in agreement, but also those zones where the cultures gradually wane and fade away. In this agreement, the final relics of former continuous common boundaries of the whole region are manifested.

When Graebner adds here (p.134) that the single relations must penetrate into *all* the departments of culture, that is a requirement that applies for the culture circles of *all* types and degree of difficulty and follows from the nature of the culture circle in its existential order (see above, p. 177).

There is no real reason outside of the word "culture circle" to introduce the term "circle of cultures" as a sum of single cultures, as Lebzelter (6) wants to do; a culture circle can fall into such single cultures in the course of time. But the imporant thing originally was its internal unity.

β. *The External Geographical Form of the Culture Circle*

The difficulty of establishing a culture circle as such is also greater or less, corresponding to the geographical form of the diffusion of its parts. Graebner (p. 134 ss.) mentions four cases here:

1. "Those culture circles stand out in bold relief with the greatest degree of clearness and certainty, which, like the West African culture circle, cover a somewhat great compact region" (see in this regard also above, p. 178).

2. "Matters are less clear in cases of dissociated culture circles."

a. "When the objects and forms of a great culture circle appear insularly outside of and near the compact region of diffusion, there can be no doubt concerning the coherence of the first to the united region of distribution and, hence, not of the explanation*, that we have here to deal with detached parts of a great unity." Graphically represented:

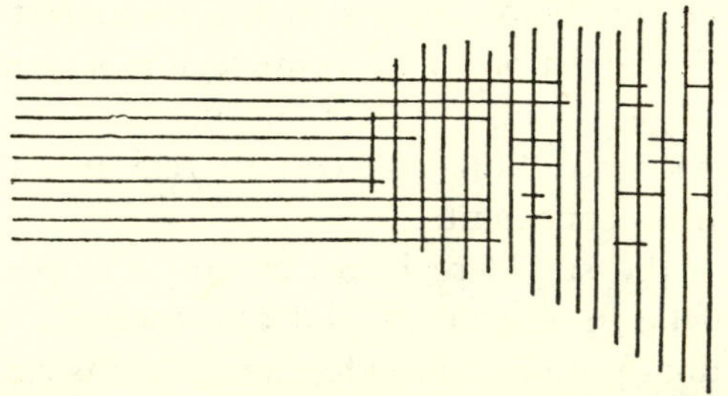

* Professor Schmidt's improved version of an unintelligible text of Graebner is given here. He thinks the confusion in the text (in this case) is due to a typographical error—Translator's note.

b. "The situation is hardly more difficult if the territory of the complex is broken up at one or several places by corridors of lesser intensity or absolute disappearance of the characteristic elements."

Graebner gives, as an example, the two mother-right regions of New Brittany and the Northern Solomon Islands on the one hand, and the New Hebrides on the other. These are broken up by father-right districts of the Central and Southern Solomon Islands, but here traces of mother-right elements function as criteria of continuity.

c. "Matters are substantially more difficult in such culture circles, which, consequent upon some historical event or other, are actually torn asunder into relatively small and scattered pieces. To work them out, it is not only necessary to establish and elaborate the conditions of diffusion with the utmost care, but also the criteria of relationship must be extensively and cautiously applied. In this matter it is always correct to base far-reaching conclusions, at least at first, only upon actually clear coincidences of diffusion."

For an example, Graebner chooses the totemistic culture circle in Melanesia, which is considerably scattered. He describes this in all its details. In its very self, through its many firmly localized totem clans, this culture circle is disposed to such a disintegration in the case of the invasion of a culture circle with widely extended associations, like the mother-right-agrarian culture.

Graphical representation:

γ. *The Single Elements as Content of the Culture Circle*

As already indicated above (p. 182), every single culture element of the different regions of distribution (if it is to be accounted an element of a culture circle comprising these single districts) must, as a criterion of quality, demonstrate its historical relations to the same culture elements of the other regions of diffusion through characteristic similarities and confirm and certify its appurtenance still more through the criterion of quantity and the auxiliary criteria.

But in many cases it still remains difficult to certify in detail the appurtenance of an element to a culture circle:

First, because the degree in which an element becomes assimilated is very different according to the local intensity of the whole culture and in its own significance over against the competing elements.

Second, because the culture circles themselves in the regions of more intensive occurrence are often not sharply delineated, but they are often superimposed reciprocally upon each other.

Third, because our knowledge of the state of affairs is often very defective.

Thus, it is inevitable that in single cases the appurtenance of a culture element to a certain culture circle remains doubtful and, for the time being, must be reckoned an insoluble problem. "The very important methodological principle must be applied in such cases: nothing uncertain is to be taken as certain." The use of hypotheses is allowed here also, but in a given case we must remain conscious of this hypothetical character.

Graebner then gives a number of rules, according to which the appurtenance of an element to another culture circle can be declared either uncertain or probable or certain (p. 138).

I. Uncertain are:

1. "All phenomena or forms which appear only in a territory where several culture complexes are of uniform value," because precisely this equal value takes away the bases for a decision.

2. "Further, all the discrete presences in an otherwise apparently monochromatic culture district. The reason for the last assertion is that we cannot raise the claim to exhaust the number of culture circles elaborated up till now, nor to grasp all the culture phenomena present in them."

II. "The highest *probability* of culture association lies in the case of coherence; that means, if a doubtful phenomenon appears in a certain constancy externally bound to a phenomenon whose appurtenance is certified." Here also belong the "coherences" already established as such by Tylor (see above, p. 132).

III. "A form or an element can pass for *certain*":

1. "If in a sufficient number of cases it has its main distribution (with special regard for the intensity) within the relatively homogeneous district of the whole culture (here, naturally, the decision is often left to a certain intuitive feeling)."

2. "If its diffusion corresponds to characteristic diagnostics of the whole culture"; *e.g.,* also agreeing with the zones of deterioration.

3. "If objects stand in a strictly logical, psychological, or essential relation with definitively established elements of a culture (and only with them), so that its appurtenance to other complexes appears unthinkable"; *e.g.,* the "mother-earth" theme in the mother-right-agrarian culture.

c. The Culture Area and Its Relation to the Culture Circle

The culture area is a special product of North American ethnology and was only applied later to African ethnology by an American, M. J. Herskovits. (7) He did not however find followers there or elsewhere.

α. *The Culture Area Itself*

A. L. Kroeber gives us a short but very instructive history of the culture area in his article "The Culture Area and Age-Area Concepts of Clark Wissler." (8) He shows that it was already used in North American ethnology in the nineties of the last century and that after the evolutionistic display of museum materials had given way, the objects were arranged according to culture areas. After 1900 this arrangement came into vogue for the cartography of cultures. The full exposition and development of the idea, however, was first given by Clark Wissler in his book, *The American Indian* (1st ed., New York, 1917): "In short, the culture area was both formulated concretely and examined as to its meaning. The standardization, although by no means hard and fast, appeared so sound that it has been generally accepted by anthropologists, modified or supplemented only in details and the theoretical findings have been never seriously attacked." (9) Wissler's contribution was the emphasis upon the culture centers in the culture areas as points of certain productivity and dispersion within the culture areas.

Kroeber sees the reason for this in the fact that the concept of the culture area arose in America and remained in the Americas, which are smaller and were more sparsely populated, by what was essentially a single race producing very advanced civilizations: "This comparatively uniform and undocumented mass of native New World culture almost necessitated a static, descriptive approach." (10) In this connection he says: "It is probably no accident that the diffusionist historical explanation of both the Graebner-Foy-Schmidt school and the Rivers-Smith-Perry school, which make almost no use of culture areas as such, but attempt to account for most of prehistoric culture, originated in Europe; that they have had almost no following in America; and that they have not even been countered by rival theories here." (11)

This, however, does not fully clarify the distinction between the culture area and the culture circle. This difference can be grasped more easily if we proced from the term "culture area." In the first place, it indicates an area; *i.e.*, a (geographical) region in which there is a culture. I cannot agree with Kroeber (p. 248) on this point when he writes: "Anthropologists have not been wholly happy in their terminology. They speak consistently of *culture areas,* whereas it is the content of these areas, certain culture growths or aggregations, that they are really concerned with, the areal limitation being only one aspect of such an aggregation." It was certainly not so in the beginning, for then the "area" stood in the foreground and only later "the content of these areas" stood out. Even where Kroeber defends Wissler (p. 253) against the criticism that he is an environmentalist, he quotes the following statement of Wissler: "While the environment does not produce the culture [still he must continue with the following words of Wissler] it [the environment] furnishes the medium in which it [culture] grows, and when once rooted in a *geographical* [12] area, culture tends to hold fast."

β. *The Culture Area Differentiated From the Culture Circle*

The difference, therefore, between the culture area and the culture circle consists in this: the culture area is the equalization of cultures different in kind and origin, brought about in a certain "area" without the necessity of having an organic permanent connection effected. This last point, however, is essential for the culture circle.

The second difference is this: the culture circle consists of elements which enter into all the essential, indispensable cultural domains, while the essential thing for the culture area is the combination of characteristic individual features.

Third, the culture circle differs from the culture area because, while the culture circle can exist both when the present and the past are fully intact, as well as when the present and the past are incomplete, fragmentary, or superimposed upon each other, the culture area indicates essentially only the collection of characteristic culture elements of the present in an area existing today. The culture circle is independent of time; the culture area is essentially a concept of something which has contemporary existence.

Finally, in connection with the foregoing, there is another difference; namely, a culture circle can be present in different parts of a continent or of the earth, separated from one another, essentially identical, while a culture area exists only once and that in one particular area, which naturally occurs only in this one place upon the earth.

Because of the last two reasons given, the culture area cannot be used as a methodological means to investigate temporal depths. Sapir admits this defect (see above, p. 39); and also Wissler felt this and endeavored to supply the want by means of a distinction between a "center" and "margins" within the culture area. We have seen above (p. 47 s.) how much success he had in this venture. The culture circle, on the other hand, is a very effective methodological means to carry out this investigation of time depths, which could not exist at all or function without it. Kroeber recognized this and criticized Wissler's idea of the culture area: "They [the culture areas] are not equivalent in culture historical significance, but are of different orders," and further: "In short, the culture areas codified by Wissler are unduly uniformized as to size, number of included tribes, and implied level. They remain essentially descriptive; their historical potentialities have only begun to be exploited." (13)

According to my opinion, it follows from the very nature of the culture area as such that its application can never go very far. Kroeber confirms this, when he, after he had endeavored to justify the culture area, sees himself compelled to confess: "The two concepts, however, have been brought into little relation so far." When he then says that "The concept of the culture center seems to hold the potentiality of co-ordinating these two approaches; it can give the culture an historical depth and can synthesize discrete age area findings so as to be interpretable in generalized areal as well as in temporal terms," then it must be said that the age area should certainly not stand alongside the culture area, but methodologically it must go before it if it is to be legitimate. The culture area, however, precisely does not possess this methodological vitality.

2. THE CULTURE STRATUM AS THE GREAT UNITY IN THE SUCCESSION OF TIME

A. The Establishment of the Chronology From the Contact and Mixing of the Culture Circles

α. *The More Numerous Possibilities for Obtaining Chronological Measures*

We have already pointed out above (p. 177) that the culture circle puts more numerous and better means into our hands to establish the (relative) chronology of the single culture strata and, hence, to give the firm indispensable foundation to the culture history of peoples without writing. We mentioned, first of all, in general that with the culture circle we can advance into considerably greater time depths than we can with a single culture element and a small unity, because the culture circle often requires thousands of years for its formation and crystallization.

We had especially emphasized that, since the boundaries of a culture circle are more extensive than the province of distribution of a single culture element, it offers more occasions for marginal acculturations along these borders by coming into contact with forms of other cultures. If Graebner is right in stating (p. 140) that these contact forms are to a great extent secondary, because they can be formed by the younger local forms of the culture circle in question, then the great length of the boundary still affords an opportunity for the development of different local forms, the whole of which can nevertheless to a certain extent reflect the general nature of the culture circle. At any rate, the character and the older form of the culture circle stands out all the clearer, the more contact forms of different kinds are subtracted, as we have recognized as necessary (above, p. 180).

But also the region of a culture circle which in comparison with the district of diffusion of single culture elements is very extensively spread out, as already emphasized (above, p. 177), offers more occasions for forming crossings and mixed forms and, thus, gives more numerous possibilities to get measures of time.

β. *Time Measure Obtained From Cases of Crossing Cultures*

1. Graebner here offers the following rule (p. 140): "Whenever the territory of a culture unity or a special circle of forms of such a unity is cut asunder by another complex, then the last mentioned culture, at least in this particular region, is the younger"; *i.e.,* it can be relatively older in another culture circle, it all depends upon its position there—but here it is not so.

Graebner calls the fundamental concept of this methodological rule "very simple"; *i.e.,* obvious. In general, it is; but there must still be an objective means for establishing that the one culture is actually the dividing one and the other the divided, and that the situation is not rather the case, that the supposedly separated culture is in reality the one which (later) surrounds the alleged separating culture on two sides. That is certainly excluded if a real (complete separation) has taken place, if two parts of a culture are held apart through a culture lying in the middle of the *entire* length of its distribution and still further beyond that, which is graphically represented thus:

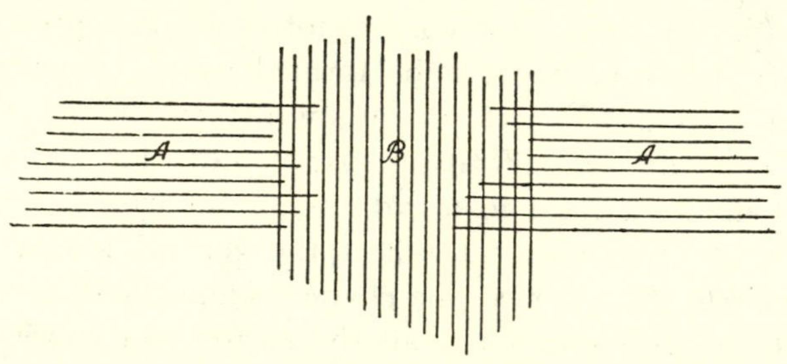

2. H. Pinard amplifies this rule by two others (14):

The first is: "The culture divided by another culture is so much the older, the more frequently it has been crossed by alien cultures." That is evident if he means the greater age of the culture intersected over against *all* the cultures intersecting it has to demonstrate the relative age. Every one of the intersecting cultures must be demonstrated with regard to the other intersecting cultures by a comparison with them.

The second amplification reads: "The intersected culture is all the older, the more differentiated it is in each of the fragments thus formed through the interjection." That would indeed show that the whole time gone by since the entrance of all the crossings is quite considerable. Whether also the time span between the single crossings is greater is not determined by this rule, but must be established in another way.

γ. *Time Measures Obtained From Cases of Superposed and Heterogeneous Cultures*

1. Graebner here proposed the following rule: "Likewise, wherever a complex is overlaid by another, *i.e.*, where the former existence of a culture is attested by the rudimentary existence of its elements within a delimited territory of another culture, the overlaying culture is the younger. The opposite is impossible because no culture complex can diffuse itself sporadically and in jumps, but can only do so continuously."

This rule is all the more evident when the fragmentarily diffused culture appears directly bordering on a large territory of continuous diffusion (case a); but it remains valid also in case such a region is lacking (case b). Here is a graphical representation of the two cases:

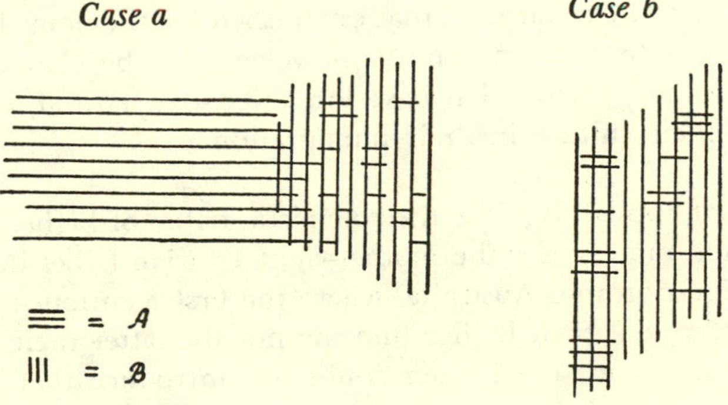

2. Graebner adds a departure from this rule (p. 141): "An exception is thinkable only in case the diffusion of the culture is very rapid and superficial, say, by nomad tribes, and is followed by almost complete absorption. Such a case occurs naturally very seldom under older and more primitive circumstances, and its possibility is easily recognizable in the form of the respective culture."

Graebner does not give any characteristics of this species. We might propose these three: *1*, the number of culture objects in the rudimentary districts is not great. 2, They are quite heterogeneous; *i.e.*, originating from different cultures. *3*, In the whole extension of rudimentary diffusion they present few variations.

Fr. Kern had already pointed out such a nomadic diffusion for the Indo-Germanic peoples migrating into Europe. O. Rydbecke gives a more clear and concrete case in the Indo-Germanic people migrating into Sweden who are characterized by the battle ax and cord-ornamental beaker pottery. (15) The first and second characteristics are explained by the peculiarity of the nomad herder culture: small stock of articles because of difficulty of transport and superabundance of (alien) culture objects, which have been acquired through robbery or trade. The third characteristic results from the hasty transition through the region by means of mount and draft animals.

3. A similar exception as that established for the nomad shepherd tribes by Graebner must, however, also be claimed for such (primary) tribes that have lost the entire natural foundation of their culture in their immigration.

That applies, *e.g.*, for the totemistic tribes of higher hunting and more so for the mother-right-agrarian tribes in their immigration into Australia, where the first mentioned could not carry out their higher hunting nor the latter their horticulture. Hence the former could not introduce their fixed round hut with its conical roof, nor the latter their rectangular house with a gable. Of course, they lose quite a bit of their strength through these differentiations, and cannot maintain themselves numerically. If the tribes of Primitive culture into whose territory they intruded are still quite vigorous, they will also in part absorb the intruders through their aboriginality. Hence, the region first conquered by these fuse again into islands; the tribes of the Primitive culture, however, also mix their culture with that of the intruders.

We then obtain the following age grades, beginning with the oldest: *1*, the old unmixed Primitive culture (A_1); *2*, the immigrating culture (B_1); *3*, the recently advancing Primitive culture (A_2); *4*, mixture of the Primitive culture with the immigrating culture (AB).

4. Another exception of this kind which, of course, is only possible in later, higher culture, results where immigrants with highly developed means of travel wander through without halting on the way, then settle at a certain place more or less permanently and in turn, under the absorbing effect of the cultures which they met, break up again into fragments.

Examples of this kind are the numerous German municipal and land colonies in the Slav and Magyar regions of the East. Here the "fragmentary" islands are the younger portion.

B. The Establishment of the Chronology From the Migration From Asia to Other Countries

a. *Time Measures Obtained From Intercontinental Migrations*

1. In case one or several culture circles as a whole have migrated into a continent, an important possibility for the objective establishment of the (relative) date of this immigration results from the way in which Africa, Oceania, and America are situated with regard to the largest and central continent, that of Asia. Graebner expresses this idea thus (p. 141): "The

continents most important for the history of the preliterates, Africa, Oceania and America, are jointed to Asia with such narrow connections that, at least for land diffusion cultures, there remain but very restricted possibilities of immigration. Hence, we necessarily get a kind of stratification of the complexes following one after the other, so that the youngest complexes lie near the gate of entry and the oldest seem to be pushed into the most distant districts of the respective continents."

The words "land diffusion cultures" need more explanation. They are cultures in which the means of sea travel were not well enough developed to make long ocean journeys possible, but only permitted trips along the coast or between islands not far distant from each other.

> Such is the case at least with all Primitive cultures, which know only simple floats and bark canoes. It is true also that the totemistic hunter culture, with its simple dugout canoe, is unable to cross the sea. The plank boats of the mother-right culture, however, travel somewhat farther, whereas the herder nomads lack every kind of water transportation.

2. In the case of Africa, it is most difficult to find a satisfactory way of establishing the stratification through the junction with Asia.

For not only the Isthmus of Suez, but also the whole length of the Red Sea to Aden and still farther southward permit immigrations from Asia on a broad and consequently manifold front. Only the one fact that the oldest strata of immigrations are not to be looked for in East Africa appears also decisive here.

3. Also with regard to Oceania the situation is on the whole not any too good.

> The number and size and position of the islands of Indonesia and then of Melanesia, Micronesia, and New Guinea offer very many possibilities for migrations.

On the other hand, the situation of Australia is univocal, and that was very useful because of the great importance Australia held in most evolutionistic theories for the last fifty years.

For almost all the cultures of this continent, because of the meager development of their means of water travel, no other immigration is possible than to cross from South New Guinea over the maze of islands of the Torres Strait to land at Cape York in the northeast and then to penetrate southward through the narrow neck of this peninsula. Most probably the oldest cultures continued their journey under the pressure of subsequent waves of culture into the eastern half, which is provided with water and, therefore, with flora and fauna all the way to the extreme south and southeast, where therefore the oldest tribes are to be looked for in the Kurnai-Kulin. Only when East Australia had been inhabited did the following younger tribes branch out toward the west, where they came upon the desert and therefore went along the coast. The very last immigration, the Aranda tribes and their relatives, were forced to be satisfied with the desert region of Central Australia. (16)

4. The connection between (North) America and (Northeastern) Asia is, you might say, still more clear.

Here the present-day chain of islands of the Bering Strait, which was a continuous strip of land at the end of Miolithicum and the beginning of Neolithicum, forms the one narrow entrance to the extensive continent of America during those ancient times. Besides, South America is separated from Asia by the whole breadth of the Pacific and the tribes living farthest from the *porta invasionis,* the Fuegians, belong to the oldest tribes of the whole American hemisphere. (17)

β. *Time Measures Obtained From Intracontinental Migrations Into Regions of Refuge*

1. However, not only the greatest distance of the tribes from those points of entrance characterize their extremely high eth-

nological age, but also in cases of smaller distances other factors can bring about the same effect. Graebner writes on this question (p. 142 ss.): "Also within the continents not all parts show themselves alike favorable to culture diffusion: great fruitful river valleys and plains make it easier; mountains, deserts, swamps, etc., render it more difficult. For thus, the oldest remnants of culture maintain themselves more easily in the farthermost ramifications of river territories, outlying mountain districts, tracts of forest difficult of approach, economically poorer countries, etc. The observation of these phenomena in connection with those of scattering and superposition gives good criteria for the sequence of various cultures, even though the possibilities of immigration increase especially consequent upon maritime borrowing taking place here."

It seems to me that these words of Graebner are in part unclear and in part incorrect. It is not so much a matter of facilitation or hindering of the diffusion of culture, but rather to what place the older culture strata will be pushed by the later younger cultures. The latter are in general more advanced economically and, consequently, also greater in numbers. Therefore, they will not overlay the older cultures and mingle with them except where the older cultures cannot yield any more, but they will crowd them out and push them into so-called "out-of-the-way districts." In some cases that will be a pushing of these before themselves to the uttermost extremity, to the very end of the continent, as we have learned to know both in this chapter and the last. This propulsion takes place especially where the district is so narrow that the younger immigrating culture can cover the whole breadth and thus exercise its pressure on the whole front and, consequently, does not allow anything of the older culture to escape at the borders and remain behind. We find something of this kind on Cape York Peninsula in Northeastern Australia.

2. However, if the district of the older cultures is so widely spread out that the pressure of the younger cultures can only affect a part of it, and if this should happen to be somewhere in the middle, then an interpenetration of the territory of the

older tribes will take place and also a shunting on both sides; *i.e.*, to the outermost extremities, to the ocean shore. That is the case with the Eastern Algonkin and the North Central Californians.

These cultures shunted to the side will maintain themselves the best there, if they are protected against onrushing younger cultures by a mountain range, a desert, or by some other impassable and unapproachable regions.

We have this in the Eastern Algonkin, who are protected by the Great Lakes, and also the North Central Californians, who are protected by the Sierra Nevada and the desert of the Great Basin. A good example of this is also found in the Kurnai in Southeastern Australia, who have the Australian Alps for protection, and the Kulin as well, who are shielded by the Murray River.

Islands can also be such regions of isolation, if they are separated from other islands or the continent by a sufficiently wide expanse of water, which in turn forms their safeguard.

The Andamanese Pygmies are such a case.

In all these cases we are dealing with marginal *border recess regions.* These must be distinguished from *border regions as such,* which are border regions of homogeneous culture and, as such, frequently need special methodical treatment (*cf.*, p. 177).

3. The "uttermost ramifications of great river valleys" to which Graebner likewise attributes isolating and conserving functions (above, p. 198) [under which the upper course of great rivers with their primary source and their tributary streams are to be understood], enter into consideration here only in case we have to do with mountainous and forest districts, where also forests and mountains form the isolation strata and the deeply gorged river beds are too dangerous for water travel and so could not become regular water routes. But also widely

branching river deltas can become such recess districts if they happen to form the swampy marshes of big rivers, as, for instance, the Nile, Amazon, etc.

"Economically poor countries" only then become "regions of retreat" if all other regions are already occupied, so that there remains no other choice, as, *e.g.*, with the Bushman in South Africa and the Aranda in Central Australia. Therefore, they also fall into more recent times and are also thereby recognizable that they produce a more or less complete stunting of the immigrating culture, which is only incorrectly designated as characteristic of extreme primitivity.

c. The Establishment of the Chronology From the Direction of the Diffusion

1. The directions of diffusion also become measures of time only in case there is a sequence in the diffusion, and the investigation of the direction of the diffusion makes it easier to grasp the younger and the more recent elements in this sequence. Processes of superposition, intrusion, and encircling here offer different kinds of time measures.

α. *Time Measures Obtained From the Process of Superposition*

Graebner here proposes two rules (p. 142):

a. "In general, a culture which overlays another culture only in one part of its territory has spread thither from the region lying without the district in which they mingle."

b. "In cases of unequal intensity of the mixing, the direction of the active complex runs from districts of greater to those of lesser quantitative and qualitative intensity."

The conception of these two rules suffers from want of clearness or assumes certain postulates and, therefore, can be of no service to us in this form.

In *a,* the expression "overlays" is an inadmissible assumption: a culture, which really overlays, according to a rule above (p. 193), is the younger, and it is almost tautology to say that a culture which somewhere or other is (merely) lying at one place and "overlays" at another is the older one in the first case and the younger one in the second.

The rule *b* is not only confusing, but it is also directly inappropriate. If in a region in which the cultures mingle some districts show greater, others lesser, degrees of mixing of the (active) culture, in two cases at least we have exactly the opposite of what Graebner holds.

α. In regions where the mixing is of less intensity, the invading culture could have migrated through more quickly and eventually have become sedentary in those parts where we now find a greater intensity of mixture, because here the comingling was naturally more intense.

β. In a region where but a small amount of mixing has taken place, the original culture could have been strengthened again later and the immigrating culture reabsorbed (*cf.* above, p. 194 s.).

2. The problem, which we have here in both of the rules set forth by Graebner, is the question: If two cultures mix, how do we decide whether the border forms manifest incipient intermixture or the stages of fading disassociation? Looked at from this angle, the two rules of Graebner take on this form:

a. If two cultures mix, the one being stationary, the other migratory, the culture that migrates from without to the stationary culture and penetrates into its territory, mingles with it there and then leaves the territory again in another direction, then the district lying just in front of the point where the migrating culture entered is different from the district where it left in this: the former is still pure and untouched by the mixture with the stationary culture, while the latter is no longer pure, but carries along with it evidences of its passage through the stationary culture. From this we deduce the rule: The direction of the migrating culture runs from the region still "unmixed" to the one "already" mixed; hence, the first is the older culture and the second is the younger of the two.

b. If two cultures cross and both of them move, migrate, then there are three possibilities:

α. Both cultures are equally strong, they come to a standstill and the intermixture takes place where they bivouac.

β. Culture *A* is stronger, breaks through, and continues migrating.

γ. Culture *B* is stronger, breaks through and continues migrating. In both cases, the cultures which break through are no longer pure and unmixed. The question of time is settled in the same way as before under *a.*

β. *Time Measures Obtained From the Process of Intrusion*

1. Graebner thus formulates a third rule deduced from the direction of the diffusion (p. 142 s.): "If the diffusion of a complex lies entirely wedged between the regions of a culture or cultures displaced by it, (18) but in such a way that the circle around them is open on the one side and closed on the other, however, not secondarily so, then naturally the arrival of the intruding wedge must be looked for on the open side."

Through the subordinate clause "but certainly not secondarily closed again," Graebner himself adds a restricting condition, but does not say *how* the "certainly" should be made clear.

> As an example of secondary closing through which "an apparent return of the state of affairs can take place," he proposes in note 3 the West African culture, "which having crossed entire Africa, now lies along the Atlantic coast with a broad front, while behind it on the Indian Ocean, younger displacements of culture have brought about a strong occlusion." As reference he gives Ankerman's parallel lecture, "Kulturkreise und Kulturschichten in Afrika" *(Zeitschrift f. Ethn.,* XXXVI, p. 73). For an original situation he refers to Australia, "where . . . the territory of purer two-class culture is pushed like a wedge from the northeastern coast to the central part." Here the assumption of the point of exodus on the northeastern coast seems to be supported by the fact that at this point we have the link which connects it with the related culture provinces of Melanesia.

2. From the choice of these examples it follows that Graebner has his rule in mind principally for conditions in which a younger culture proceeds from a coastal region (*i.e.,* where there is nothing more behind it) and penetrates like a wedge into another culture. In that case, his choice of an example was not so fortunate. If we want to illustrate the rule, we must take a case where the reclosing of the circle has not proceeded from the point of origin of the wedge, but must be a case in which the region before the penetrating wedge of the immigrating culture remained closed. However, in Graebner's first example, "the West African culture broke through the region of alien cultures all the way to the Atlantic Ocean," so that we do not have a case of intrusion into the foreign district, but a passage all the way through it. Consequently, the fact that younger cultural phenomena effected a secondary closing of the point of entrance on the Indian Ocean side, an "apparent return of the original state of affairs takes place," but such a case cannot serve to illustrate an intrusion.

Nor is the correctness of this rule placed beyond all doubt. It would still be thinkable that a *younger* culture or also several cultures successively had migrated around the firmly established region of an older culture and had closed it on all sides with the exception of the basis along a strip of the coast, which the older culture had likewise firmly held. Hence, we have to produce the proof that this circummigration be excluded.

On the other hand, this proof is certainly possible for the case in which a culture penetrates into a valley already occupied by an older culture, mixes with one part of the culture present there, while another part of the older culture avoids this crossing and removes to the higher regions of the mountains surrounding the valley. The proof that this last culture group has not come over the mountains into other valleys is had, if these mountains are so high and so unapproachable from the other side, that a transition is not possible at all or only along extremely difficult ways.

γ. *Time Measure Obtained From the Process of Envelopment*

Here H. Pinard proposes the following rule (19): "The encircled culture is older than the encircling one."

This rule seems to be very decisive, for neither has the surrounded culture fallen from heaven into the region which now surrounds it, nor did it cut right through the region of the latter, since this at present does not manifest any traces of its transition.

But the same reservation is to be made here which Graebner stipulates for the rule (p. 185) he set up: The present existing complete enclosing circle could have been previously half (or three-quarters) of a circle, whereby the picture of a wedgelike intruding culture would be given that is, naturally, younger at this place than the culture into which it intrudes. If this culture affected by this intrusion be strengthened again at the point of the inroad and closes the half (or three-quarter) circle again, then in this case the enclosed culture is not the older one.

In other words, Pinard's rule has to be supplemented by the words: provided, that the ring of the encircling culture has not risen only through the subsequent restoration of a breach. That is not the case, if mixtures with the one encircled do not appear in any place in the encircling culture. This last rule is subject to a restriction, if the enclosed culture is a culture of pastoral nomads with mounts (and wagons), since their passage through the territory of the culture now encircling it can take place so quickly that it leaves (none or) very few traces behind, which can also be reabsorbed again in a short time (*cf.* above, p. 194).

3. MULTICONTINENTAL CULTURE CIRCLES

A. General Requirements for the Investigation of Multicontinental Culture Circles

We have seen what importance the direction of culture migrations can have for the determination of the chronology of cultures. It is understandable that a field of certain geographical dimensions is necessary to enable one to grasp the direction of culture migrations and that this is absolutely impossible if the field of study be small and narrow. This is the reason why the North American ethnologists, so long as they restrict themselves to North America or even to the United States alone, cannot see these things. But there can be special cases where also the extension of a whole continent is not sufficient for this comprehension, but one or several continents in which the migrating culture is also diffused must be considered in conjunction with it. Of course, in this case, the methodical principles must be tested with greater caution and the tenability of the criteria must be checked with a greater degree of accuracy, because errors that are made here have all the more disastrous effects when carried over into world-wide dimensions.

Moreover, two viewpoints are to be kept in mind which seemingly contradict each other. On the one hand, exact individual researches of smaller regions must always precede world-wide comparisons. In many cases such researches negatively explain, *a priori,* that certain connections are only apparent and do not exist in reality, but a positive result may be attained in some cases; namely, connections of this kind may become evident which were not to be seen previously. On the other hand, however, the attempt at world-wide synthetic researches must be made from time to time, because many cultural connections are only thus brought to light or, at any rate, an exact and comprehensive understanding of the problem is obtained. Graebner says here very correctly (p. 144): "Furthermore, the case we have here is just like in other sciences; namely, that some sort of anticipatory synthetic survey can produce very good results from time to time. All the viewpoints won thereby always have pre-eminent heuristic value and only obtain permanence through subsequent detailed work."

Partly, however, such synthetic surveys can already be a survey of previous detailed work, as was the case with the two famous lectures, that of Graebner himself, "Kulturkreise und

Kulturschichten in Ozeanien," and that of Ankerman, "Kulturkreise und Kulturschichten in Afrika." (20) This was also the case with regard to my lecture, "Kulturkreise und Kulturschichten in Südamerika." (21) And then, later in my lectures on the same subject in the winter and summer semesters of 1931–1932 at the University of Vienna, I was able to add not only important supplements, but also improvements of the same.

B. The Application of the Criteria in the Investigation of Multicontinental Culture Circles

a. *The Criterion of Quantity*

1. "For the application of the criterion of quantity, a question of some importance is that of the relative age of unities of comparison within the region studied. Apart from the extremely diverse abundance of the cultures in general, it is clear that the *younger* complexes having entered into the history of a region relatively recent have on the whole preserved (22) their full structure and the entire original stock of their elements better than the older culture complexes," which

a. "In the course of a long time have lost part of their territory and, hence, also of their culture forms as well";

b. "Were longer exposed to foreign influences";

c. "In the assumption of an association with distant coeval cultures were longer subject to natural variation." (23)

d. If isolated, they stood longer under the influence of inner variation and one-sided formation of specialized forms.

e. Add to this the fact that the older cultures, especially as to their material and social culture, are less rich and varied and, therefore, offer less footing for the criteria of quality than the younger cultures.

From the reasons *a, b,* and *c,* Graebner deduces a methodical rule which I can but confirm after the addition of *d* and *e*: "From this it follows that in the case of cognate relations the absolute number of agreements to be expected between the corresponding younger cultures of different regions will be essentially greater than with the older ones. Conversely, therefore, each coincidence of the latter will be of considerably greater importance than in the case of the younger ones."

2. Graebner then makes a practical application of this rule (p. 145): "When investigating the culture relations between two countries, we have to begin with the younger complexes because these contain in themselves the positively greater possibility of demonstration." This rule is certainly in place, but if it cannot be followed easily because of some reason or other (*e.g.*, if accidentally the younger cultures have been poorly investigated), then there is a rule to be followed with regard to the criterion of quality in the older cultures, which I shall give in the following section.

3. But first I must still make an important correction with regard to the criterion of quantity, and that is in point *e*, which I myself proposed above. At the time I already restricted the vouched for smaller stock of the older cultures, by claiming them "especially" for the material and social culture. This restriction I shall now make still more emphatic by asserting that it would be a purely aprioristic assertion to assume this smaller amount also for the intellectual culture of the older peoples, their literary productions (myths, legends, proverbs, fables, songs), their religion (religious ideas and forms of cult), and their moral beliefs (regulation of possessions, the family, sex life). We have already enough positive proofs of a number of these peoples (Gabun Pygmies, north central Californians, the oldest Algonkins, etc.), so that we can assume that here the intellectual culture will provide very many supports for abundant criteria of quality and, consequently, also criteria of quantity.

β. *The Criterion of Quality*

1. It is precisely when the criterion of quantity cannot be so copious, in the case of the older cultures and to a degree corresponding to this lack, that scientific certainty demands that more consideration be given to the solidity of the nature of the criterion of quality. Both may be attained in the so-called

quantitative criterion of quality, which itself consists of a number of small characteristic features. Therefore, it is precisely here that we must endeavor to work out particularly well the individual features present in every single criterion of quality by a thoroughgoing study.

Hence, if the bow and arrow are the main and often the only weapon of most Pygmy tribes, then the material and cross section and length of the bow, the preparation of the ends of the bow for the reception and attachment of the bowstring, the material and manner of attaching the bowstring, the position of the finger when shooting, also the length and material of the arrow, the manner of feathering and, finally, the manufacture of the bow and arrow—all these offer a multitude of more or less characteristic traits. If the form of the family is simple among the oldest cultures, we still have the systems of relationship and their nomenclature there; hence, also the different social and economic rights and duties connected therewith, which likewise present again a whole host of characteristic traits.

2. The circumstance, that a large number of elements have "not yet" developed in the older cultures, puts the negative criterion of quality in a particularly significant role here. I have already (above, p. 145 s.) mentioned what is to be said concerning the general demonstrative force of the negative criterion. There it has already been pointed out that by means of more thorough research the positive element of the negative criterion comes to the fore. This more thorough research is in place right here, in order to set off the real characteristic of these old cultures against the younger ones and thus also bring out the criterion of quality in all its fullness.

An example of this kind was given before (above, p. 146); namely, in the case of the absence of defensive armor. Another example is the absence of body mutilations with mythologico-symbolical or social significance (knocking out of teeth, piercing of the column of the nose, circumcision); positively, it means, that the (tribal father) mythology and social distinction have not yet gained so much power so as to encroach upon the natural condition of the body. The absence or the meager development of naturism, manism, and animism is caused by the strong influence of the monotheistic belief in a creator. The same factor and the necessity of daily rational acquisition of the means of subsistence are the positive expression for the weak development of magic.

3. After the research undertaken up to now has sufficiently established that certain things like totemism, mother-right, two-class culture, patriarchal undivided family, etc., appear only among the later preliterates, a time measure is furnished us by the absence of these things; *i.e.,* in case it also coincides with primitivity in other matters as well (see below, p. 241) and no traces of the former possession of these things are to be found among older peoples. For those peoples, among whom such an absence has been established, come *before* the later preliterates and are ethnologically older than they. Here a criterion of quality would bind two cultures weakly together, even if one of those elements were missing. This connection, however, becomes stronger through a kind of criterion of quantity, if the two of them agree with each other in this absence of several of the same traits.

γ. *The Auxiliary Criteria* (24)

1. It is precisely at this point where we are treating of the relations of culture circles of different continents, which are mostly separated from one another by great distances, that the application of the criterion of continuity would be especially useful. And, therefore, it will also take effect here all the sooner, since these great distances mostly bring with them differences in climate, fauna and flora, and of external nature in general. If now, despite these differences, the insular occurrence of elements of both culture circles appears along their connecting line, then the demonstrative force is all the greater.

On the other hand, it must be pointed out that it is not to be wondered at if the criterion of continuity is applied the least in the case of such old cultures. Even if such islands of culture once upon a time existed, the time, however, when these old cultures migrated and left those islands behind, lies so extremely far back and so many other cultures have made their way along this route that it would have been very difficult for these small isolated regions or those single culture elements to have been able to maintain themselves through so many thousands of years.

2. For similar reasons the criterion of the degree of relationship will not be applicable very frequently and, if so, only in a weaker form. The greater length of time implied in the greater distance will have effaced and assimilated many differences in the degree of relationship. But wherever such differences have nevertheless been preserved, their demonstrative force is so much the greater.

3. It is certainly unfavorable and renders the demonstration difficult that where the distances between the two culture circles that have been compared are the greatest, corresponding to the state of affairs, criteria of continuity and degree of relationship are to be least expected. This want is somewhat compensated for in some of the oldest cultures by their peculiar position with regard to Asia, which admits of only unmistakable migration routes (above, p. 203 ss.). At present, I know of no other compensation for this than to make the criteria of quality all the more characteristic and to certify and thus make the criteria of quantity all the more extensive.

c. Conclusions From the Relationship of Multicontinental Culture Circles

When once we have proof that there is a relationship between two or several continentally separated culture circles (*i.e.,* that they belong to a greater culture circle), then several useful conclusions may be drawn therefrom with regard to the single culture circles.

a. Conclusions As to the Contents of the Culture Circles

1. This applies, first of all, with regard to the individual elements which make up the content of the culture circles in question. The appurtenance of a phenomenon, which was questionable in the one or the other subgroup, can be determined with certainty through the circumstances established for the other groups.

> As an example, Graebner proposes the settling down of the man in the place of the woman he marries (matrilocal marriage). This might appear doubtful for Melanesia, the region of the so-called bow culture, as it is found there so uncertainly and sporadically, in comparison to regions of the same culture in Indonesia and America, that it would be unthinkable to regard it as an element of the bow culture at all. Let it be further added that the rarity or doubtfulness of the occurrence of matrilocal marriage, which in itself is an element of the oldest mother-right culture, rests upon this in Melanesia, that Melanesia is only a border region and not a central region of this culture. Graebner could not have recognized this fully at that time. Also, the name "Melanesian bow culture" is incorrect, because of the reason given; namely, the two-class culture is not the oldest mother-right culture, as Graebner assumed it to be. (26)

It is seen easily that the conclusion defended here is only then admissible if we are dealing with an element of a simple culture, for an element of a compound culture could belong to but one of its components and, therefore, would not necessarily be represented in all the subregions.

2. Over against this positive rule, Graebner proposes a negative one (p. 147): "It is not allowed to ascribe a phenomenon to one of the culture circles in question for which it has not been certified in the least, on the basis of the composition of one or several sister cultures, because one or several subgroups of a family could manifest special developments or particular

borrowings from without. (27) An exception would also occur here if the doubtful element is so intimately associated with one of the culture circles in question that the first is unthinkable without the second."

β. *Conclusions As to Eventual Syntheses of Culture Circles*

1. After their relationship has been demonstrated, conclusions may also be drawn from the *structure* of continentally separated culture circles, especially with regard to the question whether a culture is composed of several other cultures or not. Graebner says on this question (p. 148): "Compound cultures might of themselves be recognizable here and there from the fact that single functional elements contain two different concurring forms; for instance, several house forms, several styles of ornament and other features of this kind (each one of which goes back to its own culture). When, on the contrary, the heterogeneous elements are not of a concurring nature (a house form of one culture circle, a form of navigation from another, etc.), then the compound character of the culture is only recognizable by comparison with related conditions, but in which the different elements appear still separated in the different complexes."

> As an example, Graebner then adduces the West African culture which can be recognized as composed of the two-class culture and the bow culture (28) only by comparison with Melanesia.

2. Graebner continues the research into compound cultures (p. 148): "The mixture through which a compound culture arises can be partial or total. It is partial if the one culture has taken a part of another complex through a process of acculturation, which process, however, need not have taken place in the present region of distribution (29). It is total if two complexes as a whole have fused. In the last mentioned case, the question whether the complex had already developed its compound form when it entered upon the present distribution or whether the fusion only took place within the region, for want

of some kind of stratificatory criteria, can only then be answered with probability in favor of the primary combination, when the elements of both or all components dominate *the whole region* not only by their multifarious mixing, but also by products common to both which agree even in details."

With this rule, Graebner touched upon perhaps one of the most important and most acute problems of progressive culture historical ethnology. After the distinction between Primitive and Primary cultures which I have introduced has been accepted, (30) and the list of primary cultures can at least as to essentials pass for complete numerically, (31) the secondary and tertiary culture circles will form a particularly important subject for future research. A part of the later cultures arose through specialized differentiation of the primary cultures. Other later cultures arose through a crossing of primary (and primitive) cultures with each other. Graebner treats this last case, and here the difficult question has to be decided: Is it a case of mixtures whose ingredients are indeed the same (Primary) cultures, but which have independently developed in different parts of the world uninfluenced by one another; or did such a mixture occur at one place on the earth, grow into a new culture circle and then as such, as a new whole, migrate over the earth, of course mingling with different cultures at different places, but at the same time still manifesting a uniform kernel everywhere?

The burning question arises with regard to a peculiar mixing of totemism and two-class system of mother-right. The totem clans are here divided into two classes or, also, the two classes have become a kind of large totem clan. While in pure mother-right the full moon and the dark moon stand at the head of the two classes, in this hybrid product their places are taken by the sun and moon, whereby the first is always the higher. The sun is represented as a hawk or eagle, the moon as a raven or crow. And also the wolf, lion, and fox (?) are used to represent the sun, and the hare, rabbit, and porcupine (burrowing animals) to represent the moon.

It is still more difficult to see which is the material culture of this crossing; however, it seems to correspond to the other elements that were crossed. It is so difficult to grasp this culture, because it appears both in very primitive (Southeastern Australia, Northwestern and Northeastern North America, South America) as well as in higher cultures. In the last mentioned it is, of course, overlayed by high cultures and, therefore, all the more difficult to recognize as, for instance, in Peru, Egypt, India, and Further India.

The rule proposed by Graebner is doubtlessly correct, but it is very difficult to apply it successfully, because the region of this crossing is for the most part in a fragmentary condition.

γ. *Conclusions As to the Existence of a Culture Circle From the Stratification of the Culture*

1. A particularly valuable, but at the same time quite difficult, possibility results from comparing a culture circle with the culture circles of other great regions in order to demonstrate the presence of a culture circle there, it being impossible to determine this on the basis of the material found in a single region. (32)

In this case the single culture elements which happen to be found on a continent belong to a certain culture circle somewhere else, but are not represented in the first continent numerically sufficient to furnish a satisfactory criterion of quantity. "Even if we assume the standpoint that analagous culture elements must originally have belonged to analagous culture unities, it would, of course, be incorrect to assume that this be precisely the particular culture unity that is to be demonstrated for this or that region, because the possibility always exists that this culture unity itself results from an historical combination, so that thereby the elements in question stand in relation only to the one component of this concretion product.

"The facts of the culture stratification then lead to a certain, but broadly defined, probability"; namely, when the total of those culture elements are found on their own continent in the same sequence of the cultures present in the same region, which a certain culture circle always takes in other continents as well. "This agreement also in the stratification conditions will give a certain probability to the conclusion, that the elements of analagous layers, even if they do not belong to the same culture complex, nevertheless belong to a chronologically homogeneous group of cultures." But this probability is diminished by another possibility; namely, that a culture circle which is the older one on one continent appears as the younger in another, because certain circumstances prevented it from entering this continent earlier (*cf.* later, p. 243 s.). "On the contrary, the conclusion will be all the more cogent, the stronger are the reasons already obtained from the circumstances of the particular region which urge the assumption of appurtenance."

2. As an example, Graebner here proposes his comparison between the stratificatory conditions found in the cultures of Oceania and those of South America (p. 149), which we, at the time, felt obliged to regard as fragmentary and we still consider it a mere summary. In the southermost part of both regions, he finds elements of the Primitive culture and in the north of both regions younger mother-right phenomena. Between these two regions, he then certifies in South America "a number of scattered elements as spear-thrower, belts of bark, penis-sheath, hut with conical roof," which of themselves do not suffice to form a culture circle. In Oceania and Australia, however, these objects are parts of a complete culture circle. Since its locality in Australia and Oceania is thus found to be exactly between that of Primitive culture and "younger" mother-right and the distribution of those scattered elements in South America is likewise so situated, Graebner concludes, that the last mentioned also belong to the same complete (totemistic) culture circle as in Australia-Oceania.

But in this matter Graebner neglected to speak of another culture whose region likewise lies in Australia between the "younger" mother-right and the primitive culture, and that is the one which Graebner, however, falsely designated as the older mother-right culture, the so-called two-class culture. In this passage he does not speak of this latter culture for South America and should have at least kept the possibility in mind that those scattered elements in South America belong to that two-class culture.

In my "Kulturkreise und Kulturschichten in Südamerika" I have, of course, likewise ascribed those elements to the totemistic culture, at the same time maintaining the existence of a mother-right two-class culture also for the Andes regions. (33) The extensive advanced researches that I undertook since that time allow me now, however, to consider it as certain that there was no *purely totemistic* culture in South America, but only one crossed with the mother-right two-class culture, which in its turn probably was not independent in South America either.

We see, therefore, how the example proposed by Graebner was not entirely well selected, nor was the method used above criticism. Of course, Graebner redeemed himself somewhat by allowing "the elements of analogous strata to belong if not to the same culture complex, then certainly to a chronological group of cultures which belong together."

4. COMPLETE PICTURE AND ORIGINAL HOME OF THE CULTURE CIRCLES

A. Complete Picture of the Culture Circles. The Oldest Culture Circles

1. The full extension of the single culture circles, especially of the older ones, as well as the totality of their relations to one another, first manifests itself in the survey of the different continents. The result is, as Graebner says in his summary (p. 150) : "a very checkered picture of culture relations. On the one hand genealogical associations, on the other, a mutually variable interreaction in every conceivable stage of assimilation,

from the most extensive and *most original* culture groups [the culture circles in the proper and fullest sense of the word] to the small unities observed at present."

These variable forms could not all be given here, but only the more general types of them, for the application of which both methodical rules and practical directions have been set forth. If the directions often appeared complicated, that was only because they correspond to the culture historical reality which also in many and in most cases is extremely complicated. That this complexity often arises in the course of culture development can generally be assumed. Whence, therefore, the practical difficulty of their great complexity argues against beginning the culture historical investigation of a region at times with the youngest strata (see above, p. 206) and conversely, there is something to be said for the method "of beginning with the primitive complexes of relative simplicity," of which Graebner speaks (p. 150), in order to obtain therefrom the necessary insight into the research of later, more complicated layers.

2. Van Bulck (154 ss.) is deserving of high praise for having drawn a detailed picture of the different forms of culture stratification. This gives us a fair idea of the diversity of these stratificatory possibilities. It is impossible to paint the picture of these many variations in full at this place. I shall but briefly repeat the different forms that van Bulck treats and for the rest refer to van Bulck's exposition itself. He distinguishes:

a. "Single colored regions," regions with one culture, and these may be both very extensive regions of autochthonous or immigrated cultures as well as small remote regions of displaced and scattered or degenerated earlier strata.

b. "Multicolored regions," regions with several cultures; namely, α, regions with two strata, which lie either above each other (domination) or alongside each other (symbiosis) or confusedly (mixed culture); β, regions with one layer and heterogeneous elements from different culture regions or only from certain culture regions; γ, no layer, but special forms (high culture center — local forms, border contactual phenomena).

This whole exposition is very instructive, because it enables the culture historian to obtain a good survey of the tasks of dissecting culture strata with which he is confronted. One must note that in this chapter van Bulck does not interpolate any methodical rules. These facts all may be treated with the rules proposed by Graebner, which I have critically sifted and methodically supplemented. No essentially new ones are necessary. Van Bulck essayed a methodological exposition only in one instance, and that is the case for which Graebner gave no rules and for which I endeavored to supply the deficiency. It concerns the treatment of regions with one culture. We will have to consider this case now.

3. Although a little while ago (p. 218) we declared it advantageous to begin research with the oldest, most simple cultures, it is precisely certain ones of these that have to overcome a hindrance that at first sight seems to be insurmountable. For these in particular have been pushed back farthest, to the outermost border regions of the whole earth. Already their distances from one another are therefore the greatest and all successive younger cultures have inserted themselves between. Thus, therefore, precisely these oldest cultures do not stand in the least contact with one another and, consequently, they cannot form relations of contact, mixture, and superposition with one another, from which their relative age might be deciphered.

This is somewhat compensated for in some of these oldest cultures, in so far as they have migrated through the same gate of entrance from Asia into other continents, especially over the Bering Strait to America or over Cape York Peninsula into Australia. As seen above (p. 195 ss.), their position in this case gives the basis for establishing their relative age. Perhaps something can still be obtained from the consideration of the directions of the migration (p. 200 ss.).

We might hope that also prehistory could still salvage something from the earth. But this hope must be moderated greatly in the face of the fact that the material culture possession of the oldest cultures is all the more meager and unimportant the older the cultures are and that the outlook for their preservation stands in inverse proportion to the age of these cultures. It must disappear entirely in cultures as that of the Pygmies, who do not even understand how to fashion an implement from stone, but only do so from wood, bambo, shells, etc.

And precisely in the case of the Pygmies, the geographical discontinuity with other cultures is the greatest and their region is the most distant from that of all other primitive cultures. Under such circumstances, how will we answer the question of the relative age of the Pygmy Primitive cultures with regard to those of the Arctic, North and South America, and Southeastern Australia?

B. The Determination of the Age of an Isolated Culture Circle

Graebner does not give any rule for the case in which the age of a culture complex should be determined which does not come into direct or indirect contact with any others. Likewise, H. Pinard de la Boullaye does not give any positive direction for the solution of this problem. But I think that we can here use the rules he sets up for the case, "where we can study a territory of equal coloring; in other words, with one single culture type, which alone fills out a whole homogeneous region." (34) Pinard also declares: "Of all possible cases that is the hardest, because it offers the least opportunity for the application of the comparative method," for the simple reason is that the different strata are missing with which the comparison might begin.

Consequently, he is of the opinion that, nevertheless, there are different criteria which can clarify the matter and win a certain chronological survey. He enumerates two of them: the principle of necessary presupposition and the criterion of complexity. The first, he formulates with the words: "Each element that presupposes another is necessarily younger in age than the one which it presupposes"; (35) the second: "That culture element must be considered as the older which is the more simple one, and that element as the younger which is more elaborate and developed."

I have made use of these principles and applied them for our case in a somewhat changed form. (36) Only the second principle can be used here, because the ethnologically high age of the cultures here under comparison is already firmly established. Also, Graebner considers the "characteristic of general culture age" as a confirmation if it is joined to another argument. For him this is the criterion of the stratification.

I had given the following form to the first criterion of Pinard: "From two culture elements of the same order, the one which presupposes the change in the original state of affairs is younger than the one which does not presuppose such a change."

I applied this principle to the manner in which man in these oldest cultures treats his own body. The Pygmies leave it in its natural condition and do not undertake to change it in any way for the purpose of socio-mythological characterization or ornament. They avoid not only circumcision (or incision or subincision), but also the other initiation form of breaking out of teeth, which is practiced by the Yuin and a part of the Wiradyuri-Kamilaroi tribes in Southeastern Australia. Neither do they have the practice of tearing out body hairs, which we find in vogue among the Kulin and the other Kamilaroi tribes. Scarification (tattooing) is absent among them, but it is practiced by the Kurnai and Tasmanians, nor is the piercing of the cartilage of the nose found among them, whereas the Kurnai have this custom. If, in a long list of important points, both primitive cultures, that of the Pygmies and that of the Southeastern Australians, seem to be of the same age, but have different practices with regard to the treatment of the body, then the Pygmies thereby prove themselves to be the older, because the treatment of the body among the Southeastern Australians doubtless represents the change of an original state of affairs; namely, the natural condition of the human body.

In this respect, the Pygmies resemble the Arctic Primitive culture and the North American (the north central Californians,[37] Algonkin) and the South American (the Fuegians, all of which do not practice bodily mutilations either). But the Pygmies prove themselves to be older than these last mentioned peoples, because they do not practice any kind of stone industry, but manufacture their implements from wood, bamboo, and shells. Here a methodical principle must be applied which we can consider only as a further development of the one applied in the first case; that culture element must be considered as the younger, the manufacture of which offers greater difficulties and presupposes more experience. There is no doubt that the same must be said of the stone industry in comparison with the wood and bamboo industry.

c. Original Home of the Culture Circles

α. *General Rules to Establish the Original Home of the Culture Circles*

"A special and, in many respects, final problem is offered by the question of the original home of the different original culture unities" (Graebner, p. 150). It was understandable and objectively justified for Graebner, at the time, to express the opinion that reliable principles for the solution of these questions were missing. He proposed three criteria, but emphasized that they do not lead to absolutely certain conclusions:

a. "It is clear that a culture complex which cuts asunder two or several related cultures cannot be indigenous in its present position."(38) Certain conclusions will perhaps result from this for radial diffusions to the single continents in the case of narrow entrances mentioned above. (39)

b. "Just as certain is it that the most closely related culture groups, in the last analysis, must be referred if not to the same identical place, then certainly to places not far distant."

c. "A last and important criterion is that of the degree of relationship and of the variation of forms. It is probable that the unity or group of unities lies nearest the assumed starting point, the rest of whose members in the same family manifest variations in different directions." (40)

For the future, Graebner suggests the possibility of applying still a fourth criterion (p. 151):

d. "An essential confirmation or control of the results elsewhere obtained will perhaps, in the future, be given by anthropogeographical arguments, the questions of relation between culture and environment. Today these problems lie in a broad field; for first it must be possible to get acquainted with the old tribes of the culture before we shall be able from their appearance to decide in what sort of environment they developed."

In the meantime, however, this better knowledge of "the old tribes of culture" required at the time by Graebner has been attained to quite a degree by means of thorough research work, and, therefore, we may now examine the question more closely, "in what kind of country they may have developed."

β. *The Real Original Homes of the Single Culture Circles*

1. The question of the home of the Primary cultures could be raised in a particularly successful manner for that culture circle which I was the first to propose and which Graebner refused to recognize as such for a long time; namely, the culture circle of the (large) animal-breeding herders. The end result of the studies undertaken by the culture historical school (41) is that South Central Siberia seems to be the home of this culture circle. That conclusion was reached essentially through the progress in anthropogeography foreseen by Graebner (above, under *d*).

As a result of this progress and through the application of Graebner's criterion given above under *c*, also the home of the mother-right agrarian culture circle turned out to be the district of the eastern slopes of the Himalayas, with the river valleys of the Ganges, Brahmaputra, Irawaddy and other streams. (42)

The home of the culture circle of the totemistic higher hunters still remains doubtful. Graebner had for a long time given this culture circle credit for the discovery of animal breeding. (43) Doubtless this culture circle was closely associated with that of the (large) animal-breeding herders, but it is not identical with it. However, by following Graebner's criterion proposed above under *b* we might assume the home of the (large) animal-breeding herders was west and southwest of South Central Siberia; namely, the bordering highland region of Central Asia. Today, however, traces of it are hardly to be found outside of prehistory. (44) The original territory can by no means be "in a center of distribution with higher food gathering or hunting," as Trimborn thinks,(45) but in such a region as has an abundant fauna which is also intensely specialized. (46)

2. Finally, the home of some Primitive cultures could be established with some certainty. All the American Primitive cultures, the South American (Fuegians, Gez-Tapuya) and the North American (north central Californians, the Algonkins) once formed an old culture together with the Arctic culture (Samoyedes, Koryaks, Ainu, Ancient-Eskimo), whose habitat was somewhere in (North) Eastern Asia. To the southwest, the Pygmy culture joined it and was the first to separate from there and split up into an African and a (South) Asiatic group. On the Southeast, the preparatory stages of the later Southeastern Australian Primitive culture joined, which migrated from there over the present Indonesia and New Guinea to Australia. (47) In the working out of these facts, among others, Graebner's criterion proposed above (p. 221) under *a* also aided.

Thus, the words of Graebner (p. 151) have in fact not yet been fulfilled: "Until then, however, perhaps the vigorous ethnological culture historical research shall have brought many of its own criteria to maturity, which we today cannot imagine." However, the criteria for the most part already proposed by Graebner have proven themselves sufficient, with several corrections and supplements, to attack with success the particularly difficult and important problem of the home of the culture circles.

(1) In van Bulck, the culture circle is but lightly touched upon in a short polemic with the opponents of the "Doctrine of Culture Circle," p. 221-224.

(2) Also H. Ulrich in his "Logische Studien zur Methode der Ethnologie," *Anthropos*, XVIII-XIX (1923-1924), p. 751 s. did not come to this distinction.

(3) *Cf.* Sapir, *Time Perspective,* p. 44 s., and also below, p. 173 ss.

(4) Also recognized by Sapir, *Time Perspective,* p. 51.

(5) Fr. Boas, "The Social Organization and the Secret Societies of the Kwakiutl Indians," *Report of the United States National Museum* (1895), p. 315 ss. and "Die Entwicklung der Mythologien der Indianer der nordpazifischen Küste Amerikas," *Zeitschrift für Ethnologie,* XXVII, p. 487 ss.

(6) Lebzelter, "Zur Methodik menschheits-geschichtlicher Forschung," *Zeitschr. f. Ethnol.,* LXIV (1932), p. 202.

(8) M. J. Herskovits, "A Preliminary Consideration of the Culture Areas of Africa," *Amer. Anthrop.,* N. S. XXVI (1924), pp. 50-63; "The Cattle Complex in East Africa," *Amer. Anthrop.,* N. S. XXVIII (1926), pp. 230-272.

(9) In *Methods of Social Science,* ed. by Stuart A. Rice (Chicago, 1931), pp. 248 ss.

(10) Kroeber, *op. cit.,* p. 251.

(11) Kroeber, *op. cit.,* p. 249 s.

(12) Italics mine.—W. Schmidt.

(13) Kroeber, *op. cit.,* p. 262 s.

(14) H. Pinard de la Boullaye, *L'Étude comparée des Religims,* Vol. II (2nd ed.), p. 280.

(15) In this regard see W. Schmidt, *Rasse und Volk* (Salzburg, 1935), p. 149 ss.

(16) *Cf.* W. Schmidt, *Die Gliederung der Australischen Sprachen* (Vienna, 1919), p. 220 ss.

(17) W. Schmidt, *Ursprung der Gottesidee,* VI, pp. 171 ss., 196 ss.

(18) In the printed text is written "from them," but that must be a typographical error. "It" can refer only to the foregoing "complex" and it is impossible to refer "them" to the foregoing regions.—W. Schmidt.

(19) H. Pinard de la Boullaye, *L'Étude comparée des Religions,* II, p. 260.

(20) *Zeitschrift f. Ethnologie,* XXXVII (1905), pp. 28 ss., 57 ss.

(21) *Op. cit.,* XLV (1913), p. 1014. ss.

(22) *Cf.* above, p. 166, the Polynesian culture.

(23) Graebner, p. 144.

(24) *Cf.* Graebner, p. 136 s.

(25) See Graebner, p. 147 ss.

(26) *Cf.* W. Schmidt, "The Position of Women With Regard to Property in Primitive Society," *Amer. Anthrop.,* N. S. XXXVII (1935), p. 252 s.

(27) As an "exemplary specimen" for the inconclusiveness of this rule, Graebner adds that I "even take phenomenon like sex totemism, which has been proven only for the one tribe, the Semang, and put it among the culture possession of the 'Pygmies' in my work, *Die Stellung der Pygmäenvölker in der Entwicklungsgeschichte des Menschen."* Everyone who takes the trouble to read pp. 270, 272 s. of the book, which is the matter under discussion (Graebner does not give the page), will see that it *never* entered my mind to designate sex totemism as belonging to the essential make-up of the Pygmy. Later investigations have further shown that also for the Semang themselves it is more than doubtful; *cf.* W. Schmidt, *Ursprung der Gottesidee,* III, pp. 222 note, 278 ss.

(28) The case must be explained differently if the two-class culture of Melanesia is to be understood only as a mixture of mother-right culture with

totemistic culture, a mixture which did not exist in Africa in this form, because here totemism was quantitatively and qualitatively stronger than in Melanesia.—W. Schmidt.

(29) Only this last form should be considered a "compound form" in the real sense of the word.—W. Schmidt.

(30) W. Schmidt and W. Koppers, *Völker und Kulturen* (Regensburg, 1924), pp. 193, 298.

(31) Of course, by far, not specifically so.—W. Schmidt.

(32) *Cf.* Graebner, p. 148.

(33) *Zeit. f. Ethnol.*, XLIV (1913), p. 1049 ss.

(34) Pinard, *L'Étude comparée des Religions,* II (Paris, 1925), pp. 250 ss.; 3rd ed., p. 271 ss.

(35) Also proposed by Sapir in *Time Perspective,* p. 15 ss.

(36) W. Schmidt, Critères pour établier la position éthologique des cercles les plus anciens *(Compte–Rendu de la Semaine d'Éthnologie religieuse,* IV [1925], p. 126 ss.); *Ursprung der Gottesidee,* III, p. 11 s.

(37) Among several north central Californian tribes the piercing of the cartilage of the nose (and of the ear) is in vogue.

(38) *Cf.* in this regard above, p. 191.

(39) See above, p. 195 ss.

(40) *Cf.* Graebner, "Die melanesische Bogenkultur," *Anthropos,* IV (1909), pp. 1024, 1030.

(41) W. Schmidt, "Totemismus, viehzüchterischer Nomadismus und Mutterrecht," *Anthropos,* X-XI (1915-1916), p. 307 ss.; W. Schmidt and W. Koppers, *Völker und Kulturen* (Regensburg, 1924), pp. 124 ss. and 502 ss.; Fr. Flor, "Haustiere und Hirtenkulturen," *Wiener Beiträge zur Kulturgeschichte und Linguistik,* I (1930), pp. 1-238.

(42) W. Schmidt and W. Koppers, *op cit.*, pp. 266 ss. and 545 ss.; W. Schmidt, "The Position of Women With Regard to Property in Primitive Society," *American Anthropologist,* N. S. XXXVI, pp. 249 ss.; *cf.* also Menghin, *Weltgeschichte der Steinzeit,* pp. 278, 500, 514.

(43) *Cf.* W. Schmidt, "Fritz Graebner" *Anthropos,* XXX (1935), p. 206.

(44) W. Schmidt, *op. cit.; cf.* Menghin, *op. cit.*, pp. 196 s., 497, and W. Koppers, *Anthropos,* XXXI (1936), p. 170 ss.

(45) Trimborn, "Zur Lehre von den Kulturkreisen," *Zeitschr. f. Ethnologie,* LXV (1935), p. 117.

(46) *Cf.* also W. Koppers, "Der Totemismus als menschheitsgeschichtliches Problem," *Anthropos,* XXX (1936), pp. 159-176.

(47) See more extensive treatment of these matters in W. Schmidt, *Der Ursprung der Gottesidee,* Vol. VI (1935), pp. 196 ss., 311 ss., 361 ss. Only in this genealogical co-ordination of the single old cultures are the difficulties solved which Trimborn raises against the reality of these culture circles. His objections proceed from the arbitrary co-ordination of each of these (Primitive) cultures with some other culture arbitrarily chosen. In this correct co-ordination especially the number of criteria of quality is greater and, hence, the criterion of quantity is also stronger.

Chapter V

MEANS TO ESTABLISH THE INTERNAL CULTURE DEVELOPMENT

1. EVOLUTION AND EVOLUTIONISM

1. SINCE the culture historical movement in ethnology has continually set itself in opposition to the older evolutionistic method and striven against it on all fronts, authors have not been wanting who thought that the culture historical method does not recognize any kind of evolution. I have already mentioned what ought to be said on this question (see above, p. 10 s.). But now the moment has come in the course of culture historical methodics to show that the recognition of evolution on the part of the culture historical school is not a mere theoretical one, but that its method, and that alone, gives us the means to establish this evolution conclusively. Graebner devotes a special chapter to this subject; namely, "Series of Development" (pp. 151-161). (1) I prefer the title used above, "Means to Establish the Internal Culture Development." Also the adjective "internal" clearly expresses the difference between the cultural productions from within; namely, from the exercise of the powers of the soul, or the people, and the culture productions arising from influences exerted from without. That there are "series" in which this internal development takes place is self-evident, since it is the natural expression of the historical sequence enacted here.

Graebner again clearly declares his standpoint of opposition to purely evolutionistic constructions. He shows his disapproval that, *e.g.,* Frobenius "axiomatically lays down purely speculative hypotheses (2) of development in his culturo-genealogical treatises," and then he continues: "The contrary procedure is methodologically correct, because the developmental characteristics lying outside the questions of cultural relationship lack every objective criterion of truth, while we have at our disposal several criteria for the problems of cultural relationship, which operate very objectively and mutually control one another. The results of culture historical research into the various interrelations of culture and culture elements can therefore serve as foundation and instances of control for the treatment of questions of development, but not vice versa" (p. 152).

2. Graebner admits that here and there forms of a culture element can of themselves give the answer to the question as to which forms stood at the beginning and which at the end of the series of development. As they stand, the following principles are sound beyond doubt; namely, that "the beginnings of every development must be (firstly) simple and to a certain extent naturally founded, and (secondly) the further developments must be intelligible in a psychologically simple manner" (p. 152, s.). Unfortunately, the two regulations are not clear, not the second, as is proven by the great number of evolutionistic hypotheses which are based upon one object, each one of which is supposed to be simple and natural; not the first, for simplicity may also be a secondary phenomenon. The first regulation is also contestable in itself, especially with regard to the elements of intellectual culture, for the claim that its original forms are simple is arbitrary apriorism. Whether they are simple or rich depends upon the intellectual power of him who produced them, and nothing justifies us to exclude men of great intellectual energy from the first stages of intellectual development or to deny, *a priori,* the high importance of the mind.

Furthermore, the concept of simplicity is ambiguous. Is the seed that contains a whole tree in itself something simple? It must be admitted that as soon as something intellectual is realized or better externalized in matter, the first forms are simple and necessarily so, because for perfection and complexity both time and experience are required. Besides, it is clear that the oldest human groups must have been small and their social communities simple. However, Graebner is entirely right when he refuses "to consider such communities of people living somewhere today simply as representatives of this ancient state of affairs, and to conclude from their culture that of the original horde" (p. 153). That cannot be done categorically until their cultural relations and the genealogical groupings consequent thereon have been established by the aid of special criteria.

3. To explain and to develop this further we must go back again to what I said before (p. 138 ss.) concerning the twofold species of culture relations, which Graebner had not sufficiently distinguished, the unfavorable consequences of which also affected his treatment of the internal culture development precisely at this point. I refer to the distinction between active and passive culture relations; *i.e.,* between those which a man, a people, a culture of their own selves actively exert upon themselves, upon other men, peoples, and cultures, and those which an individual, a whole people, or a culture passively receive from alien sources. Since every culture is something psychical, and all psychical events are immanent, the first of these remain hidden from all direct observation within the inner recesses of their souls and only become observable at the moment when they come out and manifest themselves as external influences upon others.

These active culture relations must also be included, when Graebner emphasizes that only "the results of culture historical research into the various interrelations of culture can serve as foundation and instances of control for the treatment of questions of development." Indeed, we shall very soon see that these active relations alone come into consideration for a positive solution of the problems of development, while the passive relations, if not entirely, at least to a great extent, are of but negative importance here.

2. ELIMINATION OF THE FORMS EXTRANEOUS TO THE INTERNAL DEVELOPMENT

A. Distinction Between Variation and Combination

The passive culture relations which a tribe, a people, or a culture receive are influences which they experience from without, which therefore do not proceed from their inner selves. It is clear, then, that they, if it can be done, must be separated and subtracted in order to establish the purely *internal* development. All the rules which have been proposed to obtain and to subtract the contact as well as the planitional and marginal acculturations and mixed forms from the present state of culture do nothing else thereby than cleanse the culture of these external influences and replace it in its own uninfluenced self and thus fulfill the first requirement for the establishment of its internal development. All this, therefore, is preliminary work (but absolutely necessary) for the understanding of the internal development.

Graebner is only illustrating and making a special application of this fundamental idea to the present task when he here asserts that the means and results we have learned to know up till now make it possible to distinguish between variation and combination. "Variation" is nothing else but a change from within outward; hence, internal development, "combination," is the collision with alien cultures and the subsequent subjection to their influence—*i.e.,* external development.

Graebner writes here (p. 153) : "Almost every series of forms may be conceived, a *priori,* in a threefold manner. Firstly and secondly, either terminus may be taken as the starting point the other terminus being the end result." We would then have the internal development "variation" proceeding now from this end, now from the other. "Thirdly, however, we can also have a 'variation' in which a contact series arises from the interaction of the two end forms, in which case the single intermediate stages signify a gradual predominance of one or the other component." Here we would have external influence, "combination."

In the first case, it is one culture, one cultural element, which generates a series of forms parthenogenetically. In the other case, there are two or several cultures or cultural elements which produce a series of forms by their reciprocal association.

As an example, Graebner asks the question whether the development of ornament began with figured representation and developed to geometrical ornamentation or whether, vice versa, the former proceeded from the latter, (3) or thirdly, whether the two different cultures, the one with geometrical, the other with figured ornamentation, met and mingled with each other. The decisive answer to this question can only be given by detailed culture historical investigation.

B. Rules to Establish Combinatory Forms

Graebner then proposes a rule for combinatory forms which he formulates thus (p. 154): "If both end members of two different culture complexes belong to the same series of forms [this same reflection is analogously applicable to more developed conditions] and if the intermediate members appear only there where the two culture circles overlay, permeate or come in contact with each other, then there is no doubt that it is not a case of development from one extreme to the other, but it is a contact or combinatory series." It must, of course, be solidly established that this condition which Graebner requires (namely, that "both end members of two *different* complexes belong to the same series of forms") is actually fulfilled in the case in question and that we are here actually dealing with two different cultures. The proof must be brought forward that these two end members are actually different culture complexes. If this postulate is fulfilled, we have a very important methodical rule.

Graebner gives as an example the teaching of the social development from mother right to father right advanced by evolutionistic sociology, for which the following classical specimen from Australia is proposed: the continuous series of forms leading from the mother-right two-class system (of the Dieri-Urabunna) over the (half-father, half-mother right) four-class system (of the Kamilaroi-Wiradyuri and West Kulin) to the father-right local system (of the Narrinyeri-Parnkalla). Graebner can here point to one of his most splendid and most important productions, (4) when he continues: "This theory becomes simply untenable by the fact that in the South Seas the father-right totemistic local exogamy and the mother-right two-class system prove themselves to be elements of two entirely different culture complexes, and that the alleged transitional stages of development belong to the regions where the two cultures mixed, these regions being otherwise also demonstrable."

c. Methodological Treatment of Doubtful Cases

If the criterion of quantity already in general has the task of removing the possibilities for subjective differences of interpretation which could eventually still be present in the criterion of quality (above, p. 150), then that finds its application in the rule that primarily or at any rate in a case of doubt, "only such phenomena or forms . . . shall be brought into an evolutionary historical association, between which also culture historical relations have been proven" (Graebner, p. 155); *i.e.,* exactly those phenomena that have been demonstrated by the criterion of quantity as simply belonging to the same culture circle or culture complex. It is possible that, in this process, members which might determine a series of development as such, disappear the next time, so that it would be more difficult to recognize this series as such. But the same series would itself also become doubtful and uncertain through the presence of such doubtful members and would not form a solid foundation especially for the beginning of the investigation.

Graebner holds it as "theoretically quite reasonable that by means of the series established as certain in other ways, also certain intermediate members would be postulated or made probable," which had not yet been proven culture historically. Then their insertion into the series of development would "naturally be justified" and these members in a given case could "form the starting point for conclusions upon culture historical coherences not yet observed." I do not know whether such cases are actually "theoretically quite reasonable"; but, at any rate, I think that the postulation of intermediate members should give rise to more exact research into the culture historical associations of these assumptions and that only when these have been actually established may they be inserted into the series of development.

It goes without saying that this rule does not prevent us from making those necessary surveys over the stage of research from time to time in which also the doubtful and often merely probable members of the developmental series might be included; however, they must be designated as such. Through such surveys, the opportunity may be offered to other investigators who are, perhaps, in a position to produce certitude in these cases with the help of better or more copious material or because they are better trained in this matter (above, p. 205).

3. POSITIVE DETERMINATION OF FORMS BELONGING TO THE INTERNAL DEVELOPMENT

A. Active Influences As Positive Subjects of the Internal Development

Graebner then continues (p. 156): "After the crossings and contactual forms have been sifted out, the main problem of development remains; namely, the question of the succession of development." . . . According to this, it would seem as if the appurtenance of an element to an internal development would be determined simply by this negative process of subtraction of mixed and contact forms, as it were, of elements arising from the influence of foreign cultures. The part remaining after this subtraction would then represent the sum of the elements belonging to the internal development. If we also add thereto Graebner's statement that only the investigation of (external) culture relations gives objective criteria for appurtenance and chronology (above, p. 138), then we see how unfavorably the internal development would be represented in such an historical method, because it would only be established by the negative method of subtraction of the (external) relations established with the aid of objective means.

Such a disparaging appreciation must arise if we understand by culture relations only the passive changes experienced through external influences and not, as I have frequently emphasized (above, pp. 138, 226), also, and precisely so, the active influences which are an emanation and a revelation of one's very self. In fact it has been solidly established that the relations obtained by the criteria of quantity and quality and the auxiliary criteria contain not only the passive influences coming from alien cultures, but also nonetheless, the active influences. These active relations, therefore, thus participate entirely in that positive and objective character which is peculiar to the results of the culture historical method.

2. Neither is it as if the objective element would disappear with the subtraction of the passive relations, and only the subjective element of the internal development would remain, but this subtraction will only sever the similarly objective elements of the active relations, which reveal the internal development and "cleanse" it of the alien passive influences which do not belong to the stream of internal personal development, but flow hither precisely from alien cultures. Therefore, I would not call this procedure subtraction, but rather separation in so far as the relations objectively established on both sides, which till now have been considered indiscriminately, are now cut apart and the active relations subjected to a special treatment.

It is precisely by fulfilling this condition required by Graebner, namely, that only such elements should be inserted into a series of development which would have the same culture circle in common with the other elements of the series (above, p. 229), that we obtain the positive guarantee that they belong to so large an organic juxtaposition that it is broad and durable enough to be the carriers of an internal development.

The presentation of this culture circle and its elements in different temporal junctures then also offers the possibility of directly following the course of its internal development.

Whenever the research of a culture complex, of a culture circle, is already quite far advanced, another tool is obtained for establishing the internal appurtenance of an element to this culture circle and, hence, to its course of development. At any rate, according to the stage of our research, this methodical weapon at least suggests or gives some suspicion of its course of development, for at this stage of the investigation also the specific total character of this culture is already known and has put its seal upon all or almost all the ingredients (*cf.* above, p. 177).

Thus, the custom of matrilocal marriage as such is excluded from the patriarchal pastoral nomad culture, and it requires very special circumstances to explain its occurrence there only as a foreign element. In the same way, the occurrence of the cult of Terra Mater would be unthinkable both in the totemistics-father right as well as in the patriarchal pastoral nomad cultures and only understandable as an infiltrated foreign element.

B. The Importance of Passive Influences for the Internal Development

1. In this sense, I must also again restrict and correct a statement that has been made (above, p. 226); namely, that the passive influences are only of negative importance for the determination of the internal development. Strictly speaking, there are no purely passive influences in a culture. Also man, a tribe, a people, who have experienced an influence from without, do not receive it in complete passivity, but in some way or other take an active part therein and set to work upon it. This degree of activity is different for every tribe and people, and in this very factor the peculiar nature of their own culture manifests itself. The way in which they form and mold the external influence and assimilate it to their own culture plainly

shows their own inner character and the stage of their internal development. Hence, also the so-called passive influences are not merely of negative importance for determining the internal development of these influences, but they also provide opportunities for observations and elaborations in a positive sense.

The difference in the manner in which the single cultures and peoples receive and react to foreign influences is considerable. There are some peoples who accept everything foreign, but leave it as it is and eventually exhibit a cultural medley that, of course, possesses no guarantee of longer duration in the divergency of its elements. There are others which likewise accept everything foreign, but only retain whatever corresponds to their own culture and what they can make serviceable to themselves, though it be only after previous alteration. They thereby create a steady flowing source of a new supply of strength. Finally, there are others who take nothing or, at most, a minimum of foreign elements. The purpose is to preserve their own culture undisturbed. They, however, expose themselves to the danger of one-sided and poor development.

2. To express this methodologically: If we reckon up the amount of proper strength and, consequently, also of the proper internal development which was expended in each reception of influence exerted from without, then it is absolutely impossible to sever the internal development cleanly and neatly from a culture or a people. It must also be taken into consideration that one's own strength is not only used in the mere acceptance and eventual formation of the foreign element, but that this influence also can contain stimulations which release and set in motion very long series of internal development which without these impulses would have remained in their potential torpor and would never have crossed the margin of reality. The thousand examples from the culture history of peoples with written history find their numerous counterparts also in the culture history of the peoples without writings.

Consequently, even the finest methodological means will not always make it possible to determine the boundary lines between the internal development and the exterior influences.

That applies both in case of peoples with written history as well as in the case of those without it.

4. THE DETERMINATION OF THE SEQUENCE OF DEVELOPMENT

A. The Determination of the Ordinary Sequences of Development

Now we can turn again to the words of Graebner already quoted above (p. 195): "After the crossing and contactual forms have been sifted out, the main problem of development remains; namely, the question of the developmental succession in the ramifications of the development and also the insertion into the correct series of development." Corresponding to our distinction between the active and the passive influences, we supplement the words of Graebner thus: When we have established, either positively by investigation of the active influences or negatively by subtraction of the passive influences, what elements are ingredients and members of the series of development, then it is a question as to which succession of the series of the entire development they are to be inserted and which of them are to be arranged as the earlier and which as the later members of the course of development. Graebner correctly emphasizes in general that also there "the research of relations of affinity, in so far as it describes their circles at all, partly gives decisive answers offhand and partly offers, at least, important points of view" (p. 156).

α. *The Developmental Series in Partial or Special Groups*

1. Graebner proposes the following rule here (p. 156):

"It is clear that the genealogy of forms of a certain cultural element must correspond to the genealogy of the group to which it belongs. Thus, forms or circles of forms which are restricted to one single narrow culture unity or at least to a limited complex of a great group are to be appraised with overwhelming probability as special forms of this unity and, consequently, when compared to other forms which have a more extensive distribution they are to be considered younger forms."

As an example, he proposes the very peculiar magic totemism of Central Australia (including the Aranda and neighboring tribes) and correctly points out that as long as this is only proven for this restricted Central Australian region, it is not allowed to look upon it as the original form, *i.e.,* as the oldest form of group totemism spread over great expanses of the earth, but that for the present it is to be regarded as a special local form.(5)

2. Graebner himself only concedes a "great probability" to this rule, but in fact a qualifying observation must be added. The forms of a (smaller) special group are *not* to be considered as younger if a group has already very early separated itself and taken old forms of what was at the time its early age and has preserved them in its isolation, while the greatest part of the remaining groups of the culture in question had taken on other forms, be it in the internal development or from external influence. Here is a graphical representation:

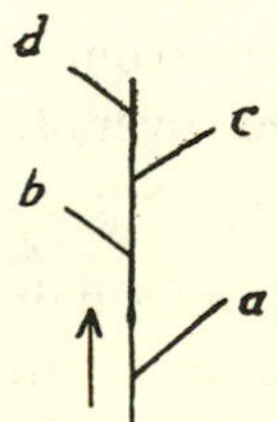

(*a* is not simply younger than the sum of *b-c-d*)

We have such a case in the Pygmies. We cannot call their special forms as (prevailing) monotheism and monogamy, later borrowings from other cultures, because they give no evidence of this. But neither can we characterize them as specializations that have come in later, if other cultures of the same or approximately the same age manifest the same features.

β. *The Developmental Series in Larger Complete Groups*

1. The following Graebnerian rule is to some extent the positive inversion of the foregoing (p. 156 s.): "The different grades of relationship of extensive culture groups give us assistance in the historical developmental evalution of their elementary forms. If a comparison is made between the culture groups and their individual complexes, the principle certainly applies that the whole is before the parts. For the whole must not only be existing, but it must also have been extended somewhat geographically before the single groups could create their special forms through variation or contact with other cultures. Therefore, the forms of an element common to the whole group must be older than the forms peculiar to one or several single groups."

In compliance with this rule, Graebner refuses to admit the role of the primitive form for the Valiha, a self-stringed bamboo instrument with idiochord zither, which Frobenius (6) (evidently for the plausible reason that here the staff and string are made from the same piece) has proposed as such, because this form is only found in Indonesia, while the staff and bow-formed instruments with single- and double-taut strings are diffused over Indonesia, Melanesia, and Africa.

2. If the greater number of single groups in which an element is diffused is of importance here for the determination of its ethnological age, the main thing is to count the single groups correctly and especially not to put the subgroups of the second degree on a par with the primary groups. A graphical representation would be:

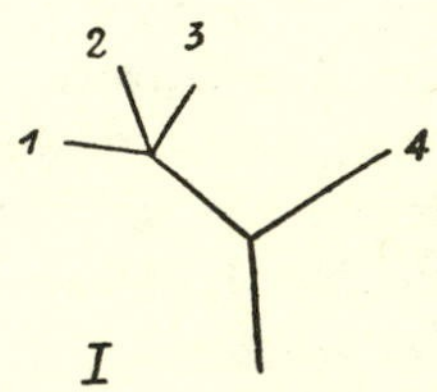

It would be incorrect in this branching of cultures in the above figures to say: 1 + 2 + 3 is more than 4. The numeration itself is misleading. The figure should be:

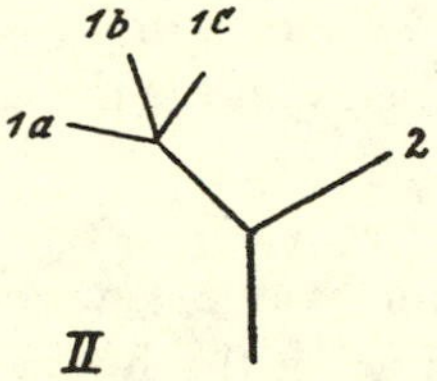

Here then it is clear 1 : 2, *i.e.,* the three groups of the second degree 1a, 1b, 1c are not more numerous than the one of the first degree.

> For this reason, Graebner refuses to have the drum form tensioned with string and wedges considered as the oldest type in the Melanesian bow culture, although it is found in the African and American and Indonesian subcomplex and is lacking only in the Melanesian, for the first three by means of other characteristics which they have in common prove themselves to be but a subgroup over against the other one, the Melanesian.

From these reflections Graebner deduces the positive general rule (p. 157 s.): "Those forms or circles of forms may, with overwhelming probability, be taken as original to a certain culture group, which are diffused in *all* subgroups of the first degree."

3. The case remains doubtful if the condition postulated in the rule just proposed is not fulfilled; *i.e.,* if a phenomenon "appears only in *one* part even though it be in the predominating part of co-ordinated complexes." The original appurtenance of this phenomenon to the total culture in question would only be tenable if it were demonstrated that it was formerly also in the other parts, but was lost later on. Such losses of even important parts are also possible in primitive cultures; Rivers has collected a number of such losses for the South

Seas. (7) Therefore, the lack of an element in a subregion is no decisive reason against its original appurtenance to the total complex.

On the other hand, only the positive proof of the actuality and not of the mere possibility, or at least a plausible reason, would allow a positive decision for the disappearance of exactly this form.

That is the case, for example, with regard to the absence of the rattan bowstring on the bow of the mother-right culture in South America. (8) The reason for this is quite evident: There is no rattan in the northern migration districts.

γ. *Synthesis*

Graebner summarized all these different rules in two general principles which, when heard for the first time, sound like mere tautology, but are not so by any means. In fact, these rules give us the main criterion for the sequence of development won from culture relations (p. 158):

1. "The forms of the older associations—and they are as a rule the more extensive ones—are naturally older than the younger ones." In other words: when certain culture relations are older than others, then also the single ingredients (or their forms) of the former are older than those of the latter.

2. "The forms belonging to a single branch of a culture group form of themselves an independent subseries of development"; that is, they cannot be attached to or inserted into the main line of development.

B. The Determination of More Difficult Sequences of Development

α. *Methodological Treatment of Groups of Forms in a Developmental Series*

1. All the rules just set up apply on supposition that "only *one* form was proper to each single complex of a culture group and only *one* form of each element to each greater unity. But

often single phenomena, such as clubs, myths, etc., will vary within one and the same historical stage of the group: instead of one form there is a whole group of forms present. Also in that case we certainly still have a criterion for the sequence of development in the inevitable association with the forms of the nearest higher unity" (Graebner, p. 159). That is to say, the multiple forms of a subgroup thereby prove themselves to be members of the course of development and, indeed, as younger members, if they can be deduced from the one form or the group of forms of the nearest higher great unity.

2. Graebner uses this opportunity to warn us against overzealous search after smooth and unilinear series of development. It is, however, always in place (I pointed it out already above [p. 236]) and here it seems especially understandable when a multitude of forms are present (p. 159): "Moreover, it must be emphasized that the tendency to take such forms within such a single developmental stage and by all means and under all circumstances arrange them in a series of development can easily lead to error. For it must be recognized that the forms of a phenomenon within a culture unity will often be united during their further development in such continuous reciprocity that they are to be considered and treated exclusively as an inseparable circle of forms. This viewpoint, of course, should not be forgotten when investigating the forms in the complexes that immediately follow in as much as under circumstances they are to be deduced not from one single form but from a complex circle of forms."

This warning is nothing else but the clarification of the fact that many phases of development do not consist in one single form, but in a great number of forms, in a circle of forms, in a veritable host of them. Neither should we attempt to find one form among them in order at all costs to propose it as the subject, *par excellence,* of the phase of development. We should rather allow the multitude and richness of forms to be recognized and regarded as the natural sequence of one mutually progressing interaction.

β. *Establishment of the Direction of the Development From Groups of Forms*

But neither is the following requisite always fulfilled; namely, "that the different parts of a total group have in common forms of an element from which, therefore, one might assume the special forms of the single complexes developed" (Graebner, p. 59 s.). The reason for this is the possibility that the common type is no longer preserved in any of the groups, but has been eliminated by the special forms, which certainly better correspond to the advanced and specialized character of the single group. That can take place the more easily the sooner the single group is formed and, therefore, the longer its characteristic has already been at work. For greater methodical certainty, let us also take the case in its most difficult form; namely, where the original form is no longer present in one of the single complexes. This is certainly possible since, *a priori,* none of the special forms bears the mark of the original form.

Graebner proposes a rule for this case (p. 160), which I give again here in other and more easily understandable words. First of all, the oldest circle of forms of the object must be established in every subgroup. By comparing all of them, we thus obtain the direction of the forms in which the common parent form lies. If then one of the special forms present corresponds to this direction, then the conclusion is justified that it, if it is not identical with the primitive form, certainly stands very near to it.

As an example, Graebner gives the wooden broad shields of the mother-right culture in West Africa, Indonesia, and Melanesia, which almost all manifest a characteristic interlacement or wickerwork, as if thereby several partial pieces should be held together. There are actually such shields put together from several boards in the Melanesian subregion of West New Brittany. It is clear that since its form of wickerwork corresponds especially to the other Melanesian forms and does not agree with those of Indonesia and Africa, that this type stands near to the original form without being identical with it.

γ. *Establishment of the Absolute Ethnological Age*

A final and (because of its far-reaching character) important criterion for the sequence of development is obtained from the association of the research into culture conditions with the knowledge of the local stratification of the culture complex. It has already been established before (above, p. 214) that merely because a culture complex precedes another culture complex in a region does not allow us to declare it by all means the older. Special circumstances could have brought it about that a culture complex which was in itself older would have been hindered for a time in its diffusion, so that only later did it come into a certain district.

However, the following rule proposed by Graebner (p. 160) is quite tenable. "But if one and the same culture appears in *all* regions in which it is at all demonstrable and *always* appears in the same chronological relations to other complexes, then this relative time sequence is not to be denied an absolute value."

The height reached by a culture in general, which has no value as an independent criterion of development, can always secondarily affect and to some extent serve as a confirmation to the criterion of stratification which possesses a primary demonstrative force in its own right (Graebner, p. 161).

(1) Van Bulck himself devotes a chapter exclusively to "Culture Development" (pp. 137-143), but makes no difference between the internal and the external development and, what is incomprehensible, does not quote Graebner's "Series of Development" (pp. 151-161) in the whole exposition, but only cites the following chapter on "Causal Problems" (pp. 166-169), so that van Bulck's whole chapter seems disarranged.

(2) *Cf.* Graebner, *op. cit.*, p. 92.

(3) *Cf.* Stephan, *Südseekunst*, p. 52 ss.; Boas, "Decorative Designs of Alaskan Needle Cases," *Proc. U. S. Nat. Mus.*, XXIV, p. 321 ss.

(4) Graebner, "Wanderung und Entwicklung sozialer Systeme in Australien" *Globus,* XC; *cf.* W. Schmidt, Die Gliederung der australischen Sprachen, (Mödling, 1919), p. 8 ss.

(5) He remarks then (note 1) with reference to an article of mine in the *Zeitschrift f. Ethnologie* (XLI, p. 345 ss.) that I have proposed this unacceptable opinion. Actually, I only speak there of the origin of this totemism of Central Australia. I myself ask the question of a radical difference between this and the totemism of South Australia, how much more then from the totemism in other parts of the world.

(6) Frobenius, *Ursprung der afrikanischen Kulturen*, p. 274 s.

(7) W. H. R. Rivers, "The Disappearance of Useful Arts," *Festschrift Till-Agnad Edward Westermarck*, pp. 110-120.

(8) W. Schmidt, "Kulturkreise und Kulturschichten in Südamerika," *Zeitschr. f. Ethnologie*, XLIV (1913), pp. 1032, 1111, 1113.

Chapter VI

DIRECTIONS FOR THE ESTABLISHMENT OF CULTURE CAUSALITY

1. THE IMPORTANCE OF THE INVESTIGATION OF CULTURAL CAUSES

A. Investigation of Causes—Final and Highest Aim

Since we have now gained a tool to establish objectively the chronology both of the external influences and the internal development, we have fulfilled the one condition required in order also to perceive the causes of both. The statement *post hoc, ergo propter hoc* is not correct, but it is absolutely correct to say *propter hoc, ergo post hoc.* In other words, the efficient cause must always precede its effect. In order to demonstrate something as a cause and something as an effect, it must be shown that the former preceded the latter.

That is the reason why we culture historical ethnologists are so intent upon the objective establishment of the chronology which Radin calls an "obsession"; because, unless the chronology has been thus established, any real research into causes is unthinkable. But investigation of causes is the final and highest aim of every science, and so ethnology would renounce its claim to be a real historical science if it would refuse to undertake the research into causes, but it would already do so by refusing to fulfill the elementary preliminary condition for this investigation into causes; namely, the objective establishment of the chronology.

Let it be kept in mind that we are referring here to the chronology of those epochs of the history of mankind, the investigation of which is the task of ethnology and of ethnology alone; namely, the times before written history. Hence, a mere scratching and scraping around on the surface is not sufficient. We must set to work with the spade and not merely turn over the surface, but deep shafts must be sunk and, if circumstances permit, a whole network of shafts must be laid, in order to come into the deepest and final time depths. What prehistory must carry out in material excavations, if it wants to establish particularly extensive successions of strata, ethnology must do in an intellectual sense. If the rules and directions of culture historical methodics in their totality seem voluminous and complicated, that comes from the problem that has to be solved; namely, to penetrate into time depths of many thousands of years, frequently of an immensely complicated cultural happening, and present it in all its reality.

The last part of Graebner's work, entitled "Kausalitätsfragen" (pp. 161-170), does not attain the depth and precision of the foregoing and needs deepening, clarification, and amplification in like proportion. Naturally, it also contains excelcellent ideas to which we shall allow their full value. The division into external and internal causality, which is doubtlessly of great importance for method, is not clear from the very beginning (p. 163 s.). Under the first caption, Graebner seems to understand not only the influences of external nature, but also the peoples as carriers of culture movements; and of the second, he gives no explanation at all. Perhaps the division is so to be understood that under external causalities are meant external events, the inner causalities being the internal motivations for these events.

B. Distinction Between External and Internal Causality

1. I consider it more useful, and as far as method is concerned more suitable, to designate as external causalities all those which work upon man from without and as internal causalities those which he himself exercises from within. This division almost agrees with the division already used for passive and active influences (above, p. 138 ss.). For both kinds we must keep well in mind that cultural causality can only be

received by human beings (external causality) and can only be effected by human beings (internal causality). That is especially to be noted of the first kind. An influence which is exercised by external nature or by human beings upon the physis of man and the man's soul does not react thereto in some way, is not a cultural causality, but remains a purely physical one. Naturally, external nature can never exercise any cultural causality upon mere objects of nature.

2. Just as this first division was taken from the subject, the bearer of the causality, so a second one may be proposed from the object of the causality, and this is of value for method. This is a division into the causality of the first origin, which could also be called creative causality, and that of the causality of later changes of an object which already exists, which may also be called modificatory causality. We would have to call the latter causality of development if it were exercised upon the same object which had been brought into existence by the causality of origin.

2. EXTERNAL CULTURAL CAUSALITY

A. External Causality Proceeding From the Natural Environment

We shall now turn to the first kind of causality and, at first, to a subspecies of it, external natural causality. It has this name because it is applied from without upon a cultural object, a human being, a tribe, a people. If it does not proceed from external nature but from man, it is for him internal causality, which he exercises (but this does not concern us here, for the time being).

First of all, concerning causality proceeding from external nature, this has already been determined by the fact that with the help of the criteria of quality and quantity and the auxiliary criteria, we may follow and establish the migrations of a cultural element or of a cultural complex and find out into what changing environment it penetrated. Here it is easy to recognize the correctness of the following rules of method:

1. All changes, which may be observed in a culture during or after the migration of this culture through a certain environment, must with all the greater certainty be ascribed to the external causality of the latter, if they indicate a utilization of, or protection against, this environment. A special case of this kind is the manufacture of implements, weapons, and clothing, etc., from materials to be found only in this natural environment. Here we are dealing with causalities of origin.

2. This influence must be all the less emphasized the more the needs of the migrating culture have already been satisfied by other environments. These demands in turn will be all the stronger, the longer the migrating culture remains in the region of the new environment and is subject to its influence. We shall have here, for the most part, modificatory causalities and in the second case there will also be developmental causalities among them.

3. The validity of the foregoing rules does not suffer if the two cultures have wandered through the same environment and do not manifest the same influence both as to quantity and quality. The reason for this is already given in the second rule; namely, it can be due to the dissimilarity of the regions through which they passed earlier and to the influences received thereby. Another and in great part still more effective reason can lie in the entirely different character and disposition of the two cultures and in the consequent different reactions to the influence of nature.

4. But an environment can not only give, it can also take away. It can exercise not only a positive, but also a negative cultural causality. Such a loss of an element of culture must be ascribed to this negative causality: *a*, if the material absolutely necessary for this element is lacking in this environment; *b*, if a profession for which an implement is necessary can no longer be practiced in this natural environment with profit or brings in very small gain; *e.g.*, fishing in case of a migration to an inland region with less numerous fishing opportunities; *c*, if the climate makes certain forms of clothing or dwelling, etc., impossible. In *b* and *c*, nevertheless, the old ele-

ment can sometimes be carried on for some time, as, for instance, the clothing of the Tungus which, originating in Central China where it is quite warm, is little fitted to their present Arctic climate. (1)

5. Each cultural element, once we are certain that it arose out of the causality of external nature, should be explained in its primary nature only from the environment in which it arose. Later environments can be adduced for the explanation of further developed or modified forms. This, however, clearly shows the importance of objectively establishing the chronology, for only the oldest forms give us the element in its original environment, or at least stand closest to it, and precisely the oldest form arose only from the oldest environment.

B. External Causality Proceeding From Man

Let us now consider the second subspecies of external causality, the one, namely, which is exercised by individuals, tribes, and peoples upon other individuals or groups. It is more diverse, changeable, and irregular than the influence from external nature and, therefore, more difficult to grasp, for here the free will of man and his culture also have their effect.

1. The reality of the causality exercised by men, etc., upon others is clear from the influences which are apparent in the latter. For here they remain foreign bodies, even though, for the originators, they are "flesh of their flesh, and bone of their bone"; they are productions of their particular culture. They are recognized as such through the criterion of quality, and this knowledge is certified and confirmed by the criterion of quantity and the auxiliary criteria. All that has been said about the handling and importance of these criteria obtains its final and most important effect here.

2. With regard to the objective chronology, we endeavor to establish for these influences, it is worthy of special notice that the article produced by the oldest influences is either identical with the original form of the article or, at any rate, stands closest to it. The order of succession of the other influences can

represent a developmental causality if it is applied to the object produced by this culture or a modificatory causality if it had one or several others for its object. Together with this we must always keep in mind here that the inner strength with which a culture reacts to the influence exercised upon it is also thereby adapted and transformed.

3. Nor should we be disturbed here if two or more cultures, which have been under the influence of the same alien culture, do not manifest the same effects. That also can have its foundation in the fact that these peoples had a different past history and were in a different culture stage when they received those influences. But it may also be due to the fact that they were of an entirely different disposition or were at the time differently inclined, more receptive, or more self-sufficient, more conscious of need or more self-confident.

c. The Importance of External Causality in the Ethnological History of Culture

1. In short, we may say that to ethnology's round of tasks also belong those variable encounters with the different environments, the collision of one group with others and the cultures peculiar to them. They have determined an important part of the external events, of the cultural history through which man passed in those remote times. For these causal factors we can also subscribe to what Graebner says of his external causalities (p. 163 s.) : "It would be folly to deny that the attainable information of external causalities in ethnology is relatively meager as compared with the varied sources open to the student of strictly historical periods of mankind. We would be foolish, therefore, not to recognize that the latter stand much nearer to the ideal of historical possibility. Indeed, in ethnology we lack the rich history of the events themselves, not to mention the much encumbered political history of the period into which they fall. Consequently, we can never expect to advance beyond a rough outline of such culture movements themselves and, at times, of the migrations of peoples. Their individual courses must, perhaps, be forever lost to us. . . ."

2. Graebner does not tell us the deepest reason for this incompetence of the ethnological history of culture, of which he speaks here. (2) It is the inability to grasp the individuals, especially the leading individuals of those distant times. The efficiency of the criteria of quality and quantity, at least up till now, has not advanced so far, because connecting links for their application are missing. A more exact and more profound working out of the tribal myths will still perhaps bring some results here; especially, a methodological investigation of the various tribal ancestor and culture hero figures. Of course, the events heaped upon one figure here are often not of one but of several periods, and we do not as yet possess the methodological means to detach one culture stratum from the other.

Even if we were able to do this, it would always be only "culture" layers; *i.e.*, collectivities, and not individuals, as in the changing tribal father of the Algonkian, who was first a bear, then deer, rabbit, buffalo, in succession, according to the principal animal of the chase of the individual periods. (3) Since we, therefore, in contrast to older ethnologists, as W. Wundt, etc., are now certain that the importance of the individual is very great also among the most primitive peoples and that here already leading individuals played a great role, (4) we must also take them more into account for those times and not calculate them collectively. Perhaps, thus precisely in connection with a more exact study of tribal myths, still more traces of individual history will manifest themselves even for the most ancient times. We have a definite case of such among the Maidu in the religious reformer Oankoitupeh, who led the people back to a higher form of religion. (5)

3. On the other hand, the comparison of ethnological with the prehistorical periods, as is carried out by O. Menghin in his *Weltgeschichte der Steinzeit,* shows how long those periods of the food gatherers must have lasted, which without any noticeable "progress" (in external culture) cover thousands (and even tens of thousands) of years. We pass over in silence the astounding speed of the historical events of modern times, for neither could that profusion of events of "early historical"

times have happened in the epochs with which we are here concerned, because there existed only very small human groups who lived thinly distributed over the earth, which was still so sparsely peopled. At any rate, the external course of events could by far not have been rich and developed, and the resonance of the individual events could also not by any means describe such broad circles and, if so, then only in a long course of time.

Of course, that does not decide the question of the plenitude and richness of psychic events of the peoples of that time, although also the small number of individuals in the single groups and the great distances separating the single groups restricted these to certain limits. The smallness of a group could especially increase the danger that the group received none of the leading individuals, (6) who are of particular importance for the awakening and preservation of intellectual life.

3. THE INTERNAL CULTURAL CAUSALITY

A. Object and Subject of the Internal Causality

In turning to the internal causality, we wish to state immediately that it is the proper and deepest kind of cultural causality. Also the external causality exercised by man contains the internal causality of the influencing agent within itself, and the two external kinds of causality, both the causality exercised by man as well as that by nature, are only then cultural causalities when the one influenced by them reacts psychically thereto.

Concerning the active culture relation, which (as we have already established [above, p. 246]) coincides with the internal causality we stated above: that, of itself, it is not directly subject to observation, since it, like everything pertaining to the soul, is immanent. Observation can only then grasp it when it manifests itself by external works. That would indeed bring the anomaly with it, that, if it is true what we said before (pp. 5, 138), namely, that the proper and deepest culture is the formation of the soul itself, exactly this culture would be condemned to uncertainty. This fear however is unfounded. Real culture of the soul, on the one hand, engenders within it a vital force, which urges on to external actualization, and, on the other hand, an inner abundance which spontaneously overflows. Further, if mortality and love also belong to the completion of the internal culture of the soul, then the first brings with it the pressure of the duty to share its own riches with others, and the inmost nature of the second is to give oneself to others.

a. *Objects of Internal Causality*

1. Accordingly, we have to distinguish three objects of internal causality: *a*, the person himself, soul and body; *b*, other persons; *c*, surrounding nature.

Man engenders artistic, social, moral, and religious conduct in his soul together with corresponding external acts and employs his own body in economic activities necessary to supply nourishment, clothing, dwelling, ornamentation, and in social or other pursuits as well.

With regard to other persons, he observes social, moral, or religious conduct or endeavors through teaching and education to create these qualities in them. With regard to certain persons, he also fulfills economic tasks of nourishing and clothing, etc.

He exercises his external causality on external nature by transforming parts thereof into his working materials (implements, weapons) for means of protection (clothes, dwelling), as means of conveyance (in order to conquer space with a less amount of strength and time), for artistic purposes, for the representation of the inner dispositions of his soul.

In all these activities, man is the efficient cause producing elements of culture, either for the first time (causality of origin), or effects changes in culture elements which he himself has produced (causality of development), or changes elements taken over from foreign cultures (modificatory causality).

2. Where, when, and how such a causality has been exercised and in what course of time the externalizations of these causalities followed will not be determined in any other way and with

any other means than through the criteria we have treated of up till now; *i.e.,* those of quality and quantity and the auxiliary criteria and their methodical application. Here is the state of affairs: there is an element of culture somewhere or other, a culture complex. Taken in itself, it offers no basis upon which to find out the subject of internal causality that caused or modified it. If at another place there is another culture element, another culture complex, which we can prove to be culture historically related to the first occurrence by applying these criteria with method, we can then conclude that both have in some way been caused or modified by the same agents of internal causality. The more numerous and varied these occurrences are, the more comprehensively does the variety of the effects enable us to infer the characteristic feature of the internal culture of the efficient agent, and, vice versa, we draw the advantage therefrom that we all the easier recognize the elements and complexes of culture which are to be traced back to the same agent entirely or in part.

β. *Subjects of Internal Causality*

1. Of course, this recognition, this establishing of applied internal causality, is obtained with the greatest ease and certainty wherever the culture product proceeds directly from this causation or the originator still offers himself for investigation; in other words, if we find it in the culture which produced it. If it was first brought there by foreign cultures, then these but naturally put their mark upon it and thereby lessen the possibility of recognition. With regard to this passage through foreign cultures, we must, at any rate, always keep in mind that elements of culture, especially single ones, never migrate alone. That applies also for articles of material culture and more so to those of intellectual culture. It is rather always man who accepts the element and passes it on either directly or indirectly.

The faculty of man for receiving and transmitting culture elements (*i.e.,* the so-called migration of culture elements) differs, of course, in degree according to the disposition of recipients and the receptivity of the given culture elements. (7)

However, since we are not giving here an exposition of the formation of human culture, but are writing a method for its investigation, we need not therefore consider these differences any further. After we have established the presence of historical relations through the systematic application of criteria, we have demonstrated that these relations have become realities. We are not for the moment concerned whether this actualization was hard or easy. The knowledge of the different degrees of facility or difficulty could increase the improbability of a doubtful case once the criteria render a particular occurrence of an historical event merely doubtful, but it could never fully justify a negative decision in the case. (8)

γ. *The Methodological Irrelevancy of the Kind of Cultural Subjects*

1. The same judgment of methodological irrelevancy must be passed on grading the diffusion of culture elements according to the character of the carriers of the culture, which van Bulck had so enthusiastically proposed treating the questions in order: Contact of peoples, migration of peoples, dominating overlays, religious proselytism, trade infiltrations, high culture radiation, influence of the individual (*op. cit,* pp. 42-122). The whole process is very interesting and instructive as a description of culture itself, but it is almost useless for the method of research.

Van Bulck's whole work arose, in the first place, from the false opinion that Graebner's "methodological criteria and principles always handle the case, in which a diffusion of culture takes place through movements of population or through elementary borrowing. He does indeed speak of other kinds of culture diffusion . . . in his *Methode,* but he again and again places movements of population in the foreground and this alone does he treat *ex professo* in his exposition of the principles concerned" (p. 493). This weighty opinion ought to have been verified by proofs, but van Bulck does not present a single one. It is, in fact, untenable. The problem of movements of population is touched upon by Graebner two or three times and more extensively when he treats of it *ex professo* (p. 162 ss.) In point of fact, Graebner did not even ask whether the culture relations arose through movements of population or in some other way, and that alone was correct methodologically.

2. For this reason, it is also wrong when van Bulck thinks: "But if we examine Graebner's *Methode* still further, unfortunately we do not find any methodological principles therein which can help us here. . . . (9) But it would be entirely wrong to take his criteria for culture diffusion through movements of population and borrowing and simply apply them here for these younger displacements of culture of which we have spoken." Van Bulck himself gives the best proof for the incorrectness of these opinions when, in the exposition of his new categories, he brings lengthy and highly informative descriptions of the culture events in question, but of methodological directions for which he had urgently asked, we do not find any trace. The great difference here between him and Graebner is clearly seen, if we compare the great abundance of methodological rules in van Bulck's chapter on "Völkerwanderung" (pp. 58-75) with the lack of such rules in the chapters devoted to his new categories (pp. 75-131). No wonder, for in the chapter on "Völkerwanderung" he had (of course, erroneously!) gathered together nearly the sum of methodological rules found in the works of Graebner, Schmidt, and Pinard; in the other chapters, he stood on his own feet.

The new categories proposed by van Bulck also lose a part of their importance as to content through a fact which he himself intimates when he writes (p. 50): "The younger culture displacements spoken of here." In point of fact, conquering overlays, religious proselytism, and radiation of high culture are of no importance whatsoever for the Primitive and Primary cultures, and they only gradually begin to be so in the Secondary cultures. Also, trade infiltration does not play a role in the primitive cultures and but a small one in the primary cultures. Influence of the individual is certainly a factor in the Primitive and Primary cultures, but till now we have no methodological means to grasp the individuals concretely (10) nor did van Bulck propose any such means (p. 129 s.).

In the following section we shall discuss what importance for methodology can be ascribed to the new categories of van Bulck in another direction.

B. Migrations of Man As Subject of Cultural Migrations

a. *Migrations of Man in General*

It still remains important whether the culture element or the culture complex has been passed on from several groups with different cultures, or whether the culture groups in which the element or the complex is at home have carried it along on actual migrations and eventually given it over directly to a foreign culture. The reason is that in the last case we naturally have a greater guarantee that the element or the complex will be transmitted in its original form, though, of course, the migrating culture, since it does not pass through a vacuum, can undergo more or less numerous and great transformations under the influence of the cultures and environments with which it comes in contact on the way.

Still it is useful to give here again the criteria which Graebner proposes for these migrations of individuals, peoples, and races (p. 162):

1. "In problems such as this [physical] anthropology can be of great aid to ethnologists in the role of auxiliary science of ethnology. Wherever somatic agreements correspond with certainty to cultural similarities, we may categorically presume movements of population. Obviously enough, the reverse does not follow, since aside from the possibility of secondary absorption of an element, a beveling of the somatic type all the way to the zero point is well thinkable in the presupposed slowness of ancient movements of population over great distances." It is indeed thinkable, but becomes actual only on condition that the migrating culture would in that case also slope off to the zero point. The case of the last van of the Arian migration in South India and Ceylon is very instructive for this case. (11)

Here physical anthropology enters as auxiliary science of ethnology and, according to the degree of quantity and quality of somatic relations which it establishes, also allows conclusions as to the number of people who were the carriers of the culture transfer. See further, below (p. 314).

2. "We may very safely conclude that a definite linguistic relationship is a strong indication of migratory movements. Indeed, we know of not one instance in which a language has been transmitted over long distances without live, direct personal contact between the peoples who spoke the language" (Graebner, p. 162). The degree of proximity of this linguistic relationship will also permit us to conclude upon the strength of the culture element which was transmitted by the migrating culture. A close relationship in language justifies the conclusion that quite a large number migrated, while a remote relationship of the language testifies that the number of the new arrivals was not great enough to have their language accepted in all its individual features. Here the settlement of the much disputed question of the relation of the Germanic languages to the other Indo-Germanic languages is of directive importance. (12)

A valuable comprehensive exposition of the role which linguistics can play in the establishment of culture relations and chronology is given by E. Sapir (*Time Perspective,* pp. 51-85; *cf.* also below, p. 281 ss.).

3. "The external dissemination without the aid of migration seems all the less probable, though not impossible, the lower the receptivity of a given cultural element." I have already mentioned (above, p. 254 ss.) how relatively unimportant the division of culture elements according to their degree of receptivity is for method. I am very pleased to see that Graebner as well has not ascribed any decisive importance to this factor.

4. "A final important criterion which follows directly from these statements is that the complete or almost complete appearance of identical culture complexes in widely separated localities is hardly thinkable without the aid of movements of population for, wherever you take the starting point of the diffusion, an external dissemination from tribe to tribe over long dis-

tances must result in the diversification and weakening of the complex, so that, near the outskirts of the movement, we may perhaps discern a few disconnected elements or weakened forms of the whole complex, but never the complex itself as a complete unit. The shorter the distance separating the two elements in question, the less weight does this argument naturally carry. Nevertheless, we may safely assume that the more complete the reappearance of a cultural complex in another locality, the less credible appears its transfer without migration" (p. 163).

β. *The Special Case of the Dominating Overlay*

1. What van Bulck calls "Dominating Overlay" does not add anything essentially new, but forms a special case of the Graebnerian rules we have just given; (13) namely, "In a certain limited region a warlike overlay dominates the culture stratum of the old residents without mixing with it and without suppressing or destroying it" (p. 75). Also van Bulck sees that the dominating overlay stands nearer to the movements of population both as to content and as to form, since in both "a real immigration of the carriers of a culture is had, and, moreover, with their complete cultural possession peculiar to themselves: economic form, religion, sociological structure, etc." But when he says that the dominating overlay is not the same in the "manner of immigration and of their subsequent cohabitation," he is mistaken.

It is, of course, an otherwise not unfrequent error (as in the estimation of the immigration of the nordic race into Germany) (14) that the dominating overlay begins with the migration of a "*small* elite group of a warlike culture of rulers." In fact, it begins with so great a number of individuals that they alone can entirely support their own economic and social culture, since they could not otherwise preserve it at all alongside the prevailing culture.

Secondly, it is erroneous to say that the migration "of a compact mass of tribes belongs to the concept of migration of peoples." This migration is supposed to suppress, split up, or destroy the local sessile culture. That is a view of the migration of peoples which van Bulck was the first to propose, but which neither lies in the meaning of the word nor was it used by other methodisers; *e.g.,* Graebner. The latter uses the word in the meaning of migration of any group of peoples, without specifying how great they are or what they do with cultures which they meet.

2. Hence, the dominating overlay is not a group *beside* the migration of peoples, but a subgroup within the movements of population. It is only a question here whether it is of any *methodological* importance to set up such a subgroup. Here also van Bulck confines himself (see above, p. 255) to the exposition of the *culture historical* importance of this grouping, which no doubt is very important as I also abundantly proved in *"Völker und Kulturen"* (p. 192 ss.). He only raises a few questions with regard to the relation of the conquering to the conquered culture, without, however, answering them. He hardly treats the relations between a dominating culture and other such cultures at all, from which comparison a still deeper knowledge of its character as well as of its ethnological age could be won. To ascertain the latter he refers exclusively to the genealogical tables of the ruling families. The historical treatment of such family tables has made it clear enough that no time depths, certainly not beyond the times of written history, can be won thereby, if they are attainable at all. Hence, from van Bulck's exposition itself there seems no sufficient reason to set up a special methodological group of "dominating overlays."

There is, however, a reason, which van Bulck himself also gives, but so fleetingly and in such a connection that its methodological importance does not stand out very prominently. I refer to the passage where he states that no mixed culture arises in the case of a dominating overlay, but that a separation remains between the upper and the lower layer. He writes (p. 79): "In this case there are 'no recent borrowings of unorganic elements,' for this condition has existed already for hundreds of years, and everything seems to indicate that the phenomenon was formerly still more characteristic." Hence, the real conclusion is that the case must be given a special methodological treatment because, besides the general rule that the age of a culture relationship is to be adjudged from the lesser or greater degree of acculturation (above, p. 170), it is necessary to add another; namely, that in this special collision of cultures, the acculturation takes place very slowly.

Of course, it would be an untenable opinion to hold that acculturation does not take place at all and that absolutely no mixture of cultures whatsoever ensues. The very fact that the one culture is dominant presupposes an enlistment of the service of the dominated culture (*e.g.,* in forced labor, surrender of products, etc.), in which case the culture of the ruling class cannot possibly remain immune. And conversely, even in the strictest separation of the ruling culture influences ooze downwards. And, finally, there is no place in the world where the separation of the dominating culture has endured for long.

It is only modally and not essentially different from other contacts of migrating peoples and, consequently, only requires a special method of investigation.

c. Empathy* As a Means for the Comprehension of Internal Causality

α. *The Importance of Empathy in General*

Having now established the human group in its culture, race, and language, which in a given case was the subject of an internal cultural causality, we have thereby already learned a good deal about the nature of this internal causality itself. But we have not as yet penetrated into its very soul and have not yet grasped the deepest cultural thoughts, feelings, and strivings of this subject of culture in their very essence.

1. In modern historiography they speak of the psychological re-experience of the events depicted, of the necessity of, so to

* Empathy is a mental state in which one identifies or feels himself in the same state of mind as another person or group—Warren, *Dictionary of Psychology* (1934). The word "empathy" was coined by the late Professor Titchener as an English equivalent for Lipps' term "Einfühlung." *Cf.* Vernon Lee, *The Beautiful* (1913), p. 63.—Translator's note.

say, living oneself into and feeling with a foreign people in time and space. Graebner very well shows the peculiar difficulty ethnology encounters because of the unfavorableness of the difference of ethnology from, *e.g.,* European history (p. 164): "There is a vast difference, however, between the position of the European historian and ours. In the description of historic events in Europe, in many cases we can not only see the events and their effects directly before us at the moment of occurrence, that is, in their immediate psychic reality, but, in addition, besides the events, we can also meet the people who are their subjects and objects. In the observation of the overwhelming mass of ethnological facts, on the other hand, we can perceive their effects alone. And the causes of these effects, moreover, date back to remote ages, while the subjects of these effects can be nothing more to us than mere abstractions of man, conceived after the image of living races, and, at best, slightly modified by our vague concept of what constitutes primitive life (primitivity)."

What Graebner says here of the abstractness of our idea of man "at best slightly modified by our vague concept of what constitutes primitive life" applies only to the picture of primitive man as presented by the older evolutionistic ethnology. If he wanted to say that of the picture of the man of his own culture historical ethnology, that would have been more than a mere exaggeration; it would have been a distortion.

2. It could not have been his intention to say that, because shortly after he continues thus (p. 166): "Indeed, the knowledge of culture historical relationships derived by our method is not able to give us a vivid picture of the entire culture at the moment when a new complex was created or an old one changed, not to mention the individual events that led up to it. Thanks to our method, however, we can at least determine the complex or group of which the culture element in question is a part. This factor is capable of narrowing down the number of possible explanations so much that it will in many instances actually permit of only one explanation."

I have already said before (p. 251 s.) what is necessary concerning Graebner's statement here about the inadequacy of the culture historical method to restore the individual events which have led to the creation or the modification of a culture element. An improvement in this matter, if it is to be looked for at all, is certainly not expected to come so easily and quickly.

On the other hand, concerning his subsequent assertion about the impossibility of restoring the exact state of culture at the moment a new creation or change occurred, we wish to point out that since Graebner wrote these lines (1911) unmistakable progress has been made and much more may be expected in the future. Therefore, his pessimism and skepticism on this matter are ever more and more deprived of all justification. Of course, I do not intend to say that this particular unfavorable position of ethnology in comparison with the history of modern European events will ever disappear entirely. But the improvements which have been achieved already are not inconsiderable, and it is worth the while to inspect them briefly.

β. *Empathy Into the Primitive Cultures*

The advances which the new ethnology has made in the more exact knowledge of the state of culture begin already with the Primitive cultures. The latter have experienced an influx of new material, which was itself in turn thoroughly investigated.

1. That applies in the first place to the Pygmy cultures, which Graebner was unwilling to recognize as such and among whom the many expeditions of P. Schebesta, P. Vanoverbergh and H. Trilles have made known in a striking manner not only the material culture, but also (which must strike us here particularly) the intellectual and social culture. The investigations of P. Schumacher have shown the important distinction between the Pygmies and the (Batwa) Pygmoids. This has also helped to clarify the position of the Bushmen, who have become better known through V. Lebzelter.

2. The Arctic culture, which had first been proposed by Graebner himself, has become better known and been thor-

oughly studied also. The abundance and importance of the North American Primitive culture which came upon the scene was unprecedented. This was as yet almost entirely unknown to Graebner, and here it was especially the intellectual culture that became so well known. Furthermore, I was able to establish fundamental groupings and clear time sequences of the single groups in a long list of investigations.

3. The South American Primitive culture of the Fuegians, likewise little known to Graebner, was thoroughly worked out for the first time after Graebner had left the field by Gusinde and Koppers.

4. I believe I have thrown new light upon the groupings and chronology of the Southeastern Australian Primitive culture through my extensive studies of the initiation ceremonies. (15)

Thus, therefore, the Primitive cultures have become clearer both as to content and chronology. Consequently, their characteristics stand out more than at the time of Graebner, so that the conditions for a psychological approach to these cultures have been fulfilled to a greater degree than formerly.

γ. *Empathy Into the Primary Cultures*

The Primary cultures have also made progress in this regard.

1. The culture circle of the animal-breeding herders, which Graebner still refused to accept as such and which he joined together with the totemistic culture circle, now not only stands out clear with its characteristics definitely established, but also our knowledge of its social, economic, and, somewhat less, its religious conditions has continually increased. The arrangement within this culture circle becomes ever more clear; namely, into reindeer breeders, horse breeders, camel breeders, small-animal breeders, cow breeders. This classification contains not only a chronology, but also indicates abundant new culture determinants in every direction and, hence, makes it possible to approach each of these cultures with the required psychological insight.

2. The state of the question is also very favorable for great progress in the case of the mother-right plant culture, and

radical changes seem likewise necessary in Graebner's views on this matter. From better acquaintance with the oldest forms of this culture circle which I have been able to procure, it appears that the Boomerang culture is not only not an old original culture, but is rather a secondary mixture of a father-right Primitive culture with an ancient mother-right culture. Furthermore, the two-class culture, which Graebner considered the oldest mother-right culture, is but an oceanic special culture and an extreme border culture. The characteristics of this culture circle thus stand out more than they did formerly. Here, too, the situation called for a psychological approach to the soul of woman in this culture. The most recent research we think has also made this possible. (16)

3. The totemistic culture circle of hunting with advanced technical devices participated the least in this progress. Nevertheless, much material has also been gathered here and many explanations of single facts have been made. Soon we can hopefully expect another important advance in the external knowledge and intimate understanding of this culture circle from the Vienna Institute for Ethnology. It is announced in the inquiry of W. Koppers, "Der Totemismus als menschheitsgeschichtliches Problem" (*Anthropos,* XXXI [1931], pp. 159-176).

δ. *Progress Made With the Collaboration of Prehistory*

In addition to all this, great progress was made with the co-operation of prehistory, for the latter has been likewise directed along culture historical lines by O. Menghin and Dr. Heine-Geldern, and, so to speak, approached the findings of ethnology from the opposite side. They proceed from protohistorical times, the oldest periods of written history, which already have an absolute chronology for those time depths. That, of course, has its limits as soon as the egress of the Neolithicum backwards has been reached.

But also the relative chronology which may be inferred from thereon retrogressively and which reaches back prehistorically into the younger paleolithicum (miolithicum), ethnologically into the tertiary and secondary cultures, gives a firm foundation to chronology and thereby also to the investigation of causes and, hence, also greater certainty.

This progress, of which Graebner could hardly have had any idea, has been made especially for Oceania and South and East Asia through the investigations of O. Menghin and Dr. Heine-Geldern. French and Dutch investigators had gallantly prepared the way in Indo-China and Indonesia. At present, Dr. M. Oka has undertaken to spread these advancements to Japan, Dr. Slawik for Korea and Dr. Fürer-Haimendorf for Australia, on the one hand in regions where high cultures prevail and on the other hand into regions where the Primitive and the Primary cultures prevail. In the latter cultures, through the cooperation of prehistory, chronologies of greater certainty have been gleaned to some extent for other places as well.

This progress obtained for ethnology with the aid of prehistory also facilitates a psychological and sympathetic approach to these cultures, because the Primitive cultures are thus brought nearer to the cultures with written history, which stand nearer to us psychically. Furthermore, their establishment of a more exact chronology has also thrown much light upon the peculiarity and different phases of these cultures.

D. Determination of the Mental Basis of the Internal Causality

α. *Principal Rules for the Establishment of the Internal Cultural Causes*

1. This short survey of the progress made since Graebner in the knowledge of mankind's cultures as to their content and relationships had to be given here in order to be able to correct satisfactorily and to restrict the former diffident remarks of Graebner concerning the possibility of knowing the exact state of the culture of ancient times. This has also been done in order to evaluate correctly the positive rule which Graebner added, the importance of which is now all the greater.

To the question of the real internal causality, the dispositions of the soul, which were the ultimate subjects of this causality, Graebner gives the following answer; or, to be more exact, for the establishment of this causality he proposes the following methodological rule (p. 167): "A cultural phenomenon can be interpreted only through the ideologies of the culture group of which they are part." Here it is also clear how important it was before anything else to determine the various relationships of these phenomena by applying the criteria and thus be able to show their cultural interdependence. For the procedure which was usually followed in the heyday of evolutionism was wrong; namely, to make use of the present natural environment only for the one purpose of explaining the causal relations of these phenomena and to neglect the present cultural environment itself almost entirely. A big list of these trite "interpretations" are so weakened by this rule that they do not even require another blow. (17)

2. But neither is the progress made since Graebner's time merely along quantitative lines, nor does it refer to external things alone. They have to do rather, as I have already pointed out to some extent, with the internal aspect of the culture. For it is precisely and principally the intellectual culture of the more ancient periods that has become much better known. Add to this the fact that the culture circles are now grasped with ever increasing certainty in their totality and consequently in their specific psychical character.

We are reminded of the latter when we hear Graebner speak of the "ideologies of a culture group." That is, of course, dry intellectualism which is by no means suitable for the internal nature of the older cultures. Here the *whole* character of the soul must be taken into consideration: thought, feeling, will, conscious as well as the subconscious sentiments of the soul. All these elements together determine "the soul" of a culture and today we can already positively grasp this "soul" of the different cultures considerably better than in Graebner's time. In the case of some of these cultures we can even venture to speak of the knowledge of their "Weltanschauung" ("view of life").

I but recall how the creation idea dominates all the religions of the old peoples of North America; how among the Yuki group it forms the foundation of the entire education of the young; how it has the same importance in the Maidu group, and is also embodied in significative ceremonies; and how among the Algonkians this creation idea is celebrated by elaborate and significant feasts. (18)

3. Another improvement upon Graebner, at first apparently of an external character, is certainly of great methodological importance. Of it Graebner says that, if in compliance with this rule we have determined the culture complex to which an element belongs and the causal explanation of this element is to be looked for, in the disposition of the soul of this complex only "the number of possible explanations will have been narrowed down so much" that in many instances it will permit of only one or practically only one interpretation. Hence, we have come so far in some cases that we know not only the great culture circles, but even their subdivisions, which to some extent already present further developments of the first. We are also in a position to specify more definitely the complexes to which an element is assigned, so that the possibilities of explanation are still more limited so as to admit of only one solution.

The importance and significance of Graebner's methodological rules will doubtlessly increase through the additions and the more exact cultural determinants with which our efforts have supplemented them.

β. *Two Additional Rules for the Establishment of Cultural Causes in Greater Detail*

Graebner enlarges upon the rules he proposed and also adds a negative formulation. These are so illuminating that they can be given without any further comment (p. 167 s.):

1. "This restriction [that a culture phenomenon can be interpreted only from the ideologies of the cultural group of which it is a part] will allow a certain flexibility, to be sure, but this

flexibility can at best be very slight; namely, the elements in question may have been derived from an older culture. For, to be precise, the origin of a phenomenon or form of culture can always be assumed to fall within a period that is ended when the new phenomenon or form of the subgroup to which it belongs (19) is complete, but which begins when the mother complex undergoes its first modification. The roots, therefore, at least of the earlier manifestations of the daughter group, must be sought in the conditions surrounding the mother group. In a certain sense the whole principle appears as an amplification of the principle given for the evaluation of the series of development, (20) an amplification on the basis of the organic association of the single complexes and facts. Thus, it is clear that even seemingly new phenomena do not, as Athene, spring full clad from the head of Zeus. They evolve gradually from earlier phenomena and ideas and must be viewed in the widest sense as nothing more than mutations and continuations of older culture possessions."

Properly speaking, the whole sixth volume of my *Ursprung der Gottesidee* is nothing else than the application of this rule: I endeavored first of all to investigate the first origins of the elements of the single Primitive cultures, to find out whether or not they are the forms proper to one of these earlier Primitive cultures and then to explain them principally from this particular culture. However, for the rest of the elements found more or less in *all* Primitive cultures we ought to have recourse to the oldest common religion still present in the single Primitive cultures and explain these elements from this religion common to them all.

2. Graebner formulates also the negative inversion of his positive rule (it is not easy to understand why he calls it a "significant illustration of the general criterion") in the sentence (p. 168): "That by its very nature no phenomenon of culture can be derived from a group or complex which is culture historically younger than itself."

In point of fact it is very simple: if a cultural phenomenon is older than a certain culture complex, then this phenomenon existed already before the complex and was due to a different cause. Hence, it could not have been engendered by a later cause at all, as it had already been posited by another. This later cause was only able to modify this cultural phenomenon, which had been brought about through an older cause in the whole region of its occurrence or only in one of its subdivisions. Then it would have produced younger forms and, in the latter case, special forms.

This negative conception of Graebner's rule is directed especially against that mania of evolutionistic ethnology which wants to derive a cultural element offhand, from its *last* natural (and cultural) environment, without even asking whether it did not already exist before it came to this environment; or, whether it had not been caused elsewhere already and then by way of migration, during which it was perhaps exposed to all kinds of modifications, it came into its present natural and cultural environment.

The French school of Durkheim should have considered all these possibilities before it assumed the "formes élémentaires" among the Aranda of Central Australia not only for the "vie religieuse," but also for the social life and other departments of culture. But, of course, one must first of all investigate these earlier relations and migrations painstakingly, as Graebner was forced to do for the social forms in his "Wanderung und Entwicklung sozialer Systeme in Australien" (21) and other works. I myself had to do the same thing with regard to the languages in my work *Die Gliederung der australischen Sprachen* (Vienna, 1919) and for the religious conditions in my *Ursprung der Gottesidee* (I, pp. 306-487; III, pp. 567-1110).

E. Examples to Illustrate Internal Causality

a. *Two Negative Examples of Graebner and Their Rectification*

Graebner proposes two examples to illustrate his rules (p. 166 s.):

1. "Thus, we might perhaps make use of the well-known question as to the origin of the squatting burial position. It has frequently been asked whether burial [in mother earth] is supposed to imitate the fetal position [in the mother's body] or [because of fear of them] serve the purpose of shackling the dead [in order to prevent their return]. This question could be decided simply by demonstrating that the culture group in which the crouching burial position first appears is, as a matter of fact, not given to the fear of the dead."

This example suffers from its consideration of the one negative side alone. Even if the squatting burial position actually did appear for the first time in a culture in which the fear of the dead is not known, the positive explanation for the extraordinarily characteristic form of the squatting burial position would still be missing. This explanation is only then given when the culture, in which it is first found, considers the earth as "mother," a necessary postulate for the conception of the squatting burial position as fetal position. I have already proven that none of the primitive cultures practice the squatting burial position. (22) The conception of the earth as "mother" is unknown to all of them, for neither does it occur among the animal breeding herders nor among the totemistic hunting cultures. It appears and is perfectly understandable too, in the mother-right agrarian culture. It has not yet been established with full certainty whether the squatting burial position appears first in this culture but it would not be excluded *a priori.*

2. "And similarly would Pater W. Schmidt doubtlessly

be justified in his contention that the great high gods of Southeastern Australia owe their origin neither to mythological concepts nor to magic or animism, if he could prove the absence or at least the very feeble development of the three elements for the culture group in question. His proof in this case fails because these suppositions are most likely unfounded."

This example suffers from the same defect; namely, that it considers only the negative side. Even if it were proven that mythology and magic and animism were strongly represented, their positive connection with the high gods concerned would have to be demonstrated positively before we could assume the derivation of the latter from the former, whereby also the relative importance of those supreme beings for the whole life of the Southeastern Australians must be estimated in comparison with the importance of those three factors. Graebner at the time had at hand only the very first (French) edition of my investigations of these matters, which he also quotes (p. 167, note 1) and which in material and method was quite imperfect. Neither was he acquainted with the German edition of the *Ursprung der Gottesidee,* volume I (1912), which presents a complete revision of the first edition, nor the second edition of this book in 1924; still less, the volume III of this work (1931), in which I once more very thoroughly handle the religions of the Southeastern Australians; nor finally volume IV (1935), in which I carry out a synthetic comparison of the old Primitive cultures, wherein naturally the Southeastern Australians have also been treated (pp. 309-367).

I have summed up in volume VI (pp. 319-321) what I have been able to establish by detailed investigations of each regarding the naturism, animism, manism, and magic of the Southeastern Australians and their high gods. The conclusion is essentially a negative one. The final summary reads (p. 321): "Taken all in all, the Southeastern Australian Primitive culture in its most ancient form precedes those times and cultures in which naturism, animism, manism and magic attained their greatest development. Over against this the totality of the characteristics of the Supreme Being which stand out so clearly in the religion of the Southeastern Australians as well as the significant functions of creation and control of morality make of the Supreme Being such a characteristic well-defined impressive figure that it can be placed alongside the most definite figures of this kind in the other Primitive cultures, and therefore it is impossible to derive them from these later phenomena." Hence, I can pass over the polemic of Graebner's statement without another word.

β. *A Positive Example*

1. To supplement the two inadequate examples which Graebner gives, I will substitute a positive one. I say inadequate because they are purely negative. My example concerns the primitial offerings, which in some cultures, Primitive and Primary, are offered to the Supreme Being; in others, to the ancestors. Which is the older: the latter, in which the Supreme Being, in agreement with Spencer's manistic theory developed evolutionistically from gifts to deceased ancestors, or the former, in which the second form only arose later, passing through the stage of tribal father and tribal mother? Then, too, one must ask from what spiritual disposition did this practice of making primitial offerings to the Supreme Being arise?

First of all, it can be established with all certainty that the primitial offering certainly existed in the greatest part of the oldest cultures, when there was as yet no mention of any gifts or offerings to the dead, (23) while the primitial offerings to the dead turn up first in the Primary culture circle of the mother-right agrarian horticulture and its variants of more recent times. From which it may be negatively established:

1. The primitial offering to the Supreme Being in Primitive culture cannot be deduced from that offering to the dead in the mother-right culture circle.

2. The primitial offering of the Primitive culture offered

to the Supreme Being cannot be derived from any kind of (food) offering given to the dead.

From which idiologies and dispositions of Primitive culture the primitial offering to the Supreme Being positively arose, we find out through the facts (1) that this offering comprises only the means of sustenance, the means to prolong life, which (on the stage of food gathering in the Primitive culture!) must be sought for anew every day by hunting and plant gathering; (2) that it is the small but especially valuable pieces of the captured animal that are offered; (3) that in the Primitive culture the belief in the creative power of God flourishes. For it is in this culture that he is the highest lord and owner of all things, especially, however, of the means of existence. The primitial offering is correspondingly nothing else but the recognition of this supreme right of ownership of the Creator, thanksgiving for the means of sustenance granted hitherto, and a petition for continuous largesse for the future. That this is actually the meaning and purpose of the primitial offering is additionally attested to by the text of the oral prayers with which many tribes accompany their primitial offerings, (24) and which likewise, on their part, are direct testimonies for the inner psychic attitude of these oldest cultures toward the Supreme Being, their Creator and God. This psychic attitude *of belief,* submission, gratitude, and petition is the last internal cause of the primitial sacrifice, and the latter is nothing else but the psychological-cultural expression of this psychic attitude.

(1) *Cf.* above, p. 149.

(2) He treats it very shortly afterward (p. 166).

(3) Schmidt, *Ursprung der Gottesidee,* V, p. 703 s.

(4) R. H. Lowie, "Individual Differences and Primitive Culture," *Schmidt Festschrift* (Vienna, 1928), p. 495 ss.

(5) Schmidt, *Ursprung der Gottesidee,* II, p. 160 ss.

(6) W. Schmidt and W. Koppers, *Völker und Kulturen,* p. 59 s.

(7) That the elements of intellectual culture are, in general, less easily transferable than those of material culture is a point of view which I had indeed advanced in common with the great majority of ethnologists. Graebner calls my opinion "decidedly fallacious" (*op. cit.,* p. 162, note 3) and as counter-

argument proposes "the well-known phenomenon of the migration myths and the far-reaching dispersion of religious ceremonies which has been proven to exist in Australia." Graebner gave no proof that the "migration myths" took place without migrations of men or of culture, and from my considerably intimate acquaintance with the religious ceremonies of Australia I know of no "extensive diffusion" of them without folk and culture wanderings, while material objects of culture may undoubtedly be distributed without such movements of population.

(8) By this I withdraw my previous criticism of Graebner's *Methode* from this standpoint. *Cf. Anthropos,* VI (1911), p. 1029 ss.

(9) In the new categories proposed by van Bulck.

(10) *Cf.* above, p. 251.

(11) *Cf.* v. Eickstedt, "Arier und Nagas," *Hirt-Festschrift,* I, pp. 363 ss., 381 s., 401 s.

(12) *Cf.* W. Schmidt, *Rasse und Volk* (Salzburg, 1915), p. 154 ss.

(13) van Bulck, *op. cit.,* pp. 75-83.

(14) *Cf.* W. Schmidt, *Rasse und Volk* (1935), p. 228.

(15) *Ursprung der Gottesidee,* III, p. 1062 ss.

(16) *Cf.* W. Schmidt, "The Position of Woman With Regard to Property in Primitive Society," *Amer. Anthr.,* N. S. XXXVII (1935), p. 249 ss.

(17) *Cf.* here also P. H. Pinard, II, p. 295 ss.

(18) *Ursprung der Gottesidee,* II, p. 739 ss.

(19) One might ask himself whether the "to which" ("dem") which can only refer to "conclusion" ("Abschluss" in Graebner's text) might not better refer to "the subgroup" in which case it should be "der"—W. Schmidt.

(20) *Cf.* above, p. 220.

(21) *Globus,* XC (1906), p. 181 ss.

(22) *Ursprung der Gottesidee,* VI, pp. 82, 90, 242, 317 s., 384 s.

(23) W. Schmidt, *Ursprung der Gottesidee,* VI, pp. 70 ss., 82, 241, 277, ss., 318, 383.

(24) W. Schmidt, *op. cit.,* p. 445 ss.

CHAPTER VII

THE METHOD OF ETHNOLOGY AND ITS AUXILIARY SCIENCES

1. ETHNOLOGY AND PSYCHOLOGY

A. INSUFFICIENT APPRECIATION OF SCIENTIFIC PSYCHOLOGY BY GRAEBNER

IF IT is certain that the essence of culture is of a psychical character, and if that is theoretically and practically confirmed by research into the internal causality, then naturally the attention of ethnologists will be directed in a special way to that science which deals with the soul; namely, psychology. The question arises as to what position ethnology ought to take toward it. Graebner is of the opinion (p. 169) that: "In these questions, psychology and indeed both individual as well as group psychology will be one of the most prominent aids to ethnology. Obviously, the psychic determinants of a cultural phenomenon or culture historical process can never fall outside the general psychological possibilities, the study of which belongs to psychology."

It is superfluous that he then adds "naturally, the historian does not have to wait until a certain problem has been solved by the psychologists." If the culture historical decision is actually dependent upon the solution of this problem, then he has simply to wait, that is all. It is a want of appreciation of real psychology to protest that "the psychological investigation with its main emphasis upon the average, the typical may in certain instances be inapplicable to the individual historical processes." For, first, he himself had also recognized individual psychology as an auxiliary science of ethnology. Second, psychology ceases to be a science of the soul and mind and becomes a natural science if it devotes itself only to the study of the average and the typical or only wishes to establish "laws," as F. Kruger endeavors to do in his psychology of development, which his teacher, W. Wundt, already has emphatically refuted. (1)

Graebner then supplements this negative appraisal of psychology positively when he continues (p. 169 s.): "What the ethnologist therefore needs *most of all* [2] is a thorough practical acquaintance with the human soul, an understanding of human nature in its most subtle ramifications. These attributes cannot be acquired as can the knowledge of scientific data. They are native gifts developed through careful cultivation; they make possible:

"1. In the first place:
"a. A highly versatile understanding.
"b. The power of abstraction unfettered by personal intellectual environment.
"c. The conception of the great number of possibilities, the consideration of which tends to prevent one sided conclusions.
"2. Such versatility has, in addition:
"a. The power to make us think and feel as a part of the particular cultural conditions we are studying, no matter how foreign its terms may be to our environment.
"b. The power to put us on kindred terms with the particular matter that we are studying." (3)

Some beautiful and useful things have been collected and expressed here by Graebner in a few words. But let us pass over the fateful necessity of the innateness of this ingenuous natural psychology. For, is not the task of psychology precisely to contribute a great or perhaps the greatest share to that advanced "training by means of education," which has been recognized by Graebner himself as necessary? I think that precisely the three minor tasks which Graebner gives first (under 1 a, b, and c) belong to the most proper field of scientific psychology: to be on the alert to observe all the riches of the life of the soul and to point out the many possibilities that present themselves there to unfetter the soul from its own narrow confines and to put it back into the whole breadth and freedom of psychical life.

I would rather consider the following two points, which Graebner gives (under 2 a and b), as something inborn or as special talents. But even here scientific psychology is able to give many suggestions and directions. On the other hand, only the sympathetic immersion of oneself into the creations of the intellectual culture of a people opens the way to the world of its culture sooner than anything else.

B. General Relation of Ethnology to Psychology

I have already mentioned before (4) that this narrow limitation of the co-operation of psychology with ethnology to a "thorough practical acquaintance of the human soul" seems to me very easily misunderstandable. I fully agreed with Graebner's words on the necessity of an "abstraction from the fetters of personal intellectual environment" and pointed, and do point out again, that it is not only a case of liberation from the personal *individual* environment, but also, and more so, a case of a release from the entire environment of one's *own people* and from one's own *culture*. If culture historical ethnology wishes to comply with the demand for a psychological approach necessary for every historian, it incurs a much more difficult task than that with which the historian with writings at his disposal must cope. For the latter, in most cases, deals with men of the western culture circle, whose thoughts, desires, and feelings are, after all, of the same general character in important matters. (5) If it concerns peoples of Asiatic (or American) high culture, then for the most part there are enough written documents at hand from which one may delve into the psyche of those peoples. But since all this is missing among the preliterates, and although we do not concede to Levy Bruhl that their "âme primitive" is entirely different from our own, namely, that it is "prélogique et prénotionelle," still we see that they (some more and some less so) manifest undeniable differences from our mentality, even though they both are offshoots of one common human foundation.

The difficulties, however, greatly increase when we are dealing with preliterates of the most distant times. Here the "thorough practical acquaintance with the human soul," with which Graebner is satisfied and which is indeed obtained through one's own praxis, can no longer suffice, and we should be thankful if here the technical science of psychology comes to our aid. It is still a matter for discussion whether psychology ought to be designated as an "auxiliary science" of ethnology, as Graebner called it, or an equal sister science, which enters and carries on the work after historical ethnology has done its share in determining the place and time of the various groups. I favor the latter opinion.

The matter may, however, take place in three different ways: 1. An ethnologist trained after the method of the culture historical school who, by means of this method, has brought about the determination of the time, place, and group, makes use of psychology afterward as a *subsequent* auxiliary science. 2. A psychologist makes use of the culture historical method of ethnology as an antecedent auxiliary science and then continues with his special science, psychology. 3. Someone who is both ethnologist and psychologist first determines the place, the time, and the various groups with which he has to deal and then subjects them to a thorough psychological research.

It is almost useless to argue which of these three cases is the best and most desirable. The third case, taken as such, would be the best, but will remain the least frequent, since it is not very often that someone is equally well versed in both sciences. With regard to the other two cases, it must be said that the one or the other may be preferred according to one's talents and inclination, but each case that presents itself will be welcomed.(6)

c. Special Cases of Application of Psychology in Ethnology

As already mentioned, the co-operation of psychology with ethnology is of special importance for the establishment of the internal causality. Graebner adds another possibility of this co-operation, which he describes thus (p. 170): "This gift is of the greatest importance, however, in all those cases in which the objective methodological criteria fail to point to unquestionable conclusions; that is, we must resort to hypothesis in the absence of proof. Wherever the order of development of several forms or of the culture group to which a given phenomenon belongs cannot be objectively established, our problem becomes one of psychical causality."

This last expression, "psychical causality," seems to me to be entirely out of place here. Psychical causality is *always* had whenever a cultural effect proceeds from man (see above, p. 252), and in the present case neither more nor less than elsewhere. It seems that Graebner wanted to say psychological causality in contradistinction to culture historical, but that also would be wrong. The situation is such that where objective systematic criteria offer *no unquestionable* conclusions, they reveal *several possibilities*. Here then psychology can be of use in the following ways: 1. From its results it can suggest still other possibilities to the ethnologist, and he, having had his attention thus called to them, can, perhaps, with the aid of ethnological media, prove them to be such. 2. In the midst of this great multiplicity of possibilities, to recognize one of them as the more probable. (See above, p. 277.)

The rule which Graebner adds to these cases is, of course, perfectly correct: "Whenever none of the given possibilities of solution is obviously dominant, we must apply the *ceterum censeo* of all unprejudiced science; we must by no means endeavor to force a solution at any price, but—while not relinquishing our personal opinions—we must dispassionately weigh all possibilities and, in the end, admit honestly if the present state of the science precludes a positive answer to our question." But there still remains what I said at the beginning of these investigations: "It is essential to every science that it strive after certainties, that it aim at certitude, and a science that consists of mere hypotheses and theories would not be a science" (above, p. 1).

3. A third field of numerous cases for the co-operation of

psychology opens up wherever the criterion of quality belongs to the intellectual culture. It consists in grasping correctly the real nature of this criterion; *i.e.,* that special characteristic which determines its essence. That is especially the case with regard to the compound quantitative criterion of quality, when from among the single traits of which this criterion is composed, psychology is able to discover the principal, the essential, one, which by its absence would cause the criterion of quality as such to cease.

We have a further case of this kind whenever a criterion of quality shows many variants in the single complexes, and we are now able to determine the real essential one among all these variants. In such cases it often happens that this essential character does not consist in some external form, but in a concept.

Already in my first criticism of Graebner's *Methode,* I proposed as an example of this kind a criterion of quality which Graebner, together with other ethnologists, designates "platform burial," and I have shown that it is not exactly the exterior manner of burial, but the purpose, to preserve the corpse (apparently) incorrupt, which forms the criterion of quality. (7)

Another example of this type are the different kinds of diving, in order to bring up earth from the depths of the sea, in the creation myths of the North American and North Asiatic peoples. Here the basic idea is not some external form or other, but the pedagogical teaching of wisdom and power of the Creator, which stands out alone and is superior to all, (8) as is manifested in the creation of the world.

2. ETHNOLOGY AND LINGUISTICS

A. Language As an Element of Culture

a. The Criteria of Quantity and Quality in Linguistic Relations

Graebner (p. 111) had already pointed out to the representatives of elementary and convergence ideas that we have always easily admitted genetic correspondences in language without any regard to distances and also in cases of discontinuous diffusion. He has also shown that language is only one culture element among others; that also considering the possibilities of diffusion we could not give it a unique position; and, finally, that the criteria according to which historical relations are to be determined are also the same for language.

We can certainly agree with him, but it is incorrect when Graebner designates these criteria in the following way: "The criteria of relationship, however, are none other than the two we spoke of: that of form in grammar and phonetics and that of quantitative concordance in a purely lexicographical respect." Graebner here simply identifies the two elements distinguished in language: the formal and the significatory, with the two culture historical criteria, that of form or quality and that of quantity. The formal elements of a language are found in its grammar and phonetics, the significatory in its vocabulary. But methodologically, both the formal as well as the significatory elements can provide criteria of form or quality, and each category in itself can produce criteria of quantity by a process of accumulation.

Hence, the following sentence of Graebner is incorrect: "Single concordances of words must not be taken as proofs for genetic connection, for this the accumulation of parallels is necessary, and to obtain a complete proof the relationship of form must also be demonstrated." In the first part of this sentence, Graebner himself states that also "single word concordances" can make up a criterion of quality, which, according to the second part of the sentence, only becomes conclusive through accumulation; *i.e.,* by becoming a criterion of quantity. Both taken together of themselves constitute a valid proof for historical relationship, which in itself does not need any "completion." When Graebner, in the third part of the sentence, demands that "the relationship of form be demonstrated" for "completeness," he errs if he means that the relationship of the linguistic form is absolutely necessary for the demonstration of historical relationship. It is required for the demonstration of a special kind of historical relationship; namely, for internal relationship or descent.

β. *Change of Language and Change of Culture*

With that we have touched upon the special character of language relationships which causes the language more easily to separate itself from the other cultural elements; and, therefore, language cannot be used offhand as proof for general cultural relationships. We are face to face with the twofold fact that people can change their language without giving up the essence of their culture and, vice versa, that they can preserve their language alongside vast changes in culture.

A very old example of this kind is the loss of native language among the African and Philippine Pygmies. A more recent example, and of an entirely different kind, is manifested in the acceptance of the Bantu languages on the part of the Hamitic aristocracies in Ruanda and the neighborhood. Far-reaching examples of another kind again are offered by the Melanesation of many Papuan tribes in the South Seas and the Arawakanation and Tupization of so many Indian tribes in South America. The examples of the second kind, the preservation of language alongside the acceptance of foreign cultures, are so numerous that it is not necessary to cite any.

The reasons why, in the first kind, the language and not the culture is given up, and the culture and not the language in the second, have not been sufficiently studied as yet. But this is a special task more for the history of culture in general than particularly for its methodics. As far as method is concerned, it is only of interest to know in what way the one and in what way the other can be established and how each, as such, can be applied with method.

The methodological difference between the two, as far as the language itself is concerned, consists in this, that in the first case the language is a product of external origin; in the second, the result of undisturbed continual inner development. The first kind reveals itself in the fact that the concordances with the new language frequently betray themselves in the vocabulary; but, on the other hand, concordances are to a large extent lacking in phonetics and grammar, the inner form of the language. In this case, the former suffice for the valid proof of external borrowing of the new language. In the second kind, we find not only the preservation of the internal language form, but also of the vocabulary, and in the last only more or less numerous "strange words," which, through their outer and inner makeup, reveal the recent date of their borrowing even to macroscopical observation. These words are mostly "culture words"; that is, words for those elements of culture which are of foreign provenience for the speakers of the language in question.

γ. *Establishment of Different Kinds of Linguistic Relationships*

The statement made frequently that mere similarities of words do not as yet prove relationship is also very inaccurate, and several distinctions must be made.

First, it must be established whether real word identities are present. It is precisely in language that the case of convergence can more easily be applied, because of the limitation of developmental possibilities of material means of speech, vowels, and consonants. Hence, for this reason too, the change in sounds can allow entirely different words from entirely different starting points (*i.e.*, from entirely different languages) to become identical or almost identical sound forms.

With the aid of the rules for sound and word formation of the language in question, it must first be established linguistically and historically whether it is really a case of word identification.

Second, if these are actually present, but *only* these, and we find no identifications of the form of the language in phonetics and grammar, then a relationship exists, but only through external borrowing, which is all the stronger the more numerous these word identifications are.

Third, if there are not only very many word identifications present, but also concordance in the internal language form, we then have a proof for the internal relationship; *i.e.*, one based upon a linguistic relationship, which is perhaps only slightly disturbed by recent borrowings of some words.

There is yet a fourth case, which lies between the third and fourth (because we often do not know whether we should reckon it with the one or with the other). We have such a case when languages have mixed to such an extent that not only has a great number of the words been taken over, but several parts of the internal language form have also been accepted. Such a crossing can doubtless only take place if the two languages concerned have mingled undisturbed for a long time. The result in this case might almost be called a new language.

> One of the most striking cases of this kind seems to me to be the origin of the German languages in North Europe from a comingling of the immigrating Indo-European languages with languages of the Megalith and Cromagnon people already settled there. (9)

This detailed exposition suffices to demonstrate in broad outlines that language is one of the elements of the entire culture and, indeed, a particularly important element of the mental culture. It has also shown that linguistic relationships are to be determined with the same criteria as the other culture relations. We have also seen special technicalities which must be observed when applying them to a culture. This is not the place to enter any further into the methodics of linguistic research itself, since linguistic research has grown into a great independent science, of which Paul (10) says that the method of no other culture science could be brought to such a perfection as that of linguistics. To this, Graebner remarks with modest pride (11): "I hope that such judgments may experience noteworthy restrictions through the greater development of ethnology for which I have endeavored here to lay the foundation." We wish to assure him that this hope is on the way to fulfillment.

B. Linguistic Phenomena As a Means for Establishing Cultural Relations

Precisely because the development of a language frequently proceeds along different lines from the other departments of culture, both the concordances as well as the discordances in language can in many cases help to establish general culture relations, so that it will pay to take up the matter here.

a. Nature and Diffusion of Culture Words

1. One of the most obvious and most frequented methods is to determine the distribution of the so-called culture words and to graph this distribution on tables. Even if every word, in the last analysis, is a culture word, nevertheless, those words which indicate very important elements of the external as well as internal culture have a special claim to this name. The presence of these words indicates the presence of the things designated by them. In many cases, however, they are also of chronological importance; for instance, if the terminology of the language is older than the form of the objects which have in the meantime undergone further development or if, on the contrary, the object has remained the same, but a young nomenclature has been taken over from a region where the object is more highly developed. If we find nomenclature of a foreign language, we may in many cases rightly infer therefrom a foreign origin also of the thing referred to.

This is the movement of "Words and Things" started or at least advanced by R. Meringer's magazine of the same name, which found a most important re-echoing in the different national atlases of words of folklore distribution. (12) Investigation of names of places and their distribution is a specialized department of this research. As the end result of all these investigations, we look for and in many cases also obtain a cross section of the culture of a certain time, illustrated by the culture words that have beeen found therein.

2. Naturally, such a cross section of an historical period is

very valuable for ethnology if this period lies before the times illustrated by written documents, for it would then be very akin to ethnology itself.

> The most significant example of this kind is the derivation of the old Indo-German culture from its languages, as, *e.g.*, we find in O. Schrader's great work, *Reallexicon der indogermanischen Altertumskunde,* (13) a second and up-to-date copy of which was recently published by A. Nehring. It is true that many reservations are to be made with regard to this linguistic archaeology, *e.g.*, that the absence of a word does not yet with full certainty mean the absence of the objects and that the presence of a word does not give us any information as to when it took root. These difficulties, however, cannot call its real worth into question. In the department of ethnology, the work of Frederici ought to be mentioned here: *Eine melanesische Wanderstrasse;* in which, however, a somewhat better knowledge of linguistic conditions might be desired. Investigations of this kind, however, can and should be more frequently undertaken.

β. *The Diffusion of Linguistic Families*

The geographical diffusion of linguistic families and their different and diverse subgroups is certainly of great importance for the history of culture. If we find an internal relationship, we may rightly assume that the same culture also migrated with the language. Wherever this internal relationship is very intensive and extensive, we also have a migration of the same culture carriers. For in such folk wanderings not only is the mere distribution of culture words of interest, but also the distribution of the formal language characteristics of the grammatical forms of substantives, verbs, etc., is important, because therein do we find the history of the language and hence of the intellectual culture as well.

When a migrating language group enters a new environment, in which there are no or very few people with other languages, it is very interesting to observe what nomenclature the new objects receive, how the latter mingle with the former terms or suppress older similar ones.

But should it come into a new culture environment where the people speak another language, in that case it is still more significant to observe what takes place; whether the immigrating or the local language conquers, which one is suppressed, which is overlain, which mixes, and in what ratio the vocabulary and the internal language form mingle.

γ. *E. Sapir's Treatment of Language As an Element and Index of Culture*

These principles and their application are excellent tools for establishing temporal and spatial relations between cultures and have been thoroughly treated by E. Sapir in the second part of his work, *Time Perspective in American Culture, a Study in Method.* This part is more significant than the first, which we have already treated before (above, p. 38 s.). This strong emphasis of linguistics for the establishment of cultural relationship is indeed an echo, and not the worst, from that time when American ethnology, both in North and in South America, took linguistics as the main foundation for the exposition of ethnological groups and culture relationships. The effects of this period, which continued longer in South America, were not always happy, but we can gratefully accept it here in Sapir's work, and I only feel sorry that I can give but a short description of its contents.

What I briefly stated above (under 1 and 2) Sapir treats extensively in the chapter "Geographical Distribution of Culture Words" (pp. 67-85). First of all, he shows how loan words are recognized from their morphological and phonetical material and which chronological rules can be won from the distribution of culture words and their phonetic changes (pp. 68-75). An exposition of chronological directions comes next. These result from the distribution of linguistic stocks and their subgroups as well as their phonetic and morphological elements (pp. 75-85). Before this, he gives a valuable treatment of culture historical aids, which can be obtained by investigating culture words and place names (pp. 51-62). After this, there follows a second treatise concerning the similar value obtainable from the grammatical treatment of forms (pp. 62-66). Numerous examples, especially of North American languages in which Sapir is so perfectly at home, abundantly illustrate the observations and rules he offers. (14)

c. The Language Circles Established by Linguistics

α. *W. Schmidt—the Linguistic Families and Circles of the World*

1. In the first part of my work, *Die Sprachfamilien und Sprachenkreise der Erde,* (15) after a general introduction on distribution, origin, and development of language and linguistics, I endeavored to present shortly, but as comprehensively as possible, what we know concerning the family stocks and single languages all over the world in so far as present-day research has constructed them. I also added references to the corresponding literature (pp. 1-267).

In the second part, *Sprachkreise und ihr Verhältnis zu den Kulturkreisen* (pp. 269-544), I tried to reach still greater groupings, which I called "Sprachenkreise" ("Language Circles"). With their aid I endeavored to penetrate into still greater time depths of the history of language.

2. In this work I did not use the comparison of vocabularies, for the laws of sound change and morphology necessary for these have been completed for only very few language stocks. However, without the knowledge of these laws certitude cannot be reached through this comparison (*cf.* above, p. 284). Thus, I had to be satisfied with the comparison of elements of the internal language form, which have the advantage that they are more firmly connected with the mind and are not so easily lost entirely.

But also here, because of the meagerness of material and research, I could only make use of a certain number. Of the sounds, I investigated the occurrence of the normal vowels a, e, i, o, u and the abnormal vowels ö, ü, as well as the distinction between surds and sonants, implodent and fricative consonants and finally the forms of the initial and the final syllables. To aid in making comparison from the grammar, I included the formation of numbers of pronouns and nouns (dual, triad, plural), the inclusive and the exclusive form of the first person plural (and dual and triad) of the personal pronouns, the different kinds of genitive formations of substantives, and the numeration systems. From the syntax, finally, I included the fundamental element of the position of the unaffixed genitive of substantives (whether standing before or after) with its effect upon the position of the possessive pronoun of substantives, the pronominal subjects and objects (accusative) of the verb, and the position of the adjective with regard to nouns.

β. *The Different Language Circles*

Investigations carried out with this purely linguistic material and according to this purely linguistic method yielded the following language circles:

1. Primitive Language Circles—characterized in sounds by normal vowels a, e, i, o, u, lack of abnormal vowels ö, ü, absence of fricative consonants and of the difference between surd and sonant consonants. In grammar, we find high development of the number (dual, triad) of nouns and pronouns, small development of numerals (not beyond the simple pair system); distinction between inclusive and exclusive form of the first personal plural (mostly); no grouping of substantives in syntax: anteposition of the genitive, of the possessive, and of the pronominal subjects; postposition of adjective. I omit here the exposition of the subgrouping of the Primitive language circles (*op. cit.,* p. 507 g.).

2. Primary Language Circles—which divide into a southern, a northern, and a central language circle.

a. The Southern Primary Language Circle, which is found almost exclusively in the southern parts of the world, has no ö, ü sounds; the occurrence of surd and sonant, implodent and fricative consonants remains doubtful: in initial and medial syllables no accumulation of consonants; in the final syllable only vowels or at most only liquid and nasal consonants. In grammar the dual (and triad) are missing and also the inclusive and exclusive of the personal pronoun, likewise the classificatory groupings of substantives; the difference between masculine and feminine is only secondary. In the numerals the quinary vigesimal system is bound together with the pair system. In syntax the anteposition of the affixless genitive, possessive, and pronominal subject is the rule; this anteposition has spread to the adjective also. The striving after uniformity and categorization prevails throughout these languages. With regard to the grouping of these languages into an older and younger, see *op. cit.*, p. 510.

b. Northern Primary Language Circle arose in the North and only lately came South. In sound we meet here with the abnormal vowels ö, ü, the distinction of consonants into sonant and surd, shut and fricative consonants, simple and compound consonantal final syllables. In grammar the dual of nouns and especially of pronouns mostly occurs together with the singular and the plural. The difference between inclusive and exclusive is missing. Most of these languages make use of the division of substantives into masculine, feminine (and neuter). The numerals show the (unadulterated) decimal system. In syntax the anteposition of the genitive in itself is in use, but in the several subgroups it partly breaks down in its effects. The accusative and the adjective have here brought their position into harmony with that of the genitive. In some languages partly anteposition, partly postposition is the rule.

c. Central Language Circle has moved farthest from the primitive languages, especially in the change of the position of the genitive and later it strongly influenced the other two primary circles, especially the northern. In sound it received the ö, ü from the northern circle. It also has the difference between sonant and surd, shut and fricative consonants; the initial and ultima syllables can occur with a vowel or a single consonant. In grammar we find the dual together with the plural and inclusive and exclusive of the personal pronoun, especially in the older languages; the numerals have the quinary decimal system, while the substantive has classifications into animate and inanimate, masculine and feminine. In syntax the anteposition of the genitive of the substantive has changed into postposition and also the possessive prefixes have changed into possessive suffixes and, hence, the previous suffix character of the language has gone over to one of prefixes.

3. From the crossing of the Primary Language Circles among themselves (and also with the Primitive Language Circles) the Secondary and Tertiary Language Circles arose, for a closer consideration of which I refer to my work cited above (pp. 521-528).

D. Parallelism of the Culture Circles of Ethnology and the Language Circles of Linguistics

a. *The Facts of the Ethnological Linguistic Parallelism*

In the further course of my investigation, I endeavored to demonstrate that the language circles worked out by the culture historical method in rough outline run parallel with the culture circles of ethnology (pp. 528-540), whence it follows that the Primitive language circles correspond to the Primitive cultures, the southern Primary language circle to the Primary totemistic culture circle of higher hunting, the northern Primary language circle to the Primary nomadic culture circle of animal breeders, and the central Primary language circle to the Primary mother-right culture circle of horticulture.

What I then wrote at the beginning of this investigation, I may here once more repeat (p. 272): "In many cases, we will only be able to give suggestions for advantageous arrangement of the problem, because the necessary preliminary work has not as yet been done, at least not as profoundly and broadly as is required for the setting up of the largest and most extensive groups. For this reason, we must put the greatest restrictions upon ourselves precisely with regard to syntax, since reliable sentence material does not exist at all for a very great number of languages and in others thorough investigation is missing entirely." Therefore, as I here point out, a comparison of the word conditions could hardly be made at all. Hence, I do not allow any doubt to arise that I hold the parallelization here of language circles with culture circles to be correct only along broad outlines and that I am of the opinion that future research itself can still bring some changes.

Nevertheless, I venture to say that this parallelization within the limits suggested is sufficiently established and the importance of their content seeems to me to lie in this: we only then have "culture circles" in the fullest sense of the words when we combine these language circles with the culture circles, since all departments of culture are represented here for the first time.

β. *The Methodological Importance of the Ethnological Linguistic Parallelism*

This parallelization is methodologically important because once the presence, in whole or in part, of a language circle of linguistics has been vouched for, the presence or former presence of the culture circle in the same degree is at least probable and, consequently, it would be worth while to undertake a more thorough investigation of the matter. On the other hand, wherever the language circle is entirely absent, the presence of the culture circle also is very doubtful. In this regard, it is very significant that linguistically there are no parallels to Graebner's Boomerang culture. (16)

Second, the occurrence of a language circle similarly as in Prehistory seems to me to be able to produce both new criteria of continuity as well as new criteria of quality, which ethnology alone cannot procure (*cf.* above, p. 158).

Third, both circles can mutually explain each other and also their single elements. Of course, up till now, ethnology has done more in this regard for linguistics than linguistics has done for ethnology. I recall the absence of the ö, ü vowels, the lack of difference between sonant and surd, shut and fricative sounds in the Primitive cultures, facts that correspond to their primitive condition (p. 282 ss.). Add to this the abundant grammatical formations of numerals and the meager development of numbers, the absence of gender forms of the substantive in these languages and the origin of these classifications of nouns in the primary cultures (pp. 334 ss., 344 ss., 354 ss.), the association of the numeral system with the economic stages of the culture circles (pp. 357 ss., 379 s.), the derivation of the postposition of the genitive from the economico-social condition of the mother-right horticultural culture circle (pp. 381 ss., 453 ss., 462 ss.). On the other hand, the idioms of the individual language circles also throw significant light especially upon the psychical culture of the different culture circles, as I showed with regard to the naïve, unreflecting manner of thinking in the Primitive cultures, with regard to the lack of distinction between animate and inanimate, masculine and feminine, personal and neuter, and that these differences certainly were not strongly emphasized at that time (p. 530 s.). Thus, in the Primary language circles the presence of a mental disposition that enters more lively into the formation of language manifests itself in the development of different classifications of the substantive, in which also the emphasis in thinking and feeling, which the language circle in question ascribes to those categories (animate and inanimate, personal and neuter, masculine and feminine) is expressed in each and every case. The deepest penetration into language development, which comes through the change of location and language on the part of the man in the mother-right culture, gives a clear proof of the plasticity of a language and of the strength of the agencies at work upon it (p. 531 ss.).

Thus, we have justified our digression into this parallelization of the culture circles of ethnology with the language circles of linguistics as a contribution to method.

3. ETHNOLOGY AND PREHISTORY

A co-operation between ethnology and prehistory has always been shown, and already Graebner in his *Methode* (pp. 74-77) not only made an appeal for this parallelization, but also had shown definite ways by which this collaboration could be realized. Following these directions already in *Völker und Kulturen* (17) I tried to make a parallelization of the results produced by the investigations of the two sciences independent of each other. The provocation for this co-operation is all the greater since this parallelization on the part of prehistory has been fully realized in Menghin's great work *Weltgeschichte der Steinzeit.* By this parallelization the mutual results have to some extent been reduced to a common denominator, whereby naturally their mutual comparison has become all the easier and more profitable. I have made use of it time and again in my exposition of method.

A. The More Definite Chronology of Prehistory

Ethnology on its part profits from this co-operation by making use of the more definite chronology of prehistory and, thus, confirms or corrects its own chronological fixations, which are generally vague, and renders them more certain. Prehistory obtains this more certain time measurement relatively easy from the direct sequence of culture strata.

We should not, however, exaggerate this advantage of prehistory. First, the direct stratigraphic sequence in European prehistory is not always identical with the actual time succession, since this is not always the same everywhere and dislocations and displacements can disturb the state of affairs very much. Second, the stratigraphic sequence especially in districts outside Europe where the preliterates principally dwell (and the main field of investigation for ethnology—the science of the preliterates) in many cases has not yet been brought into certified harmony with European findings. The reason is that, to date, the intervening ice ages could not be synchronized with the European ice ages, neither as to quality nor as to duration. Nevertheless, thousands of cases of certain time sequences have been obtained from the chronology of prehistoric strata, and ethnology would be foolish if it refused to make use of these results.

But ethnology should not go so far as to neglect its own time measures and have recourse exclusively to those of prehistory, as seems to be the vogue of late in some ethnological quarters. Neither would we have the greater certitude we are striving after, which can only be effected by mutual support and which is obtained from *both* sciences. Prehistory will also suffer thereby, since the support of its chronology through that won by culture historical ethnology is by no means superfluous. In many cases, where prehistory can only obtain uncertain results, the chronology of her sister science is (positively) necessary.

B. Supplementing Finds of Prehistory

Doubtless, ethnology must accept the help of prehistory when the latter demonstrates the presence of certain cultures, and also in places where ethnology could not define them correctly or even not at all. There can be several cases of such; those of quantitative and those of qualitative signification:

1. We have such cases of quantitative signification if prehistory proves the existence of a culture at a place outside the borders of a district in which, to date, ethnology has been unable to certify notable variants in content. Thus, of course, its quantitative criterion is strengthened. Here we can also distinguish two cases:

a. The prehistorical occurrence of the culture extends beyond the ethnological territory known until now into districts beyond which this culture region is no longer represented ethnologically and then a simple quantitative enlargement of the total territory results.

b. This occurrence is established between two subregions of that culture, in which case the prehistorical occurrence of the culture serves either as an entirely new criterion of continuity or as a confirmation of an ethnological criterion of continuity already present. (18) Under these circumstances this can also become a new or a confirming criterion of the degree of relationship.

2. Cases of qualitative signification occur wherever prehis-

tory establishes variants of a culture which, up till then, have not been met with by ethnology. These new variants can arise:

a. From cultural crossings which have never been detected before.

b. Also from a new environment.

c. They may also be realizations of one of the many possibilities of development, which every culture has but need not always be actualized.

This kind of prehistoric occurrence of a culture would yield a new criterion of quality. After joining this to the criteria had up till now, ethnology would have to supplement or correct the whole picture of the culture in conformity with the newly acquired data.

This completion or correction of the whole aspect of the culture concerned, already of course an advance and advantage in itself, could also have this good effect that ethnology, in the light of the new complete picture, would likewise recognize as belonging to this culture a number of elements of its own ethnological department about which it was not entirely clear up till now. Under certain circumstances this would lead to still greater modifications of the general picture.

3. Naturally, it is not at all impossible that prehistory might get into a position that will enable it to show quite new cultures which had completely vanished and were consequently no longer determinable by ethnological means in the present population of the world. But I confess that till now a perfectly clear case of this kind has not yet come to my knowledge.

c. The Full Life of the Ethnological Cultures

If ethnology can profit from the more certified chronology of prehistory which, since it proceeds retrogressively from the oldest protohistorical cultures and can also establish an absolute chronology even for those adjoining times without written history (19), then prehistory must stock itself from the rich abundance and full life of cultures which constitute the object of ethnological research. Otherwise, it is unable to offer a faithful picture of the complete actual history of culture. It is forced to this by several reasons, most of which require special methodological treatment. (20)

1. The first reason lies in the fact that the single prehistorical finds are most frequently of a fortuitous character, which again and again makes it impossible for prehistory to describe a dissociated great surface of one culture with sufficiently numerous and appropriately arranged proofs, as would really correspond to the actual diffusion of most cultures. A very great number of prehistoric finds, to a great extent, present but a kind of haphazard sampling, which is made at random in the earth. Such a thing can therefore become methodologically dangerous, because, if these samples have not been made in sufficient numbers, or not sufficiently proportionate to the whole region, there is a danger that entirely foreign cultures or significant variants of cultures which are identical among themselves, and which likewise lie in the earth, will not be touched by these samplings, whence, of course, the whole culture of this region would be distorted.

A second reason follows from the fragmentary character of most finds of prehistory. This fragmentary condition may be of two kinds: first, with regard to the material part of the culture, and, second, much more so with regard to the intellectual culture.

a. The very material culture is fragmentary and deficient, first, because it consists of objects which were already left behind in a fragmentary condition by the testators in the first place (*e.g.*, in Kjökkenmöddlinger [Kitchen Midden] and other such waste heaps, fill in for graves) and, consequently, they were partly or completely destroyed in the course of centuries or millenia. The older the cultures are, the latter manifests its effects the stronger, and is greatest in those most ancient times when there were as yet no implements of stone, but only such of bone or horn as we find in the old paleolithic bone cultures, or only of wood and bamboo as the Pygmies have today. Of clothing or habitation of these old cultures prehistory can give very little if any information. This state of affairs, of course, does not exclude the possibility that even here in this fragmentary and deficient representation of material culture in the finds of prehistory here and there forms or variants of a culture will be found, which ethnology could not yet have obtained in its own department.

But the whole character of this condition still puts the methodological obligation upon prehistory, to keep this deficiency and fragmentariness ever in mind, even in determining the distribution of single elements, but more so when mapping out the distribution of culture complexes. Prehistory, although it is able in single cases to produce this criterion of continuity for ethnology which ethnology itself lacks (see above, p. 296), must more frequently do without the certified use of this criterion in its own department. From this obligation laid upon prehistory, ethnology when taking over the results of prehistory incurs the right and duty to check up critically whether and in how far prehistory has fulfilled that duty.

3. Prehistory is still less competent to establish the intellectual culture of peoples whose relics it has discovered. The social and moral culture is almost entirely excluded from its research. (21) In more recent times certain houseforms, *if* they are preserved, lead to poor and uncertain conclusions; for the most part, it is hardly possible to grasp them at all. The case is almost the same with regard to religious culture: the establishment of the religious culture is first rendered possible when temples, emblems, pictures of gods, etc., are found. In the old cultures, however, there are no such things as yet. Sacrifice (primitial), when it first occurs, can only be established whereever skulls and long bones of these sacrifices are preserved as relics, but wherever only flesh or parts of plants were offered, or where the sacrifice is missing altogether, even this possibility disappears.

This insufficiency of prehistory for establishing the intellectual culture must be all the more emphasized, since we now know from ethnology that, precisely in the oldest peoples, the social and moral culture, even though it is simple, nevertheless, interiorly, it is very valuable and the religious and even the formal intellectual culture manifest an astounding richness of intellectual and effective forms and elements. No excavation, be it ever so deep, ever reports anything about all these things, nor can any spade dig up any positive information about it.

D. The Organic Relations Between the Single Regions of Culture

1. It is psychologically understandable that prehistorians, aroused at this incompetency of their science, sought to remedy it. Eventually, they had to concede that there is no way by means of which they could solve this task with the tools they possess and that only one which is essentially of ethnological character can accomplish the task. This way is supposed to have been found in the culture circles of culture historical ethnology, in which a certain material culture, together with a certain intellectual culture, forms an organic unity. If the first is established, we can assume the presence of the latter. Now, since prehistory can with the means at its disposal establish the material culture, it hopes that, by having recourse to this discovery of culture historical ethnology, it can conclude to the presence also of the corresponding intellectual culture.

In this inference, however, the achievements of culture historical ethnology have not been fully applied. The latter had already established that, just as single elements of material culture can break away from the rest and take up new relationships with absolutely strange cultures, so also the intellectual culture or a part of it can separate itself from the material culture, or if the material culture separates, the intellectual culture can refrain from so doing, whence the connection binding these two departments of culture, which, though organic, need not be intrinsic when thus given up and other new connections can be made. That was one of the points over which I had long discussions with Graebner, when he held the religion of the Kurnai of Southeastern Australia to be totemistic on the basis of the weapons and implements of the totemistic character found among them. (22)

2. Hence, it is not allowed as a general practice simply to conclude from the occurrence of the material culture generally characteristic to a culture circle to the presence also of the corresponding intellectual culture. They are valid only in cases where the material culture is present entirely and in still unmixed forms, for we must then assume that the culture circle is there in such original strength and purity that also the corresponding intellectual culture cannot be absent. But precisely the fullness and characteristic quality of the material culture will again and again be found to be missing in prehistory and, therefore, the possibilities to arrive at this conclusion will not be so very frequent in this science. Hence, too, the less complete and characteristic the material culture is, the smaller will be the methodological justification for that conclusion. (23)

Moreover, it is absolutely impossible to draw this conclusion from only one element, be it ever so characteristic and significant. Therefore, also the terms "round-butted ax culture," "neck ax culture," "comb ceramic culture," etc., are to be taken *cum grano salis.* They are not sufficiently justified, even if the material culture offers a supporting or eventually a comprehensive criterion of quantity, for "culture" in the full sense of the word also includes the intellectual and social culture, and that in a more eminent place.

3. Finally, also in the establishment of chronology, prehistory can still learn from the culture historical method of ethnology. For the greater ease in establishing the time succession which we conceded to prehistory (above, p. 295), applies only for the strata of the single excavation site, which is really only a very modest beginning of the research. But as soon as prehistory takes the subsequent necessary steps and joins the strata of the different sites which belong together, it obtains the same extension of its spatial distribution that ethnology has.

In order to obtain the depths of temporal succession from this extensive spatial distribution, the external sequence of prehistorical strata does not suffice. The reason is that this sequence can manifest great differences at the different places of excavation. Here, however, those rules are entirely in place, which the culture historical method of ethnology set up for its contact and overlay phenomena, its intrusions, penetrations, encirclings, and other results of migrations. These were applied with system and exactness by ethnology sooner than by prehistory, which, of course, had already for some time given up evolutionism and proceeded along historical lines, although not always firmly and persistently.

4. The total result of our considerations cannot be anything else than this: that both in content and in method ethnology can perform valuable services for prehistory and prehistory for ethnology. Neither of the two sciences ought to refuse this assistance, even though on the other hand, of course, both of them must also be careful to undertake the main part of their investigations with their own instruments and according to their own method, in order that they may be better able to proffer each other real support. In this case also, the disputes as to which of the two sciences is more important for the universal history of man seems to be superfluous and tedious; universal history is only too glad that it has two so thoroughgoing helpmates at its disposal (*cf.* also in this regard below, p. 336 ss.).

E. Parallelization of the Results of Culture Historical Research in Ethnology and Prehistory

a. The Defeat of Evolutionism in Prehistory

1. As already mentioned above (p. 295), I myself tried quite early to bring the results of culture historical research into harmonizing agreement with those of prehistory. From the aspect of principle there must naturally be such an agreement, and culture historical ethnology will become all the more certain of its own conclusions if its results stand in harmony with those of prehistorical research. I believe that, at the time, I demonstrated such a harmony along broad lines at least with some show of probability. But, of course, my insufficient acquaintance with that science prevented such a co-operation of prehistory as would have been required to attain a more com-

plete evidence. This task should have been undertaken by a prehistorian who was orientated along historical lines.

The oldest prehistory which developed in the second half of the nineteenth century under the leadership of G. de Mortillets in France was anything else but historical. It interpreted two stratigraphic series of prehistoric finds in an evolutionistic sense: the cultures of the higher strata in any one locality had developed in essentials from the lower strata at the same place. (24) Pigorini opposed this view very vigorously in the sense of the historical idea, in the first place for Italy, and his opposition gained more and more weight through the investigations of Obermaier, Breuil, Reid Moir, Burkett, etc. Then the following opinion made great headway: the prehistorical cultures also arise each in different parts of the world and spread elsewhere through migrations and borrowings. On these journeys they meet other cultures which they either overpower or by which they are overpowered or with whom they mingle. This interpretation has gained such general acceptance that at present the narrow circle of ancient Western European prehistory has been widened by excavations made not only in Central, Northern, Southern and Eastern Europe, but also at different places in Asia, Africa, America, Australia, and the far-reaching relationships and connections between the single prehistorical cultures become ever more clear to us by means of these excavations.

β. *The Establishment of the Prehistorical Culture Circles by O. Menghin*

The immense prehistorical material collected in all these excavations and researches has now been worked out from a purely prehistorical standpoint by O. Menghin. He has been able to detect the principal culture circles which underlie this bewildering variety. These important results have been presented in his book, *Weltgeschichte der Steinzeit* (Vienna, 1931). (25)

Menghin was able to establish the following prehistoric culture circles and culture strata, which I give here in broad outlines:

I. OLD PALAEOLITHIC OR PROTOLITHIC with three culture circles:

1. *Bone Cultures*	2. *Coup de Poing Cultures*	3. *Blade Cultures*
Alpine Cultures	Prechellean	Pre-Mousterian
Sinanthropos Pekinensis	Chellean	Mousterian
Homo Heidelbergensis	Acheulean	

II. YOUNG PALAEOLITHIC OR MIOLITHIC, also with three culture circles:

1. *Bone Cultures*	2. *Coup de Poing Cultures*	3. *Blade Cultures*
Kunda	Proto-Solutrean	Aurignacian
Maglamosean	Old Campignian	

III. EPIPALAEOLITHIC

Mixture of II 1 and 3: Capsian, Tardenoisian

Mixture of II 2 and 3: Upper Solutrean, Magdalenian, Azilian

Late forms of II 2: Campignian.

IV. NEOLITHIC (it would lead us too far afield to continue this summary).

We must, however, take the older bone cultures out of this whole schema, for the basis of the classification is stone (lithicum). Consequently, the bone cultures are prelithic and should be placed before, and even Menghin calls them the oldest protolithic cultures.

γ. *Parallelization of the Prehistorical Culture Circles with the Ethnological Culture Circles*

Menghin undertook the parallelization of his prehistorical culture circles with the ethnological, and it becomes still more exact if we place the Prelithicum of bone culture before, for then it will form a parallel to the ethnological Prelithicum of the Pygmy cultures with their implements exclusively of wood (and bamboo).

The prehistorical Protolithic period with its three culture circles is found by Menghin in the Eskimoid (Arctic), Australian, and Tasmanoid cultures of ethnology. I must confess that this arrangement does not interpret the Primitive cultures of ethnology very well.

The Miolithic period of prehistory with its three culture circles is paralleled with the three Primary cultures of ethnology: patriarchal breeders of large herds, the totemistic higher hunters, the mother-right horticulturists.

The parallels to the Epipaleolithic he finds in the secondary (and tertiary) cultures of ethnology!

It is not the place here for a criticism either of the prehistorical culture circles and their chronological arrangement or of the parallelization with the culture circles of ethnology which Menghin proposed, since we are not dealing with the content of culture, but are studying ways and methods to grasp the history of culture. And it is only in interest of this purpose that I have reproduced Menghin's arrangement of his prehistorical culture circles and their parallelization with those of ethnology.

In the same degree in which both certify each other, new methodological tools are also fashioned both to confirm, to complete, and eventually to correct the spatial distribution of the ethnological culture circles. Thus, we can sharpen our whole perspective of the geographical setting, the temporal succession and causal sequences of these cultures. All that I said in general in the foregoing chapter concerning the support of ethnology through prehistory now gains both a more definite form as well as wider spatial distribution and deeper time depths through this mutual parallelization of the culture circles.

4. ETHNOLOGY AND FOLKLORE

A. The Arrangement in the High Cultures

1. In no language is the close association between ethnology and folklore so clearly expressed as in German. While non-German languages call the first "ethnology" or also "cultural anthropology" (26) and the second "folklore," in German both words are derived from the word "Volk" ("people"), in the first case from the plural: "Völkerkunde" ("ethnology"), and in the second case from its singular form: "Volkskunde" ("folklore"). The first, therefore, is knowledge of many peoples, of all peoples; the second, of one, of one's own people, wherefore in the latter case an adjective must always be prefixed: German Volkskunde (folklore), Swedish folklore, etc.

The matter does not cause any difficulty as long as ethnology deals with the primitives, for then the scope of folklore is also in agreement, since it is directed to the broad lower strata of the people, which in many respects correspond to the primitive peoples. But confusion arises when European ethnologists devote themselves to the study of non-European peoples with high culture. The difficulties are not so great as long as it is a question of high cultures that have disappeared, such as the old American cultures of Mexico, Central and South America. When, however, existing high cultures, *e.g.*, China and Japan, are studied (and are considered apart from their new Europeanized culture), then what the European ethnologists consider to be ethnology will be folklore for the Japanese and Chinese investigators, especially for the former, who have already taken up these studies quite intensively. The restriction of folklore to the civilized nations of the white race as A. Haberlandt *first* limited it (27) cannot be held any more. He admits himself that also the more highly civilized nations of Asia can have their folklore. However, this must not be understood in Haberlandt's sense; namely, merely because they have received radiations of culture from Europe, for these people have a perfectly indigenous folklore.

A solution might be arrived at if the ethnologist would confine his study of such cultures to the periods preceding the appearance of writing. But he surely does not want to relinquish the later portion of their history in theory and certainly does not do so in practice, otherwise he would lose too much of his material. He has need of these later periods of cultured peoples, because in these cultures also the deeper strata of the people are in many ways transformed through the high culture strata built on top and have all received important historical influences from foreign high cultures. Hence, they do not present the simple clear character of primitive cultures.

2. They are thereby entirely identical with the deeper national strata of our European (and American) folklore. For also these have been influenced and changed in many ways by the influences of the older strata in the course of centuries. (28) Some folklorists as E. Fehrle (29) flatly deny all creative power to the popular mind and admit it only for the individual personality. That is correct if we recognize such creative individual personalities not only for the "higher" but also for the "lower" strata; *i.e.*, for the common people. Thus, also modern ethnology rejected the false doctrine of the former evolutionistic and half evolutionistic ethnology which held that among the primitives only the community and not the individual play a role. (30) In this sense also E. Hoffmann-Krayer's statement is to be understood, that a people does not produce but only reproduces. (31)

Hence, all peoples with high culture will thus consist of three strata, whether they be European, Asiatic, African, or American; namely: 1. An uppermost layer, which is the product of high culture, but into which single disboguements of lower strata still appear. 2. A middle layer, which consists in sedimentary productions from the upper layer and products of the old primitive culture. 3. The lowest layer, which is exclusively made up of elements from the periods before written history. The strength of these different layers as well as their relation to one another are different with every people and also thereby indicate the particular mentality of a people, but somehow all three strata are always present in all peoples with high culture.

B. The Principle of Applying the Culture Historical Method in Folklore

1. This triple stratigraphic series must first be clearly defined before we can advance to the question whether and in how far the culture historical method can and should also be applied in folklore. It is obvious that this question is to be answered in the negative for the uppermost layer, for here we have written documents which clearly enough give the chronological course of events, as well as proffer the means for solving the question of causes. In the second layer these written documents must also be diligently used and scientifically applied, but whenever these are not present, the culture historical method begins to come into play. The latter alone has a place in the lowest layer. Methodologically, therefore, we do not get a threefold but a twofold division: one stratum of written history and one of prewritten history.

This kind of historization of folklore has been carried out very little up till now. Folklore is still too much under the aftereffects of evolutionism and especially of its cheap psychologization.

2. A. Haberlandt asserts, it is true, that already W. Mannhardt "had anticipated a great deal of the methodological foundation of comparative folklore and ethnology of Graebner's *Methode der Ethnologie,*" in the foreword to his *Antike Feld- und Waldkulte* (1905), and "accordingly it must be duly said to have been worked out in the field of folklore since 1876." (32) He endeavors to prove this opinion more in detail in his later work, *Die deutsche Volkskunde,* (33) where he takes the proofs from Mannhardt's introduction (1876) to the second part of *Baumkultur der Germanen. . . .*

This opinion of Haberlandt, however, is entirely without foundation. In fact, one of the main sentences of Mannhardt that Haberlandt cites springs from crass evolutionism, the principle, namely, which always explains any culture entirely in terms of the present immediate environment: "Each tradition is to be explained first from itself and its closest compass; only when this calculation does not square may we go farther and deeper backward step by step." Neither the nearest environment nor the far distant may be brought in for explanation *a priori,* but the results of the study of all the circumstances must decide the case.

The one single rule given by Mannhardt is a very poor one: "Where direct popular tradition is had, a chronological fixation and restoration of the primitive form is likewise to be striven after at all costs. This study must proceed from inner reasons along the way of analysis and with the help of analogies, which are to be sharply checked as to value and content." Practically nothing of Graebner's *Methode* has been anticipated by such poor advice. When he, however, according to Haberlandt's own words, further demands also for folklore "the methods of investigation, which natural science in its time demanded," he diverts from the right system and goes astray upon wrong paths, which cannot lead to the discovery of culture strata and their objective chronology.

3. It would have indeed been remarkable if folklore had known the culture historical method so early. Not only that, it would be inexplicable how this method could still have been so fiercely attacked in the year 1911 by the folklorists, the Haberlandts, senior and junior, as actually happened. (34) It is encouraging that A. Haberlandt now goes so far as to admit the necessity of this method for folklore, when he writes: "Today, still, such an endeavor ["psychological" interpretation] must be extensively applied where the psychological explanation of an ancient custom or ancient phenomenon of life is sought after line for line out of elementary ideologies. Still the tradition of peoples has proven itself an historically immensely entangled web, in which each thread is woven together with many others in a knot, of which one thread comes from afar, the other from near by. And the typological and psychological grouping process is being more and more re-

placed by culture historical analysis." (35) Hence, Haberlandt admits that culture historical analysis is only now beginning to influence folklore and is "more and more" replacing the older typological and psychological procedure.

C. The Application of the Culture Historical Method in Folklore in Different Countries

α. *In European Countries*

1. Such a state of affairs, namely, the gradual replacement of typology and psychology by history, was very apparent in the great compilation, *Die deutsche Volkskunde,* edited by A. Spamer. Among thirty-one authors who worked at it, there are only three with whom historical procedure and aims assert themselves: A. Helbok, "Volkskunde und Siedlungsgeschichte" (pp. 59-79), Fr. Maurer, "Volkssprache" (pp. 182-203), and Br. Schier, "Das deutsche Haus" (pp. 477-543).

In the case of the article by Helbok, the matter itself induces one to think along historical lines. Helbok very nicely shows "that the mass of contemporary culture, forms, and ways of life of a great people with regard to the origin of their thousandfold details spring from entirely different time levels" and that the investigator "cannot do without the knowledge of the historical relativity of all the single phenomena in order to go beyond them to the original meaning" (*op. cit.,* p. 59). But he certainly errs when he thinks that the matter in this regard is different in the case of the preliterates. The second article, "Volkssprache," by Maurer profits through the historical researches of linguistics and can therefore illuminate very well the events of the "fall" and the "rise" of word forms.

The historical method is applied most intensely and consciously in the third treatise, "Das deutsche Haus," by Schier. His standpoint with regard to principles is well exemplified in his own words: "In harmony with the two mainsprings of house development, the natural and the historical factors, the method of German house research must also be twofold: it must include both social descriptions and temporal developments, and it must have a cultural geographical and a cultural historical branch. (36) Both branches are so intertwined with each other that it is of no advantage to separate them." (37) In his greater work, "Hauslandschaften und Kulturbewegungen im östlichen Mitteleuropa," (38) Schier was fully conscious of his adherence to the culture historical method. (39) Everyone who has studied this excellent work with its rich and interesting results must acknowledge that his following of this method has not harmed folklore here.

Also W. Kuhn, in his work, *Deutsche Sprachinselforschung,* (40) declares himself for the application of Graebner's method in folklore.

2. In February, 1935, at the invitation of the universities of Upsala, Stockholm, Göteborg, Lund, and Copenhagen, I undertook a lecture tour of the Scandinavian countries and came in contact with the leading representatives of the well-known and excellent schools of Swedish and Danish folklore and archeology. I lectured on the culture historical method. Everywhere, especially in Upsala (Geiger, Campbell . . . etc.), Lund (v. Sydow, Rydbeck, Forssander . . .), Copenhagen (Hatt . . .) I found full approval for the furthering of a profound and extensive historization of folklore. It was acknowledged that the research into the manner and diffusion of certain single elements did not however suffice for that (criterion of quality), but that also the embodiment of a corresponding multitude of such elements (criterion of quantity) should be carried through to organic wholes of space and time (culture strata and culture circles). We were of one mind that evolutionism is incompetent to carry out these tasks and acknowledged that the culture historical method of ethnology provides us with the means to accomplish this thoroughly and efficiently.

β. *In Eastern Asia*

1. I had exactly the same experience soon after (summer and autumn of 1935), during my lecture tour in the Far East. It is not well enough known in America and Europe that in Japan under the creative and forward direction of men like

Professor Yanagida, Viscount Shibusawa, etc., folklore has attained a high stage of development quantitatively and qualitatively not easily attainable elsewhere. The sixtieth birthday of the founder of Japanese folklore, Professor Yanagida, was celebrated fittingly by a week of a double series of lectures. In the first series, a representative reported on the status of folklore in each province of Japan. In the second series, a similar report was given for every country in Europe (and America). At one of these celebrations in Osaka in October, 1935, to which I was also invited in order to speak a few words, I was able to point to the interesting fact that one of the pupils of Professor Yanagida, Dr. Masao Oka, who later devoted six years to a thorough study of the culture historical ethnology at the University of Vienna, had now come back with an extensive work on the Prehistory and Early History of Japan. In this work the happy connection between ethnology and folklore in the sense of the culture historical idea is shown to advantage.

2. The same opinion of the hopelessness of evolutionistic orientation has also spread to China among the scholars interested in ethnology and folklore. Apropos of the bewildering mass of material for folklore that has piled up in China for centuries, both in writing and actual life, the need of a directing line and more sure way to investigate this immense material was more acutely felt. The lectures on culture historical ethnology, its methods and successes, which I was invited to hold at the universities and other schools of higher education and scientific societies in Peking, Tientsin, Nanking, and Shanghai, met with very lively interest on the part of the professors as well as the students.

3. Finally, I experienced something similar in the new state, the Philippines, where I was invited to give such lectures at the two universities in Manila. Here incipient folklore has found again an entirely different and interesting object. A native-Asiatic people which had received European high culture and religion in the form of Roman-Catholic-Spanish colonization before attaining a high culture itself was, in turn, introduced to a modern German form with an Anglo-Saxon-

American impress. If the latter does not interest folklore much, the other two elements, the native Indonesian basis and the Spanish-Catholic overlay, have created a very rich store especially of religious folklore that can rival the liveliest nationalities of Europe. It is the case of an Asiatic people which, without having reached an Asiatic high culture, still offers a rich and characteristic subject for folklore (*cf.* above, p. 306).

D. Some Additional Remarks on the Use of the Culture Historical Method in Folklore

1. Thus we can speak of an international recognition of the usefulness of the culture historical method of ethnology for folklore. We have already shown above (p. 306 s.) that this has come to be applied especially to that stratum of folklorist material which comes from the period lying beyond the time of written documents. Concerning the details of this application, there is not much more to be said. A very useful preparation for it is the cartographic presentation of the distribution of the single culture elements as has been prepared in Germany by Pessler, in Sweden by Campbell, and in several countries in the great "Words and Things" atlases. For it partly imitates the two-dimensional distribution of ethnological elements and facilitates and promotes the recognition of their events and phenomena such as contact, mixture, overlay, intersection, intrusion, etc. From these phenomena culture historical ethnology obtains a tool for establishing both the spatial relations and groupings as well as the chronological sequences and through this inspection is able to grasp the diverse causal influences at work as well as the inner character of these phenomena.

This whole work, of which Br. Schier's book (mentioned above, p. 310) is an excellent example, is, on the one hand, considerably more difficult in folklore than in ethnology, because of the increased intricacy which arose through the successive imposition of high cultures of different ages upon the lower strata. On the other hand, however, this upper layer of higher culture aids folklore in reconstructing the chronological data, which at times also throw light upon the lower strata.

Here the culture historical method with the methodological tools at its disposal collaborates in the investigation and brings it to completion.

The folklorist has a great advantage over the ethnologist, because his collection of materials and also his investigation of causes concerns a living people to which he himself belongs and whose intellectual pulse he can also feel, and whose psychic life, thought, feelings, and desires awaken in him a vibrating resonance. It is also much easier for him to fulfill the condition for psychical empathy, which is necessary in order to grasp the inner development and to gain insight into the inmost psychic associations of the culture (*cf.* above, p. 261). For the psychical union between the investigator for folklore and his people also makes itself felt in the oldest elements of his culture and often enough affects precisely these the strongest, because they reach back into the deepest foundations of the culture peculiar to his people.

5. ETHNOLOGY AND PHYSICAL ANTHROPOLOGY

A. Name and Nature of Ethnology and Physical Anthropology

I suppose many were expecting to find the list of ethnology's auxiliary sciences headed by physical anthropology. This is quite natural; since the histories of the two sciences flowed along in the same channels for a time, in the course of which first ethnology was subordinated to physical anthropology and then vice versa. I have extensively treated the history of this oscillation in my article, "Die Moderne Ethnologie." (41) Here we are concerned with the end result of this alternate position which turned out differently in the different countries of Europe and America.

If we now briefly review the data, we find that Germany, Austria, Switzerland, and Italy proposed the division: ethnology and (physical) anthropology, whereby ethnology is taken to mean the science of peoples and their cultures, anthropology being the science of races and their physical characteristics. England in its turn preferred "cultural (42) anthropology" and "physical anthropology," while in North America both formulations were in vogue, that of Great Britain and that of the Continent. Since also France and Belgium, which had a temporary preference for the term "ethnography," have accepted the term "ethnology" the Central European terminology gained the upper hand. This was still more increased by the fact that the international congress for both sciences called itself "International Congress for Anthropology and Ethnology" and arranged the sittings of the two sciences in separate sections. Thus the Central European nomenclature gained the ascendancy which it will certainly not relinquish. Lebzelter, while criticizing Menghin for his proposal to replace the term "ethnology" by "ethnography" (recently he has already given it up), commits a greater error when he atavistically understands anthropology in the wider sense as the history of humanity.

The matter at stake is not the mere differences of nomenclature, but the clear division in the terminology ought also to express the different nature of the two sciences, for this difference in turn is based upon their own practical autonomy in universities and museums. Moreover, as the objects of ethnology, peoples, and cultures are something essentially mental, it must, after the nature of its object, likewise be a mental science. Anthropology, on the other hand, deals with races and their bodily characteristics and, hence, enters the ranks of the natural sciences. But just as a natural science does not become a mental science if it wants to be natural history, so neither does anthropology if it is the "natural history of the Hominidae."

The object, therefore, of ethnology is essentially different from that of physical anthropology: the object of the former is men and peoples, who through their thought, volition, and action produce works of culture, while the latter deals with physical human beings and races which can only bring about natural effects. Hence, it is essentially inadequate and therefore erroneous when Lebzelter says: "As historical descriptive disciplines, anthropology and ethnology have the same method," (43) for ethnology is not merely an "historical descriptive" science.

B. Race and Culture

a. *The Ethnobiology of W. Scheidt*

The clear distinction which has been obtained between ethnology and physical anthropology, their nature, their field of study and, hence, their methods as well, should not be taken to be a hostile opposition. This distinction only means that each should be conscious of its own character, in order that the exactness of their respective method of procedure may enable them to work together with all the greater certainty and profit.

A new distortion threatens to enter through an infringement of demarcation lines, which a number of anthropologists are inclined to perpetrate. They are supported by the singular progress they were able to make in their field through the discovery of the laws of heredity. Since the transmissibility of their characteristics seemed to give the races greater permanency, they seemed thereby also to increase in importance over against peoples as a subject of culture. (44) Anthropologists thought they could prove that also mental qualities were hereditary and, moreover, they opined this not only in single cases but for whole races. This, however, they assert, removed all distinction between mental and natural sciences and, consequently, also undermined the distinction between ethnology and (physical) anthropology. Both sciences must, therefore, converge into one, which, of course, would have two subgroups: the study of races and the study of peoples.

This new movement was announced already in W. Scheidt's work, *Allgemeine Rassenkunde als Einführung in das Studium der Menschenrassen.* (45) It appears much clearer in an article by the same author, "Rassenkunde, Völkerkunde und völkerbiologische Forschungs- und Lehraufgaben" (46) and was further developed in his work, *Lebensgesetze der Kultur. Biologische Betrachtungen zum "Problem der Generation in der*

Geistesgeschichte" (47) and *System und Bibliographie der Kulturbiologie.* (48) Scheidt calls this new science "Völker- oder Ethnobiologie." (49)

Fr. Krause has given us a thorough criticism of these attempts, and we can but agree with him in essentials. (50) He rejects the exaggerated estimation of hereditary factors over against the culture elements. He also points out that the methods proposed by Scheidt for the determination of hereditary psychical talents are untrustworthy. They are more inadequate in the case of racial characteristics and still more so with regard to the great variability, particularly, of hereditary psychical dispositions.

β. *The Problem of Psychic-Racial Heredity*

It is very instructive to see how Scheidt has asserted his conviction of the certainty of racial transmission of psychical characteristics with ever increasing insistence. As late as 1925, he declares that the attempts to establish this are "very hypothetical" and concedes only that "very many psychical characteristics have some importance as racial characters." After 1928, he admits that the research in question "is still in its primordial stages" and asserts that it is not correct to say "that racial research pronounced everything mental to be already inherent in the blood." (51) In the same year, he writes still more categorically: "Since the science has nothing to gain from the popular writings of H. F. Günther [quoted by him—W. Schmidt] . . . it might be sufficient to prove that the study of races does not by any means hold that all psychical manifestations are exclusively determined by inheritance or that all psychical hereditary dispositions are racial characters. Hence, *a priori,* there can be no talk of the study of races being important for all the tasks of ethnology or of all the results of ethnology for the biology of races." (52) But already in 1929 the following debatable principle springs full-clad in imitation of Pallas Athene from the head of Jupiter: "Nobody today doubts any more that all essential psychical dispositions are determined by inheritance." (53)

This change really occurred entirely too fast and too easily for a person to consider it to be scientifically sound. We get a very different picture of this whole question by consulting merely the summary of E. Eickstedt in his *Grundlagen der Rassenpsychologie.* (54) He is of the opinion that though the transmissibility of certain psychical characters exists, "still the analysing forms of biological hereditary research, *i.e.,* of the so-called Mendelianism . . . , mostly suffer shipwreck on the flexibility and diversity of psychical phenomena. And also those psychologists, such as Peters, Hoffmann, Pfahler and Petermann, who have thoroughly studied these problems, agree with me in this matter." (55) Besides, even genuine racial psychologists are not of one mind as to which psychical characters are hereditary. At any rate, Peters says emphatically: "Heredity can never make the personality with its entire structure apodictically understandable." (56) For him it remains an absolute mystery how the unity of the personality of the child results from the duality of the transmitting parents: "The great mystery of psychical heredity is how one results from two." (57)

In this poverty and great uncertainty which we find in the whole field of racial hereditary psychology, it is really asking quite a bit from a well-established science like ethnology to dissolve and reform itself entirely anew on the basis of such a pitiful and hypothetical science still in its very beginnings. The importance of this cultural biology for ethnology is lessened also through what Scheidt himself says: "Biological historical research . . . will be the principal task of *modern* history." (58) Ethnology, on the other hand, must still penetrate into the older and even the oldest times. And also Krause with good reason doubts "whether such research could be carried out in the case of a foreign investigator in communities of highly civilized peoples and especially with regard to peoples of unequivocally simple culture development." (59)

c. "Psychologization" of Physical Anthropology

1. We, therefore, reject the later thesis of Scheidt which asserts that "all essential psychical conduct is determined by

inheritance." We accept, however, his somewhat earlier axiom "that the study of races does not by any means propose that all [external] psychical manifestations are exclusively determined by inheritance or that all psychical hereditary dispositions are also racial characters." From the last mentioned principle we conclude with him: "Hence, *a priori,* there can be no talk of the study of races being important for all the tasks of ethnology or, vice versa, of all the results of ethnology for the biology of races." In the present, as yet, early stage of the science of races, we cannot conclusively determine for which departments of ethnology and in what measure this science can be of use. Certainly all prudent ethnologists will gratefully welcome any real scientific results the science of races produces and make use of them as valuable aids for the elucidation of some of their own problems.

Consequently, the efforts of W. Scheidt remain and will even increase in value. With these restrictions, ethnobiology can be considered an auxiliary science of ethnology as is done by Fr. Krause. (60) As to which fields ethnology will be able to enter through the aid given it by the science of races, we can only say that they lie in the direction which already such important psychologists as de Candolle and Ribot suggested; namely, intellectual characteristics underlie the transmission by inheritance least of all; the moral dispositions, however, and above all qualities bound up with bodily functions (61) are more often involved. According to our conception of the soul, heredity can only take place with regard to bodily traits, the soul as such is not inheritable. (62) An actual transmission of intellectual qualities would only take place as the result of collective influence in time and place of the soul on the bodily organs, which attach themselves there and are thence passed on as bodily dispositions.

2. Hence, not only those influences which are exercised by the physical environment upon the body come into consideration for the formation of races, but also those "which proceed from the soul" must be considered, "be they only of individual character, as personal training, education, selection, frivolity,

vice, or influences of a social nature, as quality and preparation of food, clothing and dwelling, sexual customs and laws, etc." (63) And also O. Menghin strongly emphasizes this when he rejects "a primary determination of the form of dispositions by heredity, as is imagined above all by a certain crude popular anthropology" and accepts only a secondary one. (64)

To come back to method, these events then cannot, of course, be grasped by a purely natural science, nor for that matter by a wholly psychical science. However, neither can this be accomplished by a method which is a mixture of the natural and mental sciences. This can only be accomplished by both of them entirely distinct in nature, but here joined in the application of the method of the natural and that of the mental sciences upon an event that is of mutual concern.

This "psychologization" of physical anthropology, to give it a name more clever than correct, would not therefore consist in an essential alteration in the aims of physical anthropology, but rather calls for increased interest also in events which are both physical and psychical at the same time, for the full clarification of which it calls upon its colleagues from the faculties of the mental sciences; namely, ethnology and psychology. With the same right (or wrong) we could also speak of a "physicalization" (a terrible word) of ethnology.

D. The Historization of Physical Anthropology

There is no doubt that a certain historization of physical anthropology can be carried out precisely with regard to race. It is remarkable that Lebzelter, who took up the idea of the historical character of anthropology so enthusiastically (see above, p. 315) has done the least for precisely this method of approach. Dr. J. Wölfel has accomplished this much better in his article, "Historische Anthropologie in ihrer Anwendung auf die Kanarischen Inseln." (65)

1. Wölfel understands very correctly "historical in that strict sense which separates the historical sciences from the natural sciences, and that not the general, the typical of an event, but the single, the individual character of a particular event, is

causally important. Anthropology is only then truly 'historical' when it wants to show not the biological developments and their specializations within a race, but the racial history of a certain region and its inhabitants" (p. 493). "Racial history is only called into question with the intention and in the sense of producing, with the aid of all auxiliary sciences necessary, all the conditions required to enable an otherwise strictly anthropological science to reconstruct the historical development according to which the population of a certain large or small region was evolved precisely in the present composition and arrangement of its racial constituents" (p. 494).

Wölfel rightly emphasizes the importance of the history of the settling of a certain region. The time required for this historical process is quite satisfactorily preserved also in nonliterate cultures often with numerous and characteristic skeletal remains, unless the dead were cremated. These relics make it possible to work out the different racial groups, their coming and going, their invasions and transitions, and finally the crossings and overlays of these groups. To determine all this is the task of historical anthropology. Conversely, it is the task of ethnology to determine how and in what degree the history of the cultures of this region agrees with the status, arrival, and departure of these races. In this matter ethnology builds upon the results of historical physical anthropology and it will certainly be greatly benefited thereby.

2. Wölfel (p. 495) also points out that the racial and cultural importance of one and the same event need not be at all of the same degree: "An event that produces great political changes can remain absolutely sterile as far as the history of the settlement is concerned. As, for instance, when several Norman families settled in lower Italy. Although they developed into an immense and illustrious state, the racial influence upon the population there remained insignificant. . . . A new imposed layer of a numerically small ruling class that quickly contracts matrimonial alliances with the native population can give us some indications that will enable us to define an individual type or certain characteristic features, but is of no moment

whatsoever for the racial analysis of the whole population. At the same time, an event of an economic nature that can hardly be determined with direct historical methods can instigate a great shifting in the ratio of racial composition of a population."

He gives us many useful hints for the historization of physical anthropology for determining the correct and fruitful starting point for our investigations, the significance of the ever stronger domestication taking place in the settlement and finally (and in a special way) for racial psychology. He also shows the great importance of a fixed point outside the region where the cultures cross; *i.e.*, a point where a race occurs as yet relatively pure, as, for instance, in isolated places (see above, p. 199). The Canary Islands, a region of research to which Wölfel has devoted himself and which is of such overwhelming importance for the ethnology of both Africa and Europe, illustrates this very well.

3. In comparison with the permanent settlement, the importance of a transitory migration at first sight does not seem to be so great either for physical anthropology or for ethnology. However, this is not the case. In fact, the establishment of the effects of active migrations anthropologically and ethnologically does but add to the number of difficulties already encountered. That does not therefore dispense us from investigating them, first, because, otherwise, considerable errors of a negative character could attach themselves to our judgment of cultural events and, second, from a positive point of view, we would not be able to obtain a correct estimate of cultural or racial events without this investigation. We were able to propose some rules for these important matters already in the method itself and we have seen how the migratory movements of the Indo-Germans present an important and much debated specimen of such cases (see above, p. 280 s.).

Hence, it is clear that both the "psychologization" as well as its historization brings anthropology nearer to ethnology and makes it a much more valuable auxiliary science.

6. ETHNOLOGY AND GEOGRAPHY

It has already been pointed out above (p. 8) that ethnology is a spatial science, because the development of human culture is also geographically defined and consequently is subject to a complex scheme of influences as the components of external nature themselves; namely, the flora and fauna, and the degree of approachability. We emphasized the necessary connection between ethnology and geography and especially anthropogeography when we noted how Ratzel, one of the founders of culture historical ethnology, also had a share in the development of anthropogeography. In fact, the connection between the two was so close that Ratzel had at first called his new method "geographical" (above, p. 25, note 7a). But while his successor Frobenius thought along geographical lines entirely, calling culture a product of geographical regions, Ratzel himself succeeded in attaining to the supergeographical factor; namely, the concept of man pre-eminently endowed with intelligence and free will. Thus, Ratzel was able to grasp and vindicate the real historical element of ethnology.

In consequence of his superiority, man does not subject himself to his geographical environment, but only adapts himself to it. During this process, however, he learns how to gain ever better control over his environment by acquiring an ever more exact knowledge of its potentialities and methods to exploit them in his own service. And, last but not least, man devotes himself to other interests than the mere preservation of his material life. That is the main theme *par excellence* of the entire culture history of mankind. We shall not enter upon this matter here, since we are not at the moment concerned with the contents of culture history, but rather with the methodological means at our disposal for investigating and objectively describing culture history itself.

In this respect, geography seems to be able to aid particularly along the following lines:

a. With regard to spatial and temporal culture relations.

b. With regard to the original habitat of a culture.

c. With regard to the establishment, enrichment, and poverization of cultures in the different regions to which they migrate.

d. With regard to the transmission of culture-creative principles, which arose in one region and were applied to new materials in other regions.

A. Geography and the Spatial Juxtaposition and Temporal Sequence of Cultures

a. The Spatial Juxtaposition of Cultural Relations

1. The importance of geography for the juxtaposition of cultural relations was already touched upon above (p. 8), where it was pointed out that the absolute requisite for any cultural relations at all was the simultaneous existence in *one* region. When such a coexistence has been established, it does not mean that actual cultural relations have been demonstrated; conversely, however, if such a simultaneous coexistence is proven to be impossible, these cultural relations are positively excluded. Simultaneous occupation (by two or more cultures) of one and the same geographical district means that neither was the mere distance itself so great, nor has the specific distance been made so difficult (by mountain ranges difficult of approach, swamp land, or expanses of water) as to render impossible all contact of the two or more peoples or culture provinces in question.

Both the general as well as the specific distance have all the greater effect the more meager the means of transportation at the inhabitants' disposal. Hence, both distances are of still greater significance the older the cultures in question are, for in those early stages they either did not have a great many means of travel or had only such as were very imperfectly developed.

2. This is significant especially for the criterion of continuity: If geography proves that such a geographical continuity as is

required for the mutual interaction of two cultures or two cultural elements did not exist at the prescribed time, all possibility for having a criterion of continuity in this case is excluded in this particular direction. If, nevertheless, characteristic criteria of quality are found, the requisite connection for these by means of the criterion of continuity must be sought for along another way (*cf.* above, p. 156 ss.).

Thus, for instance, since the closer relationship between the Australian and the Fuegian languages proposed by Rivet is precluded as far as direct connections by way of the sea are concerned, because neither the Australians nor the Fuegians have any means of navigation capable of conquering such immense transmarine distances, only a common point of origin can be assumed for these relationships between South-eastern Australian and Fuegian cultures, which actually do exist. This assumed point is in (North) Eastern Asia, from which place the one branch passed over Further India, Indonesia, and New Guinea, thus reaching Australia. The other branch passed over the Bering Strait and crossed North, Central, and South America and thus reached Tierra del Fuego. (66)

β. *The Temporal Succession of Cultures*

1. Geography is also of importance for determining the sequence of culture relations, and here the historical character of ethnology stands out very plainly. Apart from the internal development of a culture which takes place in the same region (of which one might doubt if it ever existed as an internal development pure and simple [above, p. 235]), every sequence of culture relationship is also connected with a large number of geographical districts. For a culture either remains in the same region and there comes under the influences of other cultures which emigrate from elsewhere, or the culture itself immigrates into other regions and comes under the influence of both the indigenous and the immigrating cultures. Consequently, the cultural stratigraphy consists in great part of a

succession of heterogeneous culture zones and an overlay which is the outcome of their impinging influences upon each other.

2. All that has been said (above, p. 199) concerning the methodological importance of refuge areas and border regions belongs here: such districts will never be primary places of origin of significant cultures and are mostly the cause of degeneration and curtailment of what were once richer cultures; at any rate, they contribute to the longer conservation of older cultures and in the course of time can even arrest the development of these cultures completely.

The rules set up for tracing the directions of cultural diffusion are fructified by geography, because, after the establishment of the general direction, the correct cultural sequence of the active and passive influences of the regions lying along the line of diffusion will also be determined.

3. In contrast to refuge areas and border regions, the travel routes on land and sea are important in another respect. These are the stretches along which travel is the easiest and, therefore, particularly busy. It is impossible to conserve the older cultures along such routes all the way to the terminus. We should much more expect frequent interchanges of cultures both spatially and chronologically, which can lead to a complexity of cultures that is often extremely difficult to unravel.

Among the different kinds of travel routes we must certainly distinguish between trade routes for commercial purposes and travel routes followed by whole groups of migrating peoples. Besides, expeditions for conquest must also be distinguished from ordinary travel routes. It is the merit of P. van Bulck to have clearly pointed out the specific methodological treatment these different modes of travel claim (v. Bulck, pp. 42-122). P. Borchardt (67) has particularly distinguished himself in exposing such trade routes with more exact research into the various hindrances that prove a barrier to travel and, consequently, lower the speed of travel along these routes.

Ocean currents are a special kind of sea route. For they can hinder cultural intercourse in their direction entirely or give great impetus thereto, especially in more ancient times.

Their importance for the investigation of culture migrations in Oceania has been clearly shown, especially by G. Thilenius. (68)

B. Geography and the Original Home of Cultures

α. *General Principles*

1. As we pointed out above (p. 222), Graebner had called attention to the importance of "anthropogeographical arguments" (the questions of relation between culture and environment) for determining the first abode of a culture. Of course, the detailed historical investigations must have preceded and have pursued the migrations of the single subcultures back to their respective points of origin with the help of the various criteria and rules. They must also make the convergence of these points of origin upon one ultimate point of origin ever more probable before we can approach geography to increase this probability to certainty, in order that with this certainty we might delve deeper into the nature of this initial appearance and ultimate origin of cultures, in so far as this is a question of external geographical causes.

When all historical investigations have been undertaken, the task of geography becomes somewhat analogous to that of psychology; namely, to give us a deeper insight into the ultimate causes of a culture (see above, p. 278). However, while in the co-operation from psychology we are concerned with the internal psychological causes for the solution of which the aid of psychology was enlisted, geography, on the other hand, should thoroughly acquaint us with the causal influences of the environment.

And even in the case of the last mentioned insight, it is not a matter of purely material influences of the external environment, for these are never the sole determining factor in the formation of human culture and of themselves do not produce a culture. Here, too, man must consciously accept this influence and change and adapt himself thereto, in order to obtain the means of sustenance and protection. Hence, the importance of geography for determining the first abode of a culture has special reference to their economic basis, which, of course, is of the greatest importance also for the other parts of the culture.

2. Graebner proposed a number of negative and positive rules to ascertain the original district of a culture (see above, p. 222) and on the basis of these I have traced the habitats of several Primitive cultures, as well as of two Primary cultures; namely, the animal breeding herders and the mother-right agrarian culture, at the same time making that of the totemistic hunters somewhat probable. In the light of these discoveries, we can propose several rules of control which may act as a check upon our other conclusions.

β. *Special Rules*

1. In general, a geographical setting which best corresponds to the nature of a culture, and is for the most part favorable to its development, should be the original abode of that culture. In a certain sense, it can be said that this kindred environment is disposed to call this culture into existence and exert a formative influence in its development. Moreover, the negative conclusion may be drawn that no complete culture, especially not that of more ancient times, has originated in economically poor and marginal refuge areas (see above, pp. 189, 326), particularly not the last, because migrations from such places were out of the question.

All of which does not mean, however, that the cultures concerned *must* have originated of inner necessity in the more favorable region, for as a cultural effect it presupposes the human mind and one which understands how to grasp and take advantage of the opportunities nature offers, and there is no reason to assume that all peoples are gifted in the same degree to recognize and exploit the potentialities of an environment. Thus, if the original district is the most advantageous one for the development of a culture, it must be assumed that the most characteristic features of the culture best developed in that region, and conversely, did not fare so well elsewhere.

2. Further, it does not follow that, if this original region is somewhat more extensive, the distinguishing characteristic of a culture with all its special features was to be found precisely in the oldest forms and in those lying nearest the more narrow region of origin. The development of this characteristic also needs time, both in a negative sense, to free itself from the aftereffects of earlier cultures, and also positively, in order to develop all its finer details.

For example, in the animal-breeder cultures, the reindeer breeders retained the extensive rights accorded the woman and child in the earlier Primitive cultures, while the horse (and cow) (69) breeders took them away. Similarly in the older mother-right cultures, the man has not yet entirely settled down with all his effects in the residence of the woman (matrilocal marriage), but he remains at his place and the woman at hers and the man visits the woman from time to time (visiting marriage). Still less has the right to court gone over entirely to the woman in the oldest phases of mother-right, but this only took place later on.

It must be noted, however, that these harmonious and progressing developments remained geographically conterminous with the smaller region of origin and, so to speak, represent the first radiation zones of distribution of this culture.

3. It is clear that the original abode of one culture, which so favorably aids its development, need not have this effect in the case of another culture; in fact, it may be very unfavorable for the latter. That is easily seen, for example, when one compares the steppes of the large herd culture with the rainy and woody valleys of the oldest horticulturists.

It is also apparent that if a culture migrates into regions which are unfavorable to its development (which can indeed only happen under the pressure of hostile influences), its characteristics are more and more obliterated, and if the unfavorableness increases, it can degenerate and eventually disappear. As far as method is concerned, such changes in a culture allow us to draw corresponding conclusions as to the character of the region through which it migrated. This brings us to the following section, which treats of the importance of geography also for the zones of the more advanced phases of development.

c. Geography and the Advanced Stages of Cultural Development

1. We demonstrated above (p. 328) that the original site of a complete, especially of an older, culture, cannot be a region of meager economic potentialities or a refuge area. We can amplify this principle by adding that in older times, *i.e.*, in the times of the ancient Primitive culture, no poorly economic districts were occupied at all, for the simple reason that at the time the earth was so sparsely populated that no tribe or group of tribes allowed itself to be pushed into such a place. There were sufficient fairly good regions into which they could betake themselves either migrating of their own free "wanderlust" or forced to do so by others. Hence, not only the original habitat but also many of the regions of the advanced phases of development were not impoverished regions, but rather offered favorable conditions and certainly influenced these advanced stages of culture development for the best. These favorable circumstances could, it is true, be specifically different from those of the original region and, consequently, would affect the culture qualitatively but not essentially.

It is not even *a priori* excluded that the case actually happened—especially for the oldest cultures—in which the more recent regions to which these cultures migrated were still more abundantly supplied and, consequently, were still more favorable to their advanced development than their original regions or, at any rate, than some of the districts they successively occupied.

Two such cases stand out very clearly; namely, the North Central Californians and the (East) Algonkians in North

America. Both of these groups of tribes, after emigrating from Northeastern Asia, crossed the Bering Strait (at that time still an isthmus). Having passed through Alaska and northern North America (Canada today), they were separated from each other by subsequent culture movements south of the Arctic seas, where they had been still united. The Californians were pushed toward the west through the northern Great Basin to North Central California. The Algonkians were forced across the Great Lake region to the Atlantic coast. It was particularly the first who found a refuge area which, though shunted to the side, was by no means an impoverished region, but rather a country extremely rich in animal and plant life, as well as a beautiful country with a pleasant climate.

2. This fact of favorable environment in the original abode and also in the regions of the first stages of advanced development (especially in the case of ancient Primitive cultures) considerably increases the applicability of the rule I proposed shortly before (p. 207). There I admitted with Graebner that the external cultural possession is not rich in the oldest cultures and, therefore, that also the criterion of quantity naturally cannot show the richness of later cultures. At that time I already restricted this interpretation precisely to the external culture possession. But if the external circumstances are rich and favorable for the production of the means of subsistence and protection, then the time and disposition are there in abundance for products of the mind and heart and also the esthetic development of the general intellectual and religious culture. We can, therefore, expect a rich and full life in the mental culture of these peoples, which though it be externally ever so simple and plain, nevertheless does not have to be without inner greatness and importance. It is clear that this general condition of affairs must also be given ample consideration in the psychological interpretation of the older cultures.

However, if we have shown that the oldest regions of the old cultures were not poorly developed economically, then we cannot reverse this principle offhand and say all such regions are of recent or of very recent origin. The principle might well be defended, however, that the greater majority of out of the way districts were occupied only recently and that the more recent this occupation is, the more marked will its stunted character be, whereby we gain another time measure. The reason for this was touched upon (above, pp. 199, 330) when we stated that such regions were only occupied by migrating tribes after all the other more promising regions elsewhere had been yielded to others.

Thus the Aranda (Arunta), as both cultural and linguistic history directly show, (70) constitute only the last of the five or six culture strata of Australia and, hence, are the youngest; since all the other better regions of Australia had already been occupied by earlier cultures, they were simply forced to be satisfied with the terrible deserts of Central Australia.

D. Geography and the Transference of Old Culture Principles upon New Material

The importance which geographay has (as we have seen above, p. 325) for establishing the criterion of continuity can now be amplified somewhat and more closely determined.

1. An opportunity to set up the criterion of continuity can be nullified or greatly diminished also through an extremely great climatic change in the region of migration with corresponding changes in the animal and plant life, because such a change in climate must radically transform the culture. Hence, if it migrates afterward, both the characteristics as well as the number of cultural connections manifesting themselves in criteria of quality decrease, and even the older criteria of continuity are also disturbed and obliterated. At the same time, however, we must distinguish whether such a change of climate took place before, during, or after the migration.

The last case is exemplified in the passage of the Bering Strait, which did not consist of a chain of islands until the end of the Miolithic Age, while previous to that an isthmus prevented the cold waters of the Arctic Ocean from going southward. This had a very significant effect upon the climate of Northeastern Asia and that of Northwestern America, so that at the time, when the oldest cultures migrated easward, not an arctic but a boreal climate prevailed, in consequence of which a large steppe and forest region arose in Alaska and Canada. (71) Such a climate, therefore, did not effect a radical change in the migrating culture, so that the connection between the cultures in America and those still in their Asiatic home remained unbroken. When the change of climate occurred later, it was unable to destroy these deep-rooted cultural relationships and, consequently, could not reduce their recognizability, even though the criterion of continuity as such has more or less lost some of its strength.

2. Migratory movements of population are of special methodological interest if they lead a tribe into a district in which the original material that was used for implements, clothing, and habitation in their first or subsequent abodes is not present. In case no substitute is found, the implement, etc., in question must, of course, be given up. Absence of such former culture possessions would indeed diminish the criterion of quantity, but it would not constitute a positive counterproof against historical associations (*cf.* above, pp. 200 s., 247 s.).

In most cases, substitutive material is found. In the latter case, numerous characteristic criteria of quantity result from the fact that, though the manner of working the former material becomes useless, nevertheless tradition is so strong that the old method is applied to the new material until in the course of time a suitable process is invented. It has already been mentioned above that the old material may also be taken over into the new regions even when it is useless there. Through the latter procedure also a new characteristic criterion of quality is obtained (*cf.* above, p. 248).

3. Those cases are also of importance for method in which only the internal principle of a profession has been taken over

to the new region and there applied to new objects, sometimes of an essentially different kind, sometimes with but minor differences.

> We have an example of this in the case of horse breeding, which doubtless was developed only once in the steppes of Central Asia with certain races of horses and was transferred later on in Europe to other races. This phenomenon, therefore, goes back to historical borrowing and not to elementary ideas.

In fact, such utilitarian borrowing is exemplified very well in the principle of animal breeding in general (in contradistinction to the principle of taming). The first animals to be used for breeding purposes were certainly the reindeer and the horse and, consequently, also other herding animals in the tundra and steppes of Northeastern Asia. The principle was later on transferred to the horned animals farther south, especially oxen. The latter were only domesticated at first, and several were kept for the religio-mythological cult (as lunar symbols because of their horns). These cultures characterized by oxen and horned animals are, therefore, not absolutely new creations, but rather historically connected sub-groups of the great culture circle of the cattle-breeding herders. Its appearance in a more characteristic form does not indicate a "crisis of the idea of the culture circle," but only the normal advance of our research into the rich abundance of the single culture circles. Something similar is to be said with regard to the borrowing of the older form of cultivation of earth-nut plants among the agrarian cultures by the younger form of grassy plants, the different kinds of grain.

7. THE POSITION OF ETHNOLOGY IN THE GENERAL HISTORY OF MANKIND

A. Historical Retrospection

If we review the auxiliary sciences of ethnology, the importance of which for method has been briefly described here, we find that, particularly, prehistory and linguistics, as sciences of the mind, partake of the character of ethnology, while folklore and anthropology are about to reform themselves accordingly. Psychology and geography still remain auxiliary sciences with the task of explanation; the former with regard to the psychic side of culture, the latter with regard to the material side of culture.

1. Of all these sciences, ethnology was the first (chronologically) to win back again its character of a mental science and was the first to vindicate it. It was only later that prehistory and linguistics followed in this matter. The first founder, already, Fr. Ratzel, defended this claim forcibly against the evolutionism of the time which described the preliterates as peoples "without history." (72) While Frobenius again fell back into this nonhistorical evolutionism, F. Graebner and W. Foy championed this claim very enthusiastically, and the last mentioned had extensive plans for spreading this idea by means of his "Culture Historical Library." (73) Their premature and mysterious illness prevented the plan from being fully realized. In my article, "Die moderne Ethnologie," (74) I pointed out the untenability of the theories of a group of older ethnologists and psychologists by showing that the nonhistoricity of the prelierates was based upon the assumption that they lack personality and leading individuals. Besides, I have brought the linguistics of the preliterates into the service of ethnology through my works on the languages of Australia and other parts of the South Seas (75) and Southeastern Asia (76) and especially in my work, *Die Sprachfamilien und Sprachenkreise der Erde*. (77)

2. After the advances made by Pigorini, Obermeier, Breuil,

Kossinna, etc., it was, above all, O. Menghin who carried out the real historization of prehistory on a large scale, both spatially and internally in his magnum opus, *Die Weltgeschichte der Steinzeit.* Since he, to some extent, fitted his science into the spatial and chronological gaps of ethnology, he widened and insured the approach to the general history of mankind considerably. By throwing light into the unwritten prehistory of the oldest high culture peoples in Egypt, Mesopotamia, India, and Eastern Asia more systematically than had hitherto been done, he established a closer and clearer connection between unwritten human history and the oldest phases of written history than ethnology could have done alone. Robert von Heine-Geldern had done very valuable preliminary work for him in India and Further India and the South Seas. The way is also being prepared for the ancient high cultures of America by Fr. Röck with his work on the calendar and astronomy of these cultures. M. Oka has finished an immense work of this kind for Japan which, however, is still in manuscript form, and a similar work is also finished for Korea by A. Slawik, which at the same time throws much light upon the prehistory of Manchuria and ancient China. The works of Dr. J. Wölfel on the Canary Islands will soon bear fruit for the prehistory and early history of Western and Northern Africa and the Mediterranean basin. The "Indo-Germanic Question," which is being so lively discussed everywhere at present (the very bibliography of which is too copious to allow its being given here), (78) has this good effect that it continues to throw new light in every direction upon the prehistory and early history of Europe and Asia.

B. The Opening of the Portals of General History

In short, the portals of the general history of mankind have now been widely opened through the fructifying connection between culture historical ethnology and prehistory with the aid of linguistics (and anthropology). No one will ever be able to close them again. It was very heartening that this state of affairs has been recognized by literary history and that an historian of the importance of Fr. Kern removed the difficulties arising from prejudices and hesitancy in that quarter and, thus, introduced the results of that fruitful collaboration to literary history. (79) It is quite understandable that during the early stage of this collaboration the opinions of the individual investigators will be different; in fact, in some cases quite opposed to one another. Nearly all these opinions must be very carefully considered, particularly at this stage of development, and they can but serve wholesome self-criticism and the most promising fructification. It would be quite suspicious if these difficulties were absent now already or even for quite a long time to come.

On the contrary, I do not consider it of much use to discuss here which (80) of the two, ethnology or prehistory, will gain the leadership in the construction of this general history. It was psychologically understandable that O. Menghin seemed to claim this role for prehistory in the grand march forward he made in his *Weltgeschichte der Steinzeit,* and even though he purposely thanked ethnology for the strong impulse it gave for the construction of his prehistorical culture circles, (81) still he wanted to depreciate it into mere ethnography. I am pleased to see that he has given up such useless attempts and I think I can assume that he now has a different view concerning the question of precedence. It was a remarkable (but still less intelligible) disinterestedness on the part of an ethnologist, Fr. Flor, when he seemed to resuscitate prehistory's claim to precedence. (82)

I do not wish to enter upon this or any similar discussions, because I consider it useless and, on the other hand, I have always furthered the closest possible collaboration between ethnology and prehistory. This has already proven very advantageous to the Vienna School of modern ethnology. But as for general history, merely the approach has been opened up and even though it be quite extensive, the task is far from completion.

Considering the advanced specialization of the immense field of literary history, it is out of the question for one single science to cover, or for one man to master, the entire history of mankind. A universal history that is humanly possible can only embrace the prehistory and early history of the peoples of the earth. And also in this broad field, a single person alone can investigate only one subregion or master one subscience and must be satisfied to follow the other fields or sciences intelligently and critically. Hence, for a very long time to come an attempt at universal history will be made from the standpoint of one or another particular science. Each one of these will have its own specific value which the other cannot have and which it ought therefore to accept as a supplement to its own exposition. (83)

c. The Enlargement of the Domain of History by the Collaboration of Ethnology and Prehistory

In order to justify the insertion of this retrospect of the genesis of ethnology as an historical science and as a contributor to the construction of general history here at the end of my exposition of its method, I consider it useful once again to point out what progress history has made both as to content and in a purely methodological respect through the collaboration of ethnology and prehistory (and linguistics). At the same time, I do not wish to touch on the question: Which of these sciences has the greater merit in this matter?

1. As to content: In contrast to the alluring but, for the most part, delusory pretenses of evolutionism, history now possesses an orderly and objectively guaranteed approach to the centuries of human history unillumined by written documents, which cover a much longer span of time than that covered by complete literary history and include movements of population which spread out over the whole surface of the inhabitable earth.

Literary history would in vain endeavor to salvage its own importance in the face of this immense period of time by declaring these long-time periods to have been stationary and poor in events and progress. Can an era be called stationary if it witnessed all those incalculable migrations which led to the many discoveries of which the later "ages of discovery" are so proud? Neither is it correct to call this part of human history unimportant for the history of the world's progress, for in this period of man's history the foundations and lengthy developments of all great cultural elements were laid: family, state, property, right, custom, morality, art, religion and "world view." All of these are factors that still have their greatest effects even in our times. Moreover, an epoch should not be called unimportant in which the great division of economico-social development into the three Primary cultures took place; namely, the mother-right agrarian, the father-right totemistic culture of advanced hunting and the patriarchal animal-breeding herders with their radical influences upon the morals, law, and religion of the entire subsequent history of mankind, together with the manifold and complicated combinations upon which they entered with one another later on.

A full and deep understanding of the times of literary history is only possible through the knowledge of these times of which we are speaking and only after both have been united do we have a true and complete history.

2. History, however, has been greatly benefited by the fruitful combination of ethnology and prehistory also in a formal methodological aspect. For by including the culture elements themselves in order to establish spatial and temporal relationships between cultures as well as their causal influences and effects, very valuable methodological tools have been fashioned. History, indeed, likewise was acquainted with these methodological media, both in principle and on a large scale, but left them to lie dormant and undeveloped. By creating the culture historical method of ethnology in one stroke of genius, Graebner abundantly paid back to history what he had received from it (he himself having come from history). The present work is but an attempt to develop this method still further.

D. The Necessity of an Independent Method for Prehistory As Well As for Ethnology

We should not overlook the fact that ethnology, which was the first to acknowledge itself as an historical science, was also the first to develop its historical method. Menghin in his *Weltgeschichte der Steinzeit,* as Koppers has already pointed out, (84) only gave the method of prehistory in broad outlines. Since then, he has written a short (85) systematic method for a subbranch; namely, tribal science. Hence, the wish becomes all the more pressing that Menghin write a thorough method for prehistory in the second edition of his great work which is soon necessary (or in a special work), as no one else can bring to such a work the knowledge of details, the general view, and ability in the degree that he can.

He would thereby merit the greatest praise not merely from prehistory, but from all interested in universal history. For if progress in the construction of universal history depends upon the intelligent collaboration of prehistory and ethnology, then it must immediately be added that the success of this collaboration is wholly and essentially dependent upon both sciences working strictly with their own material and also according to their own method. Hence, although the methods of the two have much in common, still their differences are actually great enough to demand the careful independent development of both. Only then can the results of the two sciences mutually support and supplement each other in the construction of a universal history, (86) upon which both are at work.

In its endeavor to become ever more and more a real historical science, ethnology will not forget to remain a science of the mind. Of course, the two are not contradictories, especially in the case of culture history, since all culture has in some way or other proceeded from and been fashioned by the human mind. It is also in this wider sense that I understand the definition of ethnology which, as a science of history and of the mind, I gave already in 1906: "Ethnology is a science which has for its object the study of the development of the mind and of the exterior rational activity of man in racial life." (87) For here the "development of the mind" is understood not as evolutionism but as evolution, (88) which can be internal and external. Both, however, have their historical course, the investigation and comprehension of which we are now in a position to undertake with the aid of the new means and rules of the culture historical method.

In conclusion I must add that a further development and guarantee of a culture psychological method must take place for ethnology along with the progressive development and refinement of the culture historical method itself, in order both to supplement and to render more stable the progress it has made. It is only thus that we shall one day be able to grasp culture happenings to the full extent of their complexity and their deep significance for the history of mankind.

(1) *Cf.* W. Schmidt, *Anthropos,* XIV-XV (1919-1920), pp. 608-615.

(2) Italics mine.—W. Schmidt.

(3) The special arrangement and the numeration are mine.—W. Schmidt.

(4) W. Schmidt and W. Koppers, *Völker und Kultern* (Regensburg, 1924), p. 65.

(5) Raised also by Graebner himself at another place (p. 164).

(6) *Cf.* to this whole question my depositions against G. Wobbermin in *Ursprung der Gottesidee,* I2, p. 629 s.; further, H. Ulrich, "Logische Studien zur Methode der Ethnologie," *Anthropos,* XVIII-XIX, 1923-1924, p. 738 ss.

(7) W. Schmidt, *Anthropos,* VI (1911), p. 1034 ss.

(8) W. Schmidt, *Ursprung der Gottesidee,* VI, p. 32 ss.

(9) *Cf.* W. Schmidt, *Rasse und Volk* (Salzburg, 1935), pp. 136 ss., 154 ss., 159 ss.

(10) *Prinzipien der Sprachwissenschaft,* p. 5.

(11) Graebner, *Methode,* p. 111, note 1.

(12) *Cf.* also, the article "Volsprache" by Fr. Maurer in *Die deutsche Volkskunde,* edited by A. Spamer, Vol. I, p. 183 ss.; *cf.* Br. Schier, *p.* 284 ss.

(13) Vol. II, 1st ed., 1911; 2nd ed. (especially by A. Nehring), 1917-1923. S. and A. Nehring, "Studien zur Indogerman, Kultur und Urheimat," *Wiener Beiträge zur Kulturgeschichte und Linguistik,* Vol. IV (1936), pp. 1-239; W. v. Brandenstein, "Die Lebensformen der Indogermanen," *op. cit.,* pp. 239-277.

(14) *Cf.* also, the very instructive exposition of O. Menghin on the importance of linguistics for prehistorical tribal research, *Hirt Festschrift,* pp. 52 ss., 58 ss.

(15) Heidelberg, 1926.

(16) W. Schmidt, *op. cit.,* p. 519 ss.

(17) Regensburg, 1924 (really in 1914; see Introduction, p. v.)

(18) *Cf.* Graebner, p. 120.

(19) As the investigations of Dr. v. Heine-Geldern show very nicely for Southeastern Asia and Indonesia.

(20) *Cf.* Graebner, p. 73 s.

(21) That is admitted also by Menghin *(Hirt-Festschrift* [Heidelberg, 1936], p. 48). On the other hand, one may concede to him that the trained prehistorian may be able to draw many important conclusions from fragmentary material with regard to the intellectual culture.

(22) *Cf.* W. Schmidt, *Ursprung der Gottesidee,* I2, pp. 384-393; III, pp. 638-649.

(23) *Cf.* also in this matter, W. Koppers, "Weltgeschichte der Steinzeit," *Anthropos,* XXVI (1931), p. 234 s.

(24) *Cf.* also Graebner, p. 76.

(25) *Cf.* also the shorter and more popular exposition in Menghin's article, "Die Ergebnisse der vorgeschichtlichen Kulterkreislehre," *Neue Jahrbücher für Wissenschaft und Jugendbildung,* XI (1935), pp. 71-81.

(26) *Cf.* W. Schmidt, "Die moderne Ethnologie," *Anthropos,* I (1906), p. 134 s.

(27) A. Haberlandt, *Die deutsche Volkskunde,* Halle an der Saale (1935), p. 115.

(28) *Cf.* A. Spamer, "Wesen und Aufgabe der Volkskunde," *Die deutsche Volkskunde von A. Spamer,* I (Leipzig—Berlin, 1934), p. 4 ss.

(29) E. Fehrle, "Ziele der deutschen Volkskunde," *op. cit.,* p. 623 s.

(30) An error that turns up also here and there in the contributions of several co-operators of the same compilation.

(31) Quoted by Spamer, *op. cit.,* p. 6.

(32) A. Haberlandt, "Volkskunde und Völkerkunde," *op. cit.,* p. 51.

(33) Halle an der Saale (1935), p. 119 ss.

(34) *Cf.* W. Schmidt, "Die kulturhistorische Methode in der Ethnologie," *Anthropos,* VI (1911). pp. 1012, 1015 s.

(35) Haberlandt, *Die deutsche Volkskunde,* pp. 150, 123; *cf.* also in this regard in *Die deutsche Volkskunde* by A. Spamer, p. 57 a.

(36) The cultural geographical branch is especially made use of by W. Pessler in his clever use of cartography; see his programmatic article, "Die geographische Methode in der Volkskunde," *Anthropos,* XXVII (1932), pp. 707-742.

(37) Schier, *op. cit,* p. 478.

(38) *Beiträge zur sudetendeutschen Volkskunde,* XXI (Reichenberg, 1832).

(39) *Cf.* Schier, *op. cit.,* pp. 9, 12.

(40) *Ostdeutsche Forschungen,* II (Plauen i. Vogtl., 1934); *cf.* especially p. 304.

(41) *Anthropos,* I (1906), p. 134 ss.

(42) V. Lebzelter, "Zur Methodik menscheitsgeschichtlicher Forschung," *Zeitschr. f. Ethnol.,* LIV (1932), pp. 191, 192.

(43) Lebzelter, *op. cit.,* p. 192.

(44) *Cf.* W. Schmidt, *Rasse und Volk,* p. 19 ss.

(45) Munich, 1925.

(46) *Mitteilungen des Museums für Völkerkunde in Hamburg,* XIII (1928), pp. 75-169—Scheidt, I.

(47) Berlin, 1929.

(48) Hamburg, 1932. A textbook, "Kulturbiologie. Vorlesungen für Studierende aller Wissensgebiete" (Jena, 1930) has already been published and a "popular" exposition in Reclams Library, "Kulturkunde" (Leipzig, 1931), in which he asserts that it is "not recommendable to make use of works on ethnology or folklore when one takes up the study of cultural questions, or even to render considerations of them difficult by recalling such knowledge."

(49) This theory is pushed beyond all limits by another scientist in Hamburg, who wants to carry out a complete fusion of ethnology and the study of races under the name "Bio-Ethnologie" (P. Hambruch, "Probelme einer Bio-Ethnologie," *op. cit.*, pp. 111-140).

(50) Fr. Krause, "Völkerkunde—Anthropologie—Ethnobiologie," *Ethnologische Studien*, I (1931), pp. 135-166. The incorrect exposition of the culture historical school in this article has been corrected above (p. 31 ss.).

(51) W. Schmidt, *op. cit.*, p. 38.

(52) Scheidt, I, p. 82.

(53) Scheidt, *Lebensgesetze der Kultur*, p. 67.

(54) Stuttgart, 1936.

(55) V. Eickstedt, p. 132 s.

(56) In v. Eickstedt, p. 133, note 177.

(57) W. Peters, *Die Vererbung geistiger Eigenschaften und die psychiche Konstitution* (Jena, 1925), pp. 348, 366, 368.

(58) Scheidt, *op. cit.*, p. 93; also, *Archiv für Rassen- und Gesellschaftsbiologie*, XXI (1929), p. 129 ss., where he also admits that valuable results can only be obtained on European soil, since the methods of research are so complicated.

(59) Krause, *op. cit.*, p. 157.

(60) Krause, *op. cit.*, pp. 155, 159.

(61) *Cf.* W. Peters, *op. cit.*, p. 112.

(62) W. Schmidt, *Rasse und Volk*, p. 41 ss; *cf.* Lenz, *Menschliche Erblichkeitslehre* (1927), p. 503: "The doctrine of transmission of the psychical dispositions neither presupposes nor supports the materialistic opinion that psychical events are only externalizations of the body."

(63) W. Schmidt, *op. cit.*, p. 46 s.

(64) O. Menghin, *Blut und Geist* (Vienna, 1934), p. 49; *cf.* also his appropriate remarks on the smaller importance of the racial factor for tribal relations. ("Methodik der vorgeschichtlich. Stammeskunde," *Hirt-Festschrift*, pp. 49, 62 ss.

(65) *Eugen Fischer Festband, Zeitschr. f. Morphologie und Anthropologie*, XXXIV (1934), pp. 493-503.

(66) *Cf.* W. Schmidt, *Ursprung der Gottesidee*, VI, pp. 105 ss., 163 ss., 196 ss., 311 ss.

(67) P. Borchardt, "Die grosse Ost-West-Karawanstrasse durch die Lybische Wüste," *Peterm. Geogr. Mitteil.* (1932), pp. 219-223; "Naturbedingte Kulturwege," *Anthropos*, XXI (1926), pp. 225-232.

(68) G. Thilenius, *Die Bedeutung der Meeresströmungen für die Besiedlung Melanesiens* (1906).

(69) W. Schmidt, "The Position of Woman with Regard to Property in Primitive Society," *Amer. Anthr.*, N. S. XXXVII, p. 247 ss.

(70) *Cf.* W. Schmidt, *Gliederung der Australischen Sprachen* (Vienna, 1919), pp. 17, 86.

(71) *Cf.* W. Schmidt, *Ursprung der Gottesidee*, VI, p. 27 ss.

(72) *Cf.* above, p. 25.

(73) W. Foy in the introduction to Graebner's *Methode der Ethnologie* which was published as the first volume of the "Culture Historical Library."

(74) *Anthropos*, I (1906), p. 60 ss.

(75) W. Schmidt, *Die Gliederung der australischen Sprachen* (Vienna, 1919); *Das Verhältnis der melanesischen Sprachen zu den polynesischen und untereinander* (Vienna, 1899); *Die sprachlichen Verhältnisse von Deutsch-Neuguinea* (Berlin, 1900-1901).

(76) W. Schmidt, *Die Mon-Khmer-Völker* (Brauschschweig, 1906).

(77) Heidelberg, 1926.

(78) See, *e. g.*, my *Rasse und Volk* (2nd ed.; Salzburg—Leipzig, 1935), p. 136 ss., IV (1936); and the new contributions of several authors on the "Indo-Germanic and German Question," *Wiener Beiträge zur Kulturgeschichte und Linguistik,* IV (1936).

(79) Fr. Kern, "Die Welt worin die Griechen traten," *Anthropos,* XXV (1930), pp. 195-197; "Weltgeschichte der schriftlosen Völker," *Archiv. f. Kulturgesch.,* XXII (1931), p. 21 ss.; *Die Anfänge der Weltgeschichte* (Berlin—Leipzig, 1933).

(80) *Cf.* above, p. 26.

(81) Which he then established and strengthened with the means at the disposal of prehistory.

(82) Fr. Flor, *Hirt-Festschrift,* I (Heidelberg, 1936), p. 72 ss.

(83) Some valuable suggestions for a uniform terminology are offered by Fr. Röck, "Versuch einer terminologischen Synthese der menschheitsgeschichtlichen Wissenszweige u. s. w.," *Mitteil. Anthropol. Ges. Wien,* LXII (1932), pp. 295-304. The strength of traditional historical usage is somewhat underestimated here.

(84) *Anthropos,* XXVI (1931), p. 226 ss.

(85) See above, p. 299, note 21.

(86) Some valuable ideas on the method of prehistory can be found in A. M. Tallgren, "Sur la methode de l'archéologie pre-historique," Eurasia, X (1936), pp. 16-24.

(87) *Cf.* above, p. 5.

(88) *Cf.* above, p. 7.

GLOSSARY*

I. *SCIENCES:* discussed or referred to.

Anthropogeography: was introduced by Ratzel and studies the migrations of man.

Ethnobiology: was introduced by W. Scheidt and aims to fuse ethnology with physical anthropology.

Ethnography: is a description of peoples and deals with their local traits, habits, customs, economics, religion, etc.

Ethnology or Cultural Anthropology: the science which has for its object the study of the development of the mind and of the exterior rational activity of man in racial life.

Ethnosociology or Social Anthropology: sociology relating to early times of human life.

Folklore: treats of the traditions, myths, proverbial sayings, popular beliefs and practices of the common people.

Geography: description of the surface of the earth as the natural environment of man.

History:

a. Written or literary: records of past events of literate peoples; makes use of written documents exclusively.

b. Non-written or preliterate: reconstruction of the events of those times which antedate written history either of peoples of the distant past (prehistory) or of the present-day primitives or preliterates (ethnology).

Linguistics: the science of languages.

Physical Anthropology: the natural history of man (race, physical characteristics, etc.).

Prehistory: the study of man's early history from relics and remains.

II. *METHODS*

Biological: was applied by Frobenius in his later researches and holds that culture has its own biological phases of develop-

* This glossary does not appear in the German original. It has been included here by the Translator to aid students who may use this book as a textbook.

ment and for these stages the material environment is of the highest importance. Culture is a thing for itself and man is not the creator but the mere carrier of culture.

Culture Historical: follows the principles of general history but makes use of the culture itself and its productions as methodological media to reconstruct the history of man in those times for which we have no written documents.

Developmental: same as biological.

Functional method or Structure Theory: examines the interrelations of the different parts of one culture at a time in order to find more or less fixed relations.

Evolutionistic: holds that all development is from the lower to the higher, more simple to the more complex, etc.

Geographical or geographical-statistical: the earlier method of Frobenius shows that the cultures of two geographical provinces may have very many correspondences and thus produces the criterion of quantity and develops the theory of migrations (Ratzel) into the theory of culture circles (Frobenius).

Psychological: the doctrine of the social psyche common to all peoples which produces the so-called "Elementary Ideas" (Elemetargedanken), which in turn give rise to the customs, laws, beliefs, etc., of mankind. The different geographical provinces exert their climatic influence upon man and produce different peoples and cultures (Folk Ideas: Volkergedanken).

Statistical or Quantitative: an auxiliary method which by analyzing and cartographing the various culture elements seeks to show the historical relations between these elements.

III. TERMS

A. Culture Historical Terminology

1. Causality.
   a. External: Exerted upon man from without.
   b. Internal: Exerted by man from within.
   c. Creative: Produces something for the first time.
   d. Modificatory: Effects changes in an object that already exists.
2. Criteria.
   a. We have a Criterion of Quality if characteristic similarities

are found between two culture elements, provided this likeness did not take its origin from the nature of the object in question or (when material) from the stuff out of which it was made, and we postulate an historical connection.

b. We have a Criterion of Quantity if there are many criteria of quality present which are however independent of one another.

c. The Criterion of Continuity endeavors to establish a continuous connection in the intervening areas.

d. The Criterion of the Degree of Relationship increases the cogency of the argument by pointing to an increase both as to number and strength of the resemblances in proportion as we approach the two chief areas.

3. Culture.

a. Definition: Culture consists in the inner formation of the human mind and in the external formation of the body and nature in so far as this latter process is directed by the mind. It is, therefore, immanent but only observable in its external manifestations.

b. Culture Area: The region within which a particular culture complex is found.

c. Culture Circle: A culture complex which embraces all the essential and necessary categories of human nature.

d. Culture Complex: A cluster of interlocked culture traits; often they are grouped around some special feature of the culture after which the complex is named, *e.g.*, totemistic complex, mother-right complex, etc.

e. Culture Unity: Any group of culture traits; culture complexes, strata, circles are greater culture unities.

f. Culture Whole: Term used in contradistinction to a part or certain aspect of a culture which might be given special prominence for the purpose of classification.

4. Development or Evolution.

a. Internal: From within.

b. External: Due to influences from without.

c. Unilinear or monotypic: The theory that all culture developed from the lowest beginnings in a straight line upward towards higher forms.

5. Influences.
   a. Active: Influences which an individual, a tribe, a people exert upon others.
   b. Passive: Influences which an individual, a tribe, a people receive from others.
6. Processes.
   a. Acculturation: The imparting of culture from one people to another by means of contact. This contact may be
   1—Marginal Acculturation or Contact-action: The two cultures collide and mingle only along their borders.
   2—Planitional Acculturation or Mixture: The two cultures fuse and mingle over a broad area.
   3—Borrowing: A culture element is passed on from one people to another. This may take place during the process of acculturation, trade infiltration, migrations, etc.
   b. Migrations or Movements of Population or Folk Wanderings: A large body of people move with the complete or almost complete culture in their possession. A single or a few individuals do not constitute a migration in the strict sense of the word, howsoever great the consequences might be upon their own culture or the culture of others. Migrations may take the form of
   1—Encirclement: The immigrating culture surrounds another.
   2—Intrusion: The immigrating culture pierces another like a wedge. If this should pass all the way through the sessile culture it would constitute a Crossing.
   3—Overlay or Superposition: The immigrating culture carriers establish dominion over the sessile culture and frequently hold themselves aloof socially and culturally at least for a time.
   c. Convergence: Those cases of similarity which are not to be explained from the common inborn disposition of mankind nor from historical influences, but from assimilation of originally entirely different elements through the influence exerted by a similar environment.
7. Regions.
   a. Border Regions: Strictly speaking of a culture or a continent in which special forms may be developed. Sophus

Müller considered whole Europe such a border region in relation to the higher cultures of the East.

b. Refuge Areas: A district into which a tribe immigrates under pressure from other advancing tribes. Often as not such regions are poor economically and some natural formation as mountains, rivers, deserts acts as a protection or isolating agent.

c. Monochromatic: Districts in which one culture prevails throughout.

d. Polychromatic: Characterized by a number of heterogeneous cultures.

8. Relations: Active and Passive. See Causality, Influences.

a. Culture Relations: See Causality, Influences.

b. Spatial Relations: All culture is two-dimensional and, therefore, the space factor plays an important role. The great spatial unity is the culture circle.

c. Temporal Relations: In the reconstruction of history the working out of time relations is important not only for history itself, but also for the all-important research into causes.

9. Sources.

a. Division:

a) Classification according to Origin:

1—According to Time: Contemporary and Subsequent.

2—According to Place: Native and Alien.

3—According to Manner in which obtained: Direct and Indirect.

b) Classification according to Intrinsic Value:

1—Material Sources: Survivals and Vestiges.

2—Formal or Speaking Sources: Traditions and Written Sources.

b. Collection of Sources: By fieldworker and ethnologists.

c. Criticism of Sources: As to authenticity, time and place. External and Internal Criticism.

d. Interpretation of Sources:

1—Direct or of the first degree or local. The meaning and significance that are peculiar to cultural elements here and now. This may be

a) Unilateral: The meaning of one of the phenomena of comparison is already known.

b) Multilateral or reciprocal: The meaning of neither complex is certain and a recapitulation of all the component features is necessary.

2—Indirect or of the second degree or distant interpretation: By comparative research.

10. Diagram of Ethnological Cultures according to Wilhelm Schmidt:

1. *PRIMITIVE CULTURES:* (Foodgatherers) (Preliterates)	1) Central Primitive Culture; exogamous, with monogamy. 2) Southern Primitive Culture; exogamous, with sex-totems. 3) Arctic Primitive Culture; exogamous, equal rights.
2. *PRIMARY CULTURES:* (Foodproducers) (Preliterates)	1) Exogamous, patrilineal. Totemistic, higher stage of hunting; "city" culture. 2) Exogamous, matrilineal. Horticulturists; "village" culture. 3) Patrilineal, with undivided family; to this belong the pastoral nomads who become ruling races.
3. *SECONDARY CULTURES:* (Picture Writing)	1) Free patrilineal cultures (Polynesia, the Sudan, Hither India, Western Asia, Southern Europe, etc.). 2) Free matrilineal cultures (Southern China, Farther India, Melanesia, the Northest of South America, etc.).

4. *TERTIARY CULTURES:* (Alphabet) — The oldest civilizations of Asia, Europe and America.

B. Miscellaneous

Appurtenance: of a culture element to a culture circle. A culture element is proven to belong to a certain culture circle by actual observation or deduced by analogy from other similar cultures.

Boomerang: characterizes certain Australian tribes. It consists of a flat piece of wood curved in its own plane. It is a weapon of war and self-retrieving.

Coup de poing: a large flaked instrument of paleolithic times. It has a thick blunt base for a hand grasp.

Culture Hero: a personage of mythical character in the legends of primitive tribes. He is mostly pictured as a beneficent being, a savior to whom man is indebted for the arts. Then again he may play the role of a trickster, transformer, etc. His actions may run the whole gamut from something almost divine to the lowest immorality.

Diving Motif: in mythologies of creation the Supreme Being often commands different animals to dive into the deep to supply a bit of earth from which He is then able to create the world.

Empathy (German Einfühlung): a mental state in which one identifies or feels himself in the same state of mind as another person or group.

Father-right: a community or group in which the father (or the males in general) is supreme. In such a society descent, inheritance, succession, etc., are reckoned through the father (patrilineal), the wife settles in the home of the husband (patrilocal residence), and in its extremest form it develops into a patriarchy in which the patriarch has full and absolute authority.

Initiation: ceremonies by which a tribe introduces the young at the age of puberty into full membership in the tribe. A tribe may have such rites only for boys, or only for girls, or for both, mixed or apart, singly or in groups.

Monogamy: the marriage of one man with one woman.

Monotheism: the belief in and worship of a Supreme Being as the sole creator and master of the universe. There is a controversy concerning the application of the term monotheism in religions in which other divinities are tolerated or even magical, manistic and animistic rites are practiced.

Mother-right: the woman is here supreme. Descent, inheritance and succession are through the mother (matrilineal), the man resides in the home of his wife (matrilocal residence, marriage), and may develop into the extreme form of matriarchy in which the matriarch has absolute authority. The mother's brother (avunculate) in this case often assumes the authority of the father with regard to his sister's children.

Mythology: the whole body of myths and legends of a tribe concerning cosmogony, gods and heroes, or the study of them. If the sun plays a large role we speak of solar mythology, or the moon, lunar mythology.

Primitial Offering: among some primitive tribes (especially the Pygmies) it is the custom to throw away a choice morsel of food or the first catch of the day as an offering to the Supreme Being.

Scarification: mutilation of the body, usually during the initiation ceremony. Often also for medical purposes or for the sake of adornment (tattooing).

Survivals: (to be distinguished from the "survivals" used above to designate material sources with a material substratum) a term introduced by Tylor. Survivals are older forms that are preserved even though the culture background in which they arose has become extinct or given way to a more highly developed stage.

Totemism: the practice of a social group, without regard to age or sex, of entertaining a mysterious relationship as a group to a class of animals, plants or material objects. This class of objects is their *Totem.* This genuine totemism is to be distinguished from *sex-totemism* (Southeast Australia), which rather distinguishes groups already existing (men and women) among themselves. *Individual Totemism* (Algonkians) is also a misnomer, as it consists only in relations between the individual and a group or kind of animal. Frazer here more correctly spoke of a "guardian spirit." The *Nagualism* of Ancient Mexico and Central America is another form of individual guardian spirit and not genuine totemism.

Tribe: a group of individuals with common language, customs, government, etc., and usually occupy a definite territorial region.

Two-class Culture: a mixture of mother-right and totemism.

INDEX OF SUBJECTS

D

E

F

G

H

N

R

INDEX OF AUTHORS
(Referred to or Discussed)

(In the following indexes particularly important references are in italic type.)

T

U

V

W

Y

INDEX OF COUNTRIES, PEOPLES, LANGUAGES and TRIBES

B

C